A History of Czech Economic Thought

Situated in the turbulent heart of Europe, the Czech Republic has suffered from significant discontinuity in its historical development, but its economic thinking has not until now been subject to a full analysis. This book offers a history of Czech economic thought from the late Middle Ages to the present day. It traces methodological developments and the relationship between economics and politics, and introduces not just pioneering figures in the field but also those whose lives and careers were thwarted by history, as well as Czech exile thinkers.

Identifying key themes in Czech economic thought, the volume considers which branches of economic theory have had the greatest influence on Czech thought, and explores the relationship between Czech economic thinking and wider established schools of thought.

This book will benefit students and researchers of history of economic thought, economic history, economic theory, and political economy, as well as those with a specific interest in the Czech Republic.

Antonie Doležalová is Associate Professor at the Institute of Economic Studies, Charles University, the Czech Republic.

The Routledge History of Economic Thought

7 **History of Latin American Economic Thought**
Oreste Popescu

8 **History of Norwegian Economic Thought**
Olov Bjerkholt and Pal Lykkja

9 **A History of Russian Economic Thought**
Vincent Barnett

10 **History of Scottish Economic Thought**
Edited by Alistair Dow and Sheila Dow

11 **A History of Irish Economic Thought**
Edited by Renee Prendergast, Tom Boylan and John Turner

12 **A History of Ottoman Economic Thought**
Developments before the 19th Century
Fatih Ermis

13 **A History of Italian Economic Thought**
Riccardo Faucci

14 **A History of Australasian Economic Thought**
Alex Millmow

15 **A History of American Economic Thought**
Mainstream and Crosscurrents
Samuel Barbour, James Cicarelli and J. E. King

16 **A History of Czech Economic Thought**
Antonie Doležalová

For a full list of titles in this series, please visit https://www.routledge.com/The-Routledge-History-of-Economic-Thought/book-series/SE0124

A History of Czech Economic Thought

Antonie Doležalová

Routledge
Taylor & Francis Group
LONDON AND NEW YORK

First published 2018
by Routledge

2 Park Square, Milton Park, Abingdon, Oxfordshire OX14 4RN
52 Vanderbilt Avenue, New York, NY 10017

Routledge is an imprint of the Taylor & Francis Group, an informa business

First issued in paperback 2020

British Library Cataloguing-in-Publication Data
A catalogue record for this book is available from the British Library

Library of Congress Cataloging-in-Publication Data
A catalog record has been requested for this book

ISBN: 978-1-138-91416-2 (hbk)
ISBN: 978-0-367-66635-4 (pbk)

Typeset in Bembo
by Swales & Willis Ltd, Exeter, Devon, UK

To the memory of Milan Sojka (1951–2009)

Contents

Introduction

What if Czech economic thought does not exist at all?

This question assailed me several weeks after signing an agreement for a book on the history of Czech economic thought. Indeed, no overview of the development of the field on a world scale has mentioned it until now; not even Joseph Schumpeter, himself hailing from one of the Bohemian Crownlands, included any Czech economists in his *History of Economic Analysis* (1954). The question was elicited both by the adjective *Czech* and the subject – economic thought.

In Czech historiography, Czech economic thought is traditionally identified as having emerged in the second half of the 19th century, when it began to separate away and distinguish itself from German-speaking circles (Sojka *et al.*, 1998). But the first studies reflecting Czech economic thought at the beginning of the 20th century and in the decades to follow use the territorial definition of economic thought in the Bohemian part of the Habsburg monarchy, with its complicated national structure, regardless of whether the authors were of Czech or German nationality or whether they wrote in Czech or German. In Marxist historiography after 1948, representatives of Czech economic thought were branded as propagators of Czech economic nationalism or exponents of the (Czech) bourgeoisie. Not even after 1990 did the issue of the Czech nature of Czech economic thought become a topic for discussion, and although the number of published books and studies (Vencovský, 1997) bears witness – albeit limited in time – to increased interest in the given theme among Czech historians and economists, most of them could be described as textbooks with the primary goal to introduce personalities that should not have been forgotten. In these works, Czech economic thought is defined nationally, and with few exceptions (Půlpán, Vencovský *et al.*, 2005), these books and studies are limited to 1882–1948 in terms of time.

In my book, which is the first systematic treatment of the history of Czech economic thought from the Middle Ages through to the present day, the term *Czech* is meant territorially. It therefore does not include only authors who were born Czech and wrote in that language, but all who worked on the territory corresponding to today's Czech Republic. The appellation of this territory has changed during history. Until 1918, it was called the *Lands of the Bohemian Crowns*. From 1918, all the Bohemian Crownlands (Bohemia, Moravia, Silesia) were, together with Slovakia (and until 1938 also with Carpathian Ruthenia), part of Czechoslovakia, and the name *Czech Lands* began to be used to refer to what were formerly the Bohemian Crownlands; thus today, Bohemia embraces only the western part of the present-day Czech Republic. Moreover, Czech has always used the name *Čechy* to refer to this territory. This is plural in Czech, in contrast to the Latin word *Bohemia*, which originated from the name of the Celtic tribe Boii, whose members appear to have resided in this territory between the 1st century BC and the 1st century AD, only to be pushed out by successive waves of Germanic and Slavic settlers (Teich, 1998, 3); the latter came to this territory – Czechs in Bohemia and Moravians in Moravia – in the 6th century.

In this book, the history of Czech economic thought is the history of economic thought in the Bohemian Crownlands and in the Czech Lands. Writing such a book entailed confronting the fundamental difficulty of including and excluding – that is, who truly belongs to the centuries-long story of Czech economic thought? If the criterion was to be one of a 'national' background, the message of the positive impact that the blending of cultural influences in the space of Central Europe has had would be lost. If the criterion was to be that of 'who was born in the territory', all the focus would be on the few 'stars' that would, thanks to their significance in today's economics, completely overshadow numerous others: Carl Menger and Friedrich August von Hayek were of Bohemian descent, Eugen von Böhm-Bawerk and even Joseph Schumpeter were born in Moravia. Hence my incorporation of thinkers who were active in the Bohemian Crownlands and in the Czech Lands, and who broadened the horizon of economic thought, regardless of their national background; this fully applies also to the 'socialist period', when two out of three of the most significant Czechoslovak economists mentioned in the pertinent chapter had German-Jewish roots.

In this book, economic thought is viewed not only in terms of the history of economic doctrines, but rather as the way people think as regards the economy and economic issues. The book examines the evolution of economic thought, its methodological, institutional and thematic advances. It introduces figures that are crucial to understanding the development of economic thought in the turbulent heart of Europe, which has suffered from significant discontinuities in its historical development. The majority of these economists were not economists by education; the situation began to change only in the second half of the 20th century. The majority of them were theoreticians and practical economists (*národohospodáři*) at the same time or, as the case may be, journalists; they entered public space and changed the public discourse in various ways.

The goal of the book is to explore the ideological disputes, generational conflicts and diffusion of ideas and subsequently place Czech economic thought within the broader European context. Notwithstanding the fact that the tradition of Czech economic thought has, from the European perspective, always been in the shadow of German and Austrian economic analysis, ideas have spread back and forth between Czech and European thought: The Czech Reformation had an influence on European thought; in the early 19th century the Bohemian economists were among the first who reconsidered the mathematization of economics; in the late 19th century Albín Bráf contributed to the *Methodenstreit* controversy; in the early 20th century František Čuhel and his utility theory influenced Ludwig von Mises; in the interwar period Karel Engliš's teleological theory of human behaviour was discussed in the context of the Austrian school and it resonated particularly strongly in the 1960s and 1970s amongst Czech economists living in exile in the United States. After the Second World War, the ideas of Czech economists as to economic planning in a democratic society drew considerable European interest. Czech economic thought drew international attention as a project of the reform of Socialism in the 1960s during the Prague Spring, and then again in the 1990s, as pursuit for transition from Socialism to capitalism emerged.

The book focuses on three topics and answers three questions:

- The first topic is focused on an analysis of methodological development as well as themes that are crucial for understanding the development of Czech economic thought and is based on the question as to the extent to which Czech economic thought has been a valuable part of the European tradition of economic thought.
- The second topic is focused on an analysis of Czech economic thought under various international influences and to the same extent the contribution of Czech economic thought to the development of European economic thought, and it answers the question as to what branches of European economic thought have had the biggest influence on Czech economic thought and what the mode of transfer of ideas from neighbouring countries was.
- The third topic is focused on the development of Czech economic thought in historical context and examines the question of how deep of an impact the dramatic changes in political regime in Czech history had on the evolution of economic thought and its (dis)continuity.

The book follows a chronological line, although none of the four chapters has a precise time definition. The limits of an attempt to bound a phenomenon as dynamic as economic thought are shown – as early as in the first chapter – by Comenius, who according to the time of the emergence of his works should be part of the second chapter; yet his work belongs, in its character, to the tradition of the Czech Reformation, although he attempts to connect millenarianism with his constructive rationalism. In the second half of the 17th century, which marks the beginning of the second chapter, the Bohemian Crownlands were rather the place of realization of economic ideas, not the place of their origin; as a result, economic thought began to spread in society, albeit slowly. Likewise, Josef Kaizl and Albín Bráf, who are placed in chapter three, marked by the year 1882, began their scientific activity a decade earlier, in the same way as economics began – albeit sporadically – to be taught in Czech earlier. Not even the year 1948 represents a clearly divided line as the beginning of Marxist-Leninist economics, for the teachers of the first disseminators of this thought had been economists who had arisen from the tradition of interwar Czechoslovak economics, its roots extending as far as the 19th century. But the political changes that were reflected also in the organization and realization of scientific practice can univocally be dated to the year of the communist coup d'etat.

In each chapter, the book focuses on the main themes and questions in which Czech economic thought was interested during a particular period, taking the influence of contemporary streams of economic thought and the ever-changing theoretical, geopolitical and economic conditions into account. The first chapter focuses on identifying the elements of economic thought in the writings of Czech medieval and early modern thinkers and especially of the Czech Church reformers, who reflected on the relationship between private and common property, providence and human behaviour, social justice, mercy and charity. Until the first half of the 17th century, we can find economic considerations in only a minimal number of texts. Economic thought was firmly rooted in theology and its language was theological-philosophical. Besides John Hus and Comenius, the chapter introduces the lay thinker Petr Chelčický, who was the first thinker to uncover the semantic content of used terms. At the end of the 15th century, the first book on the welfare of the state was written in Bohemia.

The second chapter covers the period from the second half of the 17th century to the end of the 19th century. The chapter questions the stereotype that economics at that time was viewed as a practical (as opposed to a theoretical, academic) discipline, whose purpose within the framework of the multi-ethnic Habsburg Empire was only as an aid in optimizing the administration of the state and explains the interdisciplinary roots of economic thought. The chapter describes the genesis of economics as a scientific field and shows that, in economic discussions, attention turned primarily towards questions concerning the applicability of the principles of Mercantilism and Liberalism in the Czech environment and support for agriculture and the emerging industrial sector. At the same time, the first fiscal and monetary theories were formulated on the distribution of wealth in society. The social question and the relationship between economics and ethics became the main subjects of theoretical debates. Besides well-known cameralists, such as J.J. Becher, P.W. von Hornigk or J. Sonnenfels, this chapter introduces the unknown pupils of the last-mentioned: Joseph Ignatz Butschek, knight of Heraltice, Leopold Ludwig Schulz von Strasznitzki and Václav Gustav Kopetz, who were the first teachers of Cameralism in the Bohemian Crownlands. Georg Franz August Count Buquoy and Alois Lexa, knight of Aehrenthal were the first in the search for formalization of economics, Bernard Bolzano and František Chleborád were original social thinkers and the first propagators of cooperative concepts in the Bohemian Crownlands.

The third chapter charts the period from the year 1882, when economics was institutionalized at the Czech part of the University in Prague and Czech became the language of economic tuition there until the year 1948, and is the widest-ranging in content. In this period, Czech economists were interested in different streams of contemporary economic thought. At the beginning, the social question, the evolution of capitalism and the distribution of wealth between the monarchy and the Bohemian Lands became the central issues of their interest. Josef Kaizl developed a new fiscal theory, František Čuhel introduced the concept of ordinal utility and Albín Bráf thought over the methodology of economics. The formation of Czechoslovakia in 1918 and the Great Depression in the 1930s introduced new challenges for both economics and economists, most notably with respect to the formation of economic policies and the relationship between the market and economic planning; the latter became a major theme in Czech economic thought and gradually replaced interest in the social question. Karel Engliš introduced his teleological theory and Josef Macek unfolded his concept of economics as a social science and promoted U-turn of economics towards active economic policy during that time.

The fourth chapter covers the years between 1948 and 1989. Despite great advances in local economic education and the emergence of new issues, domestic economic thought fell, after 1948, under the sway of Marxism-Leninism, and the only form in which major international economic ideas were addressed was when they were part of a 'critique' of non-Marxist schools of economics. Marxism-Leninism became almost exclusively the language of economics in Czechoslovakia for the long 40 years that followed. In conformity with Marxist historical materialism, economics was able to serve as a way of formulating a thesis regarding the essential evolution of capitalism into Socialism. Economic planning became a major theme in Czech economic thought. Discussion on the nature of Socialism was opened in the 1960s. The economists from the generation that had obtained its education in a Marxist-Leninist political economy participated in this discussion for the very first time. Their work, however, shows how incorrect it is to label the 40 years of economic thought in socialist Czechoslovakia as a Marxist-Leninist cliché.

The development of economic thought in the 20th century was profoundly impacted by the interference of totalitarian regimes, which led to three waves of emigration from Czechoslovakia – in the years 1938, 1948 and 1968. As a result of these emigration waves, Czech economics lost many of its experts, but emigration also led to the emergence of a specific branch of Czech economic thought in exile, where it is possible to trace stronger features of continuity than within domestic Czech economic thought.

The Epilogue emphasizes the main features of the development of economic thought after the Velvet Revolution in 1989: Czech economics opened to allow international influences in again, and students again began to study at universities abroad. One question, however, is to what extent Czech economic thought has managed, in the course of two decades, to extricate itself from the constraints of past intellectual stereotypes and limited participation in the international sphere.

The book can be read on three levels – ontological, epistemological and methodological. The first level searches for the nature of Czech economic thought as a science. It highlights the evolution of ideas as to the nature of economics and how it can be defined. From the beginning of Czech economic thought, economics is characterized as a complex science: The essence and the purpose of the study of economic facts was to not only understand but also to correct social conditions. Until the 1960s, Czech economics persevered as a highly interdisciplinary social science with a direct connection to philosophy.

The epistemological level examines the cognitive capacities of economics and its role in society. In this sense, economics gives us a better understanding of the nature of social changes, and economics itself is understood as a social science with a pervasive influence on society as a whole. It is based on the consideration that economics is closely connected to both the importance of economic questions in society and the prestige of economists within society. For example, at the end of the 19th and the beginning of the 20th century, the professional prestige of economists had risen thanks to their connection with the process of the Czech National Revival, the social and cultural movement that prepared the way towards the formation of the modern Czech nation. They were held in high esteem as propagators and supporters of national prosperity, formed a natural part of the intellectual elites and attracted the educated core of society. They enjoyed natural authority and trust. One of the reasons their status began to fade after the Great Depression and the Second World War might have been connected with the fact that economists were increasingly regarded as propagators of a particular group's interests. These shifts in perception foretold the loss of prestige and professional autonomy after 1948, accompanied also by the loss of their social position.

The methodological level explains the position of economics between theory and politics and clarifies the question of the politicalization of economics and the tools used in this regard. It is based on the consideration that, at pivotal points in the Czech history, economics even served as a powerful weapon in political struggle. It manifests itself in the teaching of economics and in the composition of the teaching staff on the one hand and in the relationship between economic theory and economic policy on the other. As we will see, for example, the fundamental discussion among Czech economists in the 1960s was focused on key topics of official reform documents published by government.

Writing this a book entailed having to confront a few problems. First, to contextualize economic thought properly. That is a crucial question when writing the history of economic thought in a country that underwent many transitions of power regimes and during the 20th century as many as three changes of ideologically different regimes. But this also means that Czech economists had a unique chance – not once, but three times within the span of a century – to participate in the changing of an economic system, and at the same time to be a part of the political power themselves. Apart from the introductory paragraphs on the political-economic development in a given historical period, the main contextualizing tools are the subchapters on how economics was taught and disseminated in the public space.

That is where the second main problem lies – that is, how to treat the ways in which the transfer of ideas to and within the Bohemian and Czech Lands occurred and vice versa. From the 14th century, exchange scholarships of Czech scholars and students at foreign universities were the most important mode of transferring new ideas. Whenever that option was not feasible, Czech economic thought became increasingly closed, and whenever it was, Czech economic thought bloomed and was a relevant part of European development. Paradoxically, the greatest blow that Czech economic thought ever suffered was an event that is in historiography perceived as an unequivocally positive step: The division of the Czech and German parts of the Charles-Ferdinand University in Prague in 1882. Carl Menger and Friedrich Wieser continued to teach at the German part, whereas at the Czech part lectures were given by two incipient associate professors, although they later became famous – nationally, within Czech society. Although all the Czech economists read and wrote in German, English and most of them in French, Italian and in Russian, they decided, under the influence of the Revivalist ethos, to write their books in Czech and for a Czech audience; as one of them wrote: 'Books in foreign language are generally useless to the nation. A science which is not presented to a nation in its language has for it the value of gold ore, hidden in inaccessible deposits in the earth' (Chleborád, 1869, I). As we will find out, the Czech audience was frequently hostile to them and the majority of them also lost the competitive pressure of world development of economic thought. What might have seemed to be strength and victory led to isolation and provincialism in a few decades; Czech economists could continue reading the works of foreign authors but nobody from abroad could read their texts.

The other issue that everyone who wishes to write a history of Czech economic thought – especially in English – must face is the correct terminology. The notion of economics itself has had a stressful history in the Czech environment. By the mid-17th century it represented the practical side of the everyday struggle for human happiness – both at an individual and state level. After that, as economics began to emerge as a specific scientific field, cameral sciences dominated, as did all the terms they used – *Polizei und Kammeralwissenschaften*, *Staatswirtschaft* and *Politische Wissenschaft* were the Central European analogies to the Western European term of political economy; although this notion was known, it was not used. The term *economics* for a scientific field was first used in 1816, but Czech practice took the translation of the German term *Wirtschaft* and introduced the term *hospodářství*, which corresponds to the English term *economy*. When the term *Wirtschaft* was supplemented with the word *nation* in the German-speaking space, Czech language also adopted it as *national economy*: the term *national-economy theory* has been used until the present to describe both the economy of the state and individuals as well as economics as a science. Eventually, the term *political economy*, too, was adopted from Germany and promoted in the mid 19th century, the meaning of the word, with only minor changes, continued until the communist coup in 1948. At that time, it began to be used with two adjectives that completely changed its meaning: The political economy of capitalism and the political economy of Socialism. The first of these froze at the level of the interpretation of economics as contained in Marx's *Capital*, the second was for a long time conserved in the Stalinist ideological milieu.

This search for the name of the discipline relates to recurrent changes in economic terminology. The formation of Czech economic terminology has always partly been a necessity, for the necessary words did not exist in common language, it was partly also a passion. When the first economic texts began to emerge in the Czech language in the first half of the 19th century, their authors (in their search for suitable Czech terms) usually used their own creativity and plunged into the formation of Czech neologisms that more or less corresponded to their own understanding of the term about which they had read in German, English or French. Such terms still have their own charm, but they can be understood only by knowing the author's whole thought concept – such as the word *prázdnění* (emptying), for leisure time. However, merit for Czech terminology should go to all those who, from the mid-19th century, taught economics in Czech, contributed to the emerging Czech-written journals, met in voluntary associations or wrote entries for the first Czech dictionaries; Czech economic terminology stabilized after the institutionalization of Czech economics in 1882 thanks to the first generation of so-called Czech national economists. The greatest innovator, however, was František Čuhel. This linguist *per se*, perhaps in every line of his text, introduces new Czech words that are difficult to match with an English equivalent; some may seem somewhat comical today, others have sexual connotations in contemporary language. His intention, however, was different from others. His concern was not to coin new terms, but to find concepts that can accurately express what they mean in economics. Most of these concepts gradually ceased to exist. A complete change in economic vocabulary was brought about by the change in the political regime after 1948, when the clichés of the political economy of Socialism became the sole language of economics. The impact was almost perfect; after 20 years, the authors of the Czech translation of what was then the 6th edition of P.A. Samuelson's *Economics* had to face a major problem with terminology: Numerous terms of political economy had already fallen into obscurity. They therefore had to coin new Czech words and terms. The same can be said of the translation of the 13th edition of the same book in the early 1990s.

So this book that treats the aforementioned issues century after century is, after all, a story of human thinking, of an endeavour to learn the nature of things. It unveils ideological disputes and generational conflicts, introduces not only pioneering figures in the field but also those whose lives and careers were thwarted by history, shows both the bravery and the smallness of human spirit, the struggles with prejudices and with objective, albeit frequently hidden, institutional obstacles. It transpires that two concepts – freedom and education – have the clearest continuity in this story: The concept of freedom not as a goal or utopian dream, but as the principle characteristic of all human action and life itself. The freedom to decide in accordance with one's reason 100 years prior to the start of the Reformation in the rest of Europe, the freedom to evaluate matters according to one's conscience and preference still prior to the emergence of the subjective theory of value. Education in Czech is the most important legacy of Czech Reformation's thoughts on a fair society in the beginning of the 15th century. In two centuries, in Comenius's work, education became the main toll to establish such a society. At the end of the 18th century, education in the Bohemian Crownlands became an instrument of state policy; Marie Theresa, the ruler at the time, considered education to be the most effective instrument in the fight against underdevelopment and poverty, and also against the retarding influence of the church and estates on society. Thanks to the influence of the Revivalists in the 19th century, belief in the importance of education for economic and social development disseminated into society as a whole.

Hence, in my interpretation, the history of Czech economic thought is a story about the endeavour to correct man and all his flaws and all human matters, the story of fighting for human dignity, the story of inquiring into the paths to useful knowledge and of searching for human happiness.

Acknowledgements

As many stories there are in the history of Czech economic thought, so does this book.

I began pursuing Czech economic thought over 20 years ago during the writing of my MA thesis. First of all, at the University of Economics in Prague, I wrote about discussions regarding the framework of the reform of the Czechoslovak economic system during the 1960s and then I followed it up at the Faculty of Arts at Charles University in Prague by writing about the history of Czech economic thought in interwar Czechoslovakia. However, I changed this second topic at the last minute to fiscal policy during that same time period and ever since then – with the only exception of the work on the virtual economic library Bibliotheca economica (www.bibliothecaeconomica.cz) – Czech economic thought has been patiently waiting for me to get back to it.

I owe the publishing house Routledge in London my thanks for putting me back on track by offering me a deal to write a book on this very topic. I am grateful to Mr Andy Humphries for finding me during that fateful spring afternoon in 2014 in Prague, to Mrs Laura Johnson, Mrs Emily Kindleysides and to Mrs Lisa Lavelle for all their patience and helpfulness and all the production team, for their responsiveness and professionalism.

I would like to acknowledge my debt to Jana Uhlíková from the Centre of Information and Library Services at the University of Economics in Prague. Without her selfless help I would not have been able to use many of the quoted books. I really appreciate the support of the director of the Institute of Economic Studies at Charles University in Prague, Dr. Martin Gregor and of the Nadace český literární fond. I owe the most to Dr. Deborah Thom and Dr. Mikuláš Teich for their invitation to stay at Robinson College at Cambridge for a year. Without the family environment that I was met with and without the excellent cuisine at Robinson and the irreplaceable Glennys, I doubt I would ever have been able to finish my work. I thank Dr Mary Stewart, Prof. Melinda Duer and Dr Brian McCabe for their interest in my work and Dr Simon Perry and Prof. Morna Hooker for their comments on my manuscript.

I will never be able to thank Petr enough for always being rooted in reality and leaving all the fantasizing to me. My loving thanks go out to my gifted son Jakub for his invaluable help with the English version of this book. And my gratefulness goes to Mikuláš Teich once again for always being so inspiring and for always being open to our never-ending intellectual discussions that I always looked forward to, for his critique of my every imprecision and for every drop of his delicious red wine that we drank. After all, how can an academic be creative without a little bit of a creative lubricant?

I dedicate this book to the memory of professor Milan Sojka, one of the founding members of the Institute of Economic Studies at Charles University in Prague, who together with professor Jaroslav Petráček, was my first teacher of economic thought during my studies of economics at the University of Economics in Prague. It was professor Milan Sojka who invited me to cooperate on the project of researching Czech economic thought when I was still a PhD candidate. Ever since then, I felt this weird sensation that I owed him a book like this. I can but hope that he was following all my endeavours with gratification and with his kind smile.

1 Between faith and freedom

The Christian roots of Czech economic thought

'Therefore, faithful Christians, search for the truth, listen to the truth, learn the truth, love the truth, speak the truth, keep with the truth, protect the truth until death; for the truth will set you free from sin, from the devil, from death of the soul, and finally, from eternal death, which is the eternal separation from God's mercy.'

John Hus (1947, 18)

From the pagan world to the state of the high Middle Ages, Czech society underwent a transformation comparable to that of the modernization of the 19th century. The transformations were accompanied by changes of ruling family lines and of the legal system, but the most fundamental transformation was the process of the Reformation, which shook not only the church but also society itself to its foundations.

From Byzantium in 863, Cyril and Methodius brought Christianity to Great Moravia, the first state unit on the territory of what is today the Czech Republic, where they introduced the Slavonic liturgy, which spread also to Bohemia, which embraces the western part thereof. Bořivoj (r. 867–889), the first historically documented Duke of Bohemia and progenitor of the Přemyslid dynasty, which evolved its origin from the mythical fortune-teller Libuše and Přemysl the Ploughman, converted to Christianity around 880. Christianity than constituted an indispensable tool for early state-building.

Still during the Přemyslid rule, the sovereign gradually ceased to have a monopoly on his rule and began to share it with the owners of individual domains. This social stratum arose from the original Přemyslid officials, entrusted with stewardship of the land which they, however, gradually 'privatized' – also with its population, including all public jurisdictions, even fiscal and judicial. This process was never enacted and gave rise to the specific Bohemian form of common law, but also to the specific position of the estates. It stemmed both from the actual disintegration of public sovereign power and from the needs of the developing market; the concept of private ownership was fixed in the concept of 'justified' possession (Třeštík, 1971). Under the last Přemyslids there began a process of territorial expansion: The influence of established Kindgdom of Bohemia extended beyond Central Europe and it became one of the important powers in Europe.

The power position of the nobility solidified after the Přemyslids had died out (1306), when the nobility implemented not only the independent election of the king, but also the separation of the direct sovereign domain from the sphere of the provincial municipality. On the basis of the election of the estates, John of Luxembourg was elected King of Bohemia (1310). In the time of the Luxembourg rule, especially that of Charles IV (r. 1346–1378), the Bohemian Kingdom became a major European power including not only Bohemia and Moravia, but also the minor provinces Lusiatia and Silesia. Housing some of the great European mining centres, Jáchymov (Joachimsthal) and Kutná Hora (Kuttenberg), the Kingdom of Bohemia was also economically a prospering country. An attempt to appoint a Czech king from the ranks of the domestic nobility was successful only once, after the extinction of the Luxembourgs, in the person of Georg of Poděbrady (r. 1458–1471); he was succeeded by the rule of the Polish Jagiellons (r. 1471–1526).

The time of prosperity was ended by a crisis in the church and the subsequent Reformation, which grew into the Hussite movement. The Reformation, the series of upheavals in the religious life of Europe during the 16th and the first half of the 17th centuries, had taken place 100 years earlier in the Bohemian Kingdom and isolated it from the rest of the orthodox Catholic world. Only at the beginning of the 16th century did the Reformation undergo another wave in neighbouring Germany and thus found its historical fulfilment. (Scribner, 1994) After initial hesitation, Luther acknowledged Hus's teaching publicly. Hus's legacy was that the Eucharistic 'Bohemian practice' was assumed by practically all reformed churches. Hus's doctrine of predestination became a common point of departure for the whole Reformation, albeit in varying interpretations. (Kavka, 1994, 139–141) The Bohemian Lands had by then already established religious tolerance; in principle, every single individual could choose their own religion; the Kingdom of Bohemia was the first land where the majority of the population on the territory belonged to reformed churches or sects. The largest of these was the Utraquist Church including, especially, peasants and burghers. Less than 5% of the population belonged to the *Jednota bratrská* [*Unity of Brethren*], and only some 15% were Catholics. (David, 2003, 579)

The multifarious dimensions of the Hussite movement transformed the Kingdom of Bohemia into a monarchy of estates. In 1526, they had elected as their King the Habsburg Ferdinand I (r. 1526–1564), brother of Emperor Charles V. Habsburg's intention was to enforce a union of the Utraquist Church with the Roman Church. A number of Silesian and Moravian princes openly rejected this and granted protection to illegal churches in their territories. Moravia thus became in the 16th century the most tolerant country and one of the most important centres of the Anabaptist movement in the whole of Europe. At the same time, one can identify growing numbers of Catholics among the aristocracy, who sought in conversion better prospects for a career at court. (Kavka, 1994, 147)

The nobility, however, was growing ever wealthier especially thanks to the growth of the manorial economy. The socio-economic interests of the nobility and sovereign house grew into a point of conflict in the rebellion of 1618–1620 which became the prologue to the Thirty Years' War. Some years after the fateful defeat at the Battle of White Mountain (1620) the Bohemian common law was abolished and Recatholicization was introduced. In Bohemia in 1627 and in Moravia in 1628, the estates were ordered either to convert to Catholicism or to leave the country. Hundreds of aristocrats and several thousand burgher families emigrated. The Unity of Brethren preserved an independent religious existence until 1656 in Lešno in Poland, where even its last senior, Comenius, was forced to emigrate.

The spiritual origin of Czech Reformation consists in recognizing the signs of the Last Days, calling attention to the imminent 'end of all time' and pointing out Christianity's unpreparedness for the Second Coming of Christ. The eschatological tendency accompanied the Czech Reformation throughout its entire duration until Comenius. Although this chapter does not concern the Reformation, writing about economic thought at that time necessarily entails being confronted by it and equally so with practical economic questions (Wood, 2002); one can hardly speak of economic thought *stricto sensu*. The reason is clear – the only science of the Middle Ages was the science of God, theology. And it was the theologians who opened the doors to the penetration of notions which were to change the face of Czech thought in issues which had hitherto been the domain of the church. When these thinkers focused on issues of freedom, equality, correct conduct, fair prices or good organization of the community, they did so always from the perspective of Christianity; the convergence point of their considerations was always the endeavour for eternal salvation. And they would clearly ask whether this premise would suit today's organization of economic relationships.

Not even the most significant representatives of that time, John Hus and Comenius, were economic thinkers, but theologians. We can find their economic considerations latently, implicitly, and only in a minimal number of texts can a more detailed explanation of economic concepts valid at the time be found. Both Hus's effort to reform the church, in the vices of which he saw a source of evil for the entire society, and Comenius's endeavour to correct human matters, were under the protection of God's Providence and were firmly rooted in the Scriptures. The most important legacy of Hus is the emphasis on the freedom of human will and education in Czech. The mystic and visionary Comenius brought the second of these legacies to perfection by placing education at the centre of any endeavour for social change. Four hundred years before it was expressed by modern social science, he discovered that the root of all evil was ignorance and illiteracy.

The publication of Hus's books would be one of the first fruits of Czech typography; in the revolutionary year of 1848, these books would be reprinted and from that time, especially thanks to the Czech National Revival, Hus would be associated with the social reform and progressive tradition in the Czech history. Even in spring 1892, however, a student who at a university meeting on the occasion of the anniversary of Comenius's birth dared to refer to Jesus Christ as the first socialist would be exemplarily punished by a Dean's warning. After the national revivalists, the communists also utilized the 'revolutionary' potential hidden in the Czech Reformation, to which they directly referred as a first revolutionary worker's movement. Hussitism would thus be subjected to merciless popular humour, such as Josef Škvorecký's (1924–2012) immortal sentence from his *The Republic of Whores* (1996), that the sources of the revolutionary tradition of the Czechoslovak People's Army were three: comrade Hus, comrade Žižka (the Hussite military commander) and comrade Gottwald (the first president of Czechoslovakia after the communist takeover in 1948).

Hus's predecessors

The economic thought of Czechs, as of other nations in Central Europe, was formed on the pagan foundations of exchange as a gift which obliges one and has a reciprocal character (Mauss, 1990). In the time of Great Moravia in the 9th century and at the beginning of Bohemian statehood in the 10th century, this is proved by voluntary payment of marriage taxes based on the idea that it is the sovereign who influences the number of descendants, or the payment of the so-called rate as compensation for protection (for peace and a good year). The same practice continued when the elected sovereign became the chief owner of all land in the country. In the interpretation of the chronicler Kosmas's Chronica Boemorum (1119–1125) by election of the prince the people placed into his hands freedom in the sense of personal freedom and the free usage of his property. This situation was changed in the first half of the 12th century: The Saint Wenceslaus (r. 921–935) who was murdered by his brother and was later canonized as a martyr, became the sovereign of Bohemia as the 'owner' of all estates in the country.

In the time of the high Middle Ages, the age-old peace was replaced by law, found by the Land Court and stored in the Land Desks, and the independence of the sovereign house decreased with the growing power of the nobility. It is therefore not surprising that the myth-emblazoned, but in policy (including economic) very practical and utilitarian Emperor Charles IV, branded, in his autobiography, the majority of the Bohemian lords as tyrants and saw himself as the guardian of justice and the community of all the good. The first Archbishop of Prague, Arnošt of Pardubice (1297–1364), had a significant influence on his considerations.

It was Arnošt who published in 1349 statutes which ordered priests to live chastely, avoid excesses, wear inconspicuous clothes and forbade them to visit taverns, have secular occupations, carry weapons and have wives or bed mates. The punishment for contravening the last point was the confiscation of so-called *obročí* (*benefices*). (Sedlák, 1915, 112) This was a fundamental punishment, for it extended to the property of the church, or more precisely, every individual priest. Since graduate priests did not have a post guaranteed in advance they had to be selected by existing parishes; and these decided according to the amounts, property or services, *obročí*, which the young priests offered. Thus specific patronal and clientelistic relationships were formed in the church. Besides benefice, the second source of the unprecedented growth of church property was the institution of *devolutiones (escheat)*.

On the other hand, towns had the resources for their economic development limited by canon law, which forbade any interest from loans: this was always usury. Whoever returned what they borrowed met their obligations fully, and it would be a sin to demand more from them.

This in substance corresponded with the general awareness that money is but a means of exchange, consumed by utility, and does not create new value of itself. Nevertheless, with the development of trade, the ban on usury was circumvented by the closure of purchase agreements in which profit above the principal was acceptable; the principal was a house or landed property. (Ibid., 65–66)

The church became an unpleasant rival to the towns, nobility and the emperor; in the second half of the 14th century it owned a quarter of all the land in the Bohemian Crownlands (Ibid., 62). King Charles IV decided to take two steps – to subject the church to social criticism and to break their educational monopoly. The end of the educational monopoly of the church was carried out by Charles IV with the establishment of Charles University in Prague – the first north of the Alps and west of Paris – as a free community of scholars. As early as a year later it became a complete medieval education facility with four faculties – those of Law, Theology, Medicine and Arts, with the last mentioned being only a step to further specialized studies at the first two faculties. In order to enable foreigners to study in Prague as well, Charles divided the academic community into four nations according to the Parisian model – Czech, Polish, Bavarian and Saxon.

Studies at the Faculty of Arts included the study of Aristotle's (384–322 BC) works and the interpretation thereof by Thomas Aquinas (1225–1274) or Albert the Great (c.1200–1280). The curriculum included not only works focused on nature, dialectics and metaphysics, but also practical philosophy including ethics, political philosophy and economics. The foundation of the study of economics was the *Nichomachean Ethics*, the *Politics* and the pseudo-Aristotelian *Oeconomia*. The connected study of theology focused on interpretation of the Scriptures and the *Sentences*, i.e. selected dictums by the Church Fathers. The Scriptures were literally interpreted according to the French theologian from the first half of the 14th century, Nicholas of Lyra (1270–1349), and the *Sentences* by the Parisian bishop from the 12th century, Peter Lombard (1096–1160).

The point of the studies was mechanical learning based on the teacher's purposeful reading out aloud; the more authors the student was able to quote by memory, the better he was considered to be. We will see that this method of learning (economics) would remain in the Bohemian Lands until the first half of the 19th century. At the beginning of the 15th century, tuition also included exercises which had the form of *questiones*, in which questions were asked and answered according to previously given rules; Plato's (427–347 BC) teaching of ideas was a great theme for *questiones* in Prague.

Likewise, Charles IV invited to Prague Konrad Waldhauser (1326–1369), known for his critique of greed, clientelism and other church practices which he branded as simony. Waldhauser was directly followed by Milíč from Kroměříž (1325-1374), born in Moravia, who developed his preaching activity in Prague. In contrast to Waldhauser, who preached in German, Milíč also preached in Czech, and the reaction to his sermons, which were supported by the authority of the Bible and Church Fathers, was immense. Mathew of Janov (1350–1393), born in South Bohemia, probably belonged to the circle of Milíč's students; in any event, however, he studied at the Parisian Sorbonne for 9 years. The principle according to which human life and self-knowledge should be directed was, according to him, the primary Truth, *veritas prima*, inscribed into every person's reason in a natural way. Thanks to this absolute criterion, everyone could control themselves and justly judge others. Vojtěch Raňkův of Ježov (c.1320–1388) became Rector of the Sorbonne in 1355 and laid down binding rules for lecturing at the Faculty of Arts. During his repeated visits to Oxford University in 1353–1354, he became a friend of Bishop Richard Fitzralph (1295–1360), who influenced John Wycliff's (1328–1384) ideas on dominion. Vojtěch's last will had a fundamental significance for further development in Bohemia. In it, Vojtěch bequeathed money to provide scholarships for studies in philosophy and theology at Paris and Oxford for students whose parents were both Czechs (Herold *et al.* 2011, 183–185). As early as the 1380s, Wycliff's works found their way to Prague thanks to these students and fell on fertile soil in Bohemia.

And finally, there was Thomas Štítný of Štítné (c. 1333–1409), a representative of the lay stream of the critique of social conditions. It was he who was the first to present in Czech – and thus to the broader social strata – a remarkable selection of Christian learning and tradition of European thought from antiquity, through Augustinianism, Neoplatonism and Patristics through to 14th century mysticism. He did so in a comprehensible form, often supplementing his texts with proverbs and stories, although his texts are likewise filled with original thoughts. In his most original work, *Knížky šestery o obecných věcech křesťanských* [*The Six Books on General Christian Matters*] (1852) he focuses both on the arrangement of society and the economic principles of its functioning.

The arrangement of society to the 'three estates' corresponds, according to Štítný, to the three-tier heavenly hierarchy: The clerical estate teaches what is to be done in life (to think about God and to pray), the estate of the lords protects the first and third estate against injustices, and the third estate is comprised of working people who tend with their work to the bodily needs of the two preceding estates. But he emphasizes that the community is not only for the lords, but the lord has been instituted for the common people and should rule wisely, with a regard for the *bonum commune* and not for his own benefit. If he thinks only of himself, he will be judged as a devil.

In this connection, Štítný criticizes the burdensomeness of taxes (he precisely captures their substance when he labels them community aid to the king), that, more than the common good, serves the king in buying out surrounding countries for his children. He similarly criticizes the nobility for tax frauds when they collect taxes in the king's name, but keep two books – one for higher sums, according to which they collect, the other for smaller sums which they return to the king. But at the time, income from the royal domains dominated among sovereign incomes; direct tax was exceptional and indirect taxes concerned only towns. Thomas also devoted attention to the lightening of coins and the economic consequences thereof.

Hus's search for the Truth

Hus's thought moved entirely along the classical lines of the great Scholastic realists and on the grounds of faith (Molnár, 1985, 17). Hus was concerned not about the freedom of conscience or the advancement of scientific knowledge, but always and only about obedience to God's Truth. His call for the poverty of the church is a call for its own identity or, as the case may be, support of the king's endeavour to change ownership conditions in the country, and not a social requirement. But all the factors which had hitherto been slumbering beneath the surface coalesced in his life. In Hus's close relationship to King Wenceslau IV (r. 1378–1419) and the nobility lies the key to the growing bravery with which Hus and other preachers and scholars embarked on the critique of ecclesiastical conditions. As a university teacher, Hus was a direct participant in the struggle over Wycliff, when Wycliff's *45 Articles* were condemned by the Charles University in 1403 – by the Polish, Bavarian and Saxon votes against the Czech one. And he was the Rector when, in 1409, the situation led to the Decree of Kutná Hora issued by Wenceslas IV, by which the proportion of votes at the University was changed so that the Czech nation had three votes and the remaining nations only one together. Wycliff was briefly 'rescued' but many university students and teachers left for Leipzig University. And therefore, after he acceded to the post as preacher at Bethlehem Chapel, he probably could not walk on any path other than that which had been prepared by his predecessors. And he had to give his name to the decades of Czech history which followed after his death.

John Hus (c. 1371–1415) was born in Husinec in South Bohemia and died as a heretic, burnt at the Church Council of Constance. He studied philosophy and then theology at Prague University. A philosophic realist and theologian, his texts were grounded not only in Plato and Aristotle, but also in the entire elite of European thought until then (Wood, 2002, 10–14). He was also inspired by Waldhauser and Milíč – he assumed many of Waldhauser's Latin university sermons literally (Herold *et al.* 2011, 166). Hus was also inspired by the call, which Mathew of Janov had sounded, for the reform of society and one cannot doubt the direct inspiration of Wycliff. He accepted – as did the majority of his Czech colleagues at the University – both Wycliff's doctrine on divine and human dominion, according to which the right to retain power and own, rule and administer the sacraments is dependent on God's mercy. And he also draws from his doctrine on universals that the common good is better than individual good. These inspirations led Hus to the view that church authority is valid only when it truthfully represents God's will (Doležalová, 1996, 31)

As a true Scholastic, Hus plays with concepts and theses which he assumes from others, in passages of thorough argumentation he hastens to quotes from the Old and New Testament whilst threatening and fulminating. His economic views can be read only between the lines. To him, economics is indeed a natural part of understanding the world and the behaviour of the individual therein; it is a part of the concern of everyday life, with fundamental consequences for eternal life.

Two facts are the key to understanding Hus's economic views. First, Hus respected the estate-stratified society in which he lived and thus also the given social order and he did not criticize it. His idea of the correction of society began and ended in the reformation of the church, or more precisely, of every individual as a member of this church. Hus was certainly not the preacher of the poor. His sermons were attended by the nobility, even the King and Queen, and he preached in German and Latin for most of his life. Only in 1402 did he also begin to use Czech, and his sermons and other texts became more popular; he used in them allegory and little verses, but especially moral instruction, sometimes bordering on threats – whether aimed at students or common people.

Second, one has to take seriously Hus's concept of Truth (Ibid.). Hus distinguished between three types of Truth: Uncreated Truth of the Scriptures – that was God; created Truth – that was Jesus Christ, and exemplary Truth. Nevertheless, he used the term *Truth* in many other meanings in his texts, which testifies to the Aristotelian–Augustinian inspiration: As a mere adverb (truly), Truth is for him a weapon, the light of life and justice, the good life and life approach, proof in the form of the Truth of the Gospel or the life of Christ, but also the correspondence of a matter with reason, the highest value and goal towards which humanity should aim. According to Hus, one can only believe in Truth; it is closer to Hebraic faith than to Greek *alatheia*, although he does not deny it; reason can approach Truth only by means of parable. At the same time, only those who use their reason to study the Bible can compare their insights with practice – i.e. with what the church passes on as dogma. And such an authority is authorized to criticize the church: Not to uproot it from the ground, but to return it to the right path. So reason commands one to embark on the path towards Truth and make it the object and sense of his or her love; love in the Augustinian doctrine of society, i.e. in favour of one's neighbours.

Hus thus makes a distinction between feelings and rational insight. Although his arguments are not very elaborated, it is clear that what obedience to Christ means to him (and before him to Mathew, and after him to Chelčický, as we will later see) was to become, two centuries later, one's obedience to one's own conscience. (Ibid., 32) And it would be the reason why Descartes (1596–1650) would not be referred to in Bohemia as an original thinker, although his works would be well known there. The Cartesian abandonment of the philosophy of being for the philosophy of mind had already taken place in Prague thanks to the rooting of philosophic traditions in the thought currents following on Augustinianism; Descartes' ideas were considered 'competitive' in Bohemia (Sousedík, 1996, 44).

But Hus was not a subjectivist calling for a tendency towards one's own (critical) reason; according to him, Truth was firmly rooted in the Scriptures, although he called for active participation in the form of the faith of every individual. And this call has its consequences in those aspects of his thought that we could call economic. A clearly economic line is evident in his concept of private ownership, alms, poverty and wealth, work and just wage or money. Hus is a man of the Middle Ages, in whom there is a strong conviction of the approach of the kingdom of heaven, for which one has to prepare; and in this sense the vanishing point of Hus's economic considerations is eternal bliss, in Hus's concept of Truth. With his life, man presents Truth about themselves and it is necessary to submit all to this; *sub specie aeternitatis*, as Hus's Aristotelian approach is named by T.G. Masaryk (1850–1937) at the end of the 19th century. Men can only attain bliss when led by the path of virtue, and this is life according to the Scriptures. Virtue is neither in beauty nor wealth, nor is it in noble birth or education, but only in morality.

To put it in other words, virtue is avoiding vice and doing good deeds. Hus focuses on distinguishing human deeds into virtuous and depraved, a critique of what is dissolute and positive instructions on how to avoid it. Yet the spectrum of vices is very broad. Among them is obsession with property, usury, boastfulness and pride, as well as not spreading the Truth. Vices include dancing, games of dice, but also marriage which presents the danger of falling into mortal sin, for reason can turn into corporeality, worries about husbandry and securing children that could prevent one from rising up to the knowledge of the Truth. Nevertheless, his greatest themes among 'depraved' activities were escheat and indulgences, and in both cases he used welfare as an argument.

Escheat not only because it is a transgression of morals and offensive to God, but also because it damages the legal awareness of people and their material prosperity. In his work *O svatokupectví* [*On Indulgences*] (Hus, 1904, V/2) Hus refuses a frequent argument of his opponents on the necessity of the cycle of goods, that the allotment of escheat keeps the church functional, using an anti-utilitarian maxim that no-one is allowed to sin, even if they were to save the whole world thereby.

Indulgence (in Czech, literally purchasing and selling sacred things) is the subject of hard and uncompromising criticism, as suggested also by the expressive language he uses for it – skinning, eating the flesh of people, it spreads like leprosy. According to Hus, indulgence is the vice whereby spiritual (eternal) things are exchanged for earthly (temporary) things. It is a specific act of exchange; he uses the term *unbridled will to exchange*, when both exchanging parties are caught in sin and anyone can participate in it – laymen, priests and the highest representatives of the church, including the pope (Ibid.). Every act of indulgence damages threefold: The person who gives, the one who takes, and finally the poor – for they are deprived of the possibility to increase their welfare. With it he ranks avarice, usury, taking gifts for clerical services, taxation (tithe) and alms, the clientelistic division of parishes and other clerical posts and any donations for which the donor receives a counter-service, including education:

> It seems to me that a large part of the people put their children to school so they can be wealthy, praised in the world, and to help their friends . . . if you learn in order to be wealthy, you are led by avarice; if you learn for worldly praise, you are led by pride; and if for bodily pleasure, you are led by lust. But if you learn for salvation, then learning is good.
>
> (Ibid., 186)

According to Hus, priests are increasing in number, for every one of them wants to be wealthy and serves mammon more than Christ. The books they 'compile' are then accessible only to the wealthy, who can multiply their goods thanks to them, and 'share none of their knowledge with the poor'. As we will see, even in the 20th century, the Czech Lands would be dominated by the general idea that (economic) education is sought after only by cunning individuals and economics only concerns accumulating money.

Hus places a far-reaching moral-rational demand on every human act and all human conduct: To consider with one's own reason what is correct and what is the way to the Truth. People are capable of this, for first, unlike animals, they do not only have to follow their own passions, but can also use reason; if they also live according to this dictate of reason, they become like angels. In this regard, the category of prudence is important, in Hus's concept a combination of Seneca's (4 BC–c. 65 AD) maxim to decide for anything, but never for anything evil, and the Aristotelian thesis that those who commit sin (are evil to themselves) cannot be beneficial to others (Hus, 1904, I/1, 233). Second, people may decide since they are free, although their freedom is limited and can also be lost by sin (Hus, 1904, I/2, 311), which he repeats after Saint Augustine (354–430), and it is also repeated by Comenius 200 years later. Comenius fully elaborates another thought of Hus's, that one builds one's judgement by education.

Hus's call to consider with reason has a fundamental place in his concept of alms as a social act. Individuals have to be capable of seeing with their reason (freedom, prudence and the endeavour for one's own bliss) whether the gift they give will truly serve good purposes. And vice versa, whether the gift they receive comes from good activity and aims towards a good goal. If we take into account that from as early as the 4th century, almsgiving was considered (as an act of mercy and aid to one's neighbour) to be one of the instruments for preparing spiritually for Easter, we understand that it was a problem which concerned every member of society. All individuals were faced with great uncertainty as to whether they did not, by giving alms or making a donation, fall into mortal sin even though their conduct was motivated by good intentions (Hus, 1904, V/2, 187). Furthermore, alms and the distribution thereof which is not for the common good is a waste of a precious resource, elicits discord and envy, and is therefore harmful, adds Hus.

Hus does not reject private ownership, but speaks of those affluent beyond their needs and criticizes the private ownership of individual priests who should only be the administrators of property entrusted to them in order to perform other tasks. They are to maintain poverty in *bezsoukromí (privacyless)*. According to Hus, church ownership is the source of clientelism and corruption. And he makes a clear distinction between these two terms and alms: Whether alms truly help the poor in need or serve the allotment of an office to one's relatives.

For Hus, the existence of poverty is part of everyday reality. He therefore does not criticize the existence of the wealthy and privileged; in substance, his concept corresponds to the argument of Clement of Alexandria (c.150–c.215) in his sermon on whether the wealthy man will be saved. The wealthy and the poor need one another (Doležalová, 2017). Wealth is justifiable if it serves good purposes, including aid to the poor – only thus is one a master and not the servant of wealth (Hus, 1904, I/2, 319.) This concept is best captured by Hus in his dying appeal from Constance to all the wealthy and poor devoted Czechs:

> I ask the lords to act mercifully towards the poor and rule them justly. I ask the burghers to conduct their business appropriately. I ask artisans to perform their work according to faith and enjoy it. I ask servants to serve their masters and mistresses faithfully. I also ask them to love theirs, not to allow the good to be oppressed by violence, and to wish the truth to everyone.
> (Novotný, 1920, 272)

At every opportunity, he exhorts the wealthy to consider whether they could not act better: In connection with escheat and inheritance, he recommends voluntarily subjecting one's decision to public checks and declaring what is to happen with his or her property after they die so that no-one will fall into the temptation of misusing it.

Hus defines poverty as a deprivation or lack of good; and like good, poverty too has a material and spiritual dimension. Because the good of the soul is dual – enlightenment of the mind and the rightness of desire – poverty of the soul is, analogically ignorance or deviation of the will from rightness. Hus does not advance any further supplementary arguments and refers only to the witness of 'Truth', that the kingdom of heaven is for the poor, and to the poverty of those who follow Christ. He thereby also substantiates his requirement for the poverty of the church, especially in connection with the taking of church tithes and indulgences. Nevertheless, in the issue of how and from what sources the living needs of priests should be secured, he gives an easy answer, that the bishop, who always manages some goods of his own, should secure this (Hus, 1904, V/2, 164).

For Hus, work had a multi-faceted form corresponding to the professional stratification of society at the time and the normative theory of the three estates. A just wage is due for all kinds of work (Ibid., 158–164), although he justifies only the side of demand, which likewise bears testimony to his positive relationship with the nobility: Employers have the possibility to deprive someone who works poorly of his or her wage and give it to someone better (Hus, 1904, I/1, 227). Hus did not reject markets, interest-free loans, compensation of damages, reasonable profit in view of costs and risks in long-distance trade. In accordance with the time, however, he rejected usury, which he considered to be any, even the smallest, interest. According to him, all market, commercial and monetary transactions should be made in the spirit of the law of God and despite human nature. The consequences for the conduct of every person are clear: Private property is in itself neutral in value, as are any work and exchange relation, the character of good or evil are given to him only by the causes and intentions of the agent: 'Desire is the root of all evil' (Hus, 1904, II/2, 322).

This reveals a sort of embryonic form of the subjective concept of value, for according to Hus, all human action is given by individual evaluation of what one has and would want to have. Also, the value which people attribute to things is always subjective, although money too has a subjective value: For sinners, no amount of money will suffice to redeem their souls, and for some it could be the road to damnation. On the examples of simony he describes the formation of exchange relations (he uses the term *measure of money*), for wealthier priests offer costlier services and gain more expensive benefices.

Hus wrote the core of his thoughts into *Šest bludů* [*The Six Heresis*] (Hus, 1904, V/2), which he had carved into the walls at Bethlehem Chapel so that ordinary people could become familiar with them. This included his thoughts on the rejection of anathema or another religious motion made by a person in sin and that it is fitting to listen to God more than man. It was precisely these thoughts that led to the revolutionizing of his followers and paved the way towards the Hussite Revolution – and the Czech Reformation. Jakoubek from Stříbro (c. 1373–1429), the first Hussite theologian, radically thought through Hus's message and interpreted it as a summons to fight. Hus's economizing thoughts were realized in Hussite Tabor, founded in South Bohemia in 1420 in an attempt to apply consistently the principle of *bonum commune est melius boni unius* there should be no poor or oppressed, no fees and taxes should be paid either to the church or establishment, for there should be no establishment anyway – Christ should rule and all communal property should be common. *Confessio Taboritarum*, the work in defence of the Taborites, written by Mikuláš of Pelhřimov (c.1385- c.1459) is, together with Hus's work *O církvi* [*De Ecclesia*] and Comenius's (Komenský) *Všeobecná porada o nápravě věcí lidských* [*General Advice for the Correction of Human Matters*], considered to be one of the three most significant intellectual contributions of the Czech Reformation.

Outside of the Reformation

Hus's legacy, however, is more colourful than the history of the Hussite movement suggests (Macek, 1965). From the economic perspective, Petr Chelčický is a fundamental thinker who brought Hus's theories into the form of the autonomous agrarian community without buyers and sinful artisans, in which everyone made a living with their own hands. Because he rejected war as a solution to social conflict, he became thoroughly unacceptable for the Hussite radical movement.

Petr Chelčický (c.1390–c.1460), a son of the South Bohemian gentry, did not have a university education. Nevertheless, he knew Hus and Jakoubek personally, and he also knew the texts of Thomas Štítný of Štítné, who inspired him to make interpretations in a comprehensible form in Czech. He radicalized Hus's requirement for life in Truth into the form of a maxim, that the antichrist is anyone who confesses Christ only in word but does not live according to the command of love for one's neighbour and does not put up resistance to evil; for him, it was especially wealthy priests and church dignitaries who were 'spiritual hypocrites'. Petr thereby added a penetrating social significance to the standard medieval thesis on the triviality of humanity: It can be surpassed only by emphasis on the spiritual dimension of being and obeying superiors only if their commands do not contravene God's commands.

In his works *Siet' viery pravé* [*The Net of True Faith*] (2011) and the *Postila* (1966), he expressed the view that not only preachers, but also spiritually advanced laymen should lead the people spiritually. This is a fundamental dramatization of the clash between the requirements of the world and one's conscience, which Hus indicated in his concept of alms. While Hus's concept is relative, Petr's demand is absolute: He deprives church authorities of their entitlement not because they live in sin, but from the very substance, and entirely rejects the institutional dimension of the church. Obedience to the law of God is revealed in the freedom of those who are able to release themselves from secular matters and authorities, rely on their own industriousness and not on others, with the exception of God. All human action has to have a moral basis – and then there will be no need for laws or governments, which are a pagan custom (although he concedes that neither is avoidable against evil).

He radically sets a new dimension of equality when he identifies the medieval division of society into three estates as being in the sharpest opposition to the Bible, based on lies and paganism. Yet he was the first thinker to uncover the semantic content of used terms when showed the real content of a particular estate (Herold *et al.* 2011, 334–336). According to him, the most serious economic consequence of the division of society is war, violence on people, which besides causing suffering, shifts resources towards supplying the military and thereby decreases the prosperity of the inhabitants and causes poverty. The second one is the production and consumption of luxury goods – food, clothing and housing.

Around 1460, the Frenchman Antonio Marini of Grenoble, who was in the diplomatic service, wrote his response to questions put to the King of Bohemia

Georg of Poděbrady *Rada o zlepšení kupectví* [*The Advice to Improve the Trade*] that concerned the welfare of the Kingdom. Four of them directly concerned economic themes: The organization of mining, adjustments of taxes and monopolies, the possibility to quantify the volume of export and import and the connected differentiation of what part of commercial profit is 'for the good of the Bohemians and for foreigners', and finally, a way to bring trade in Bohemia 'to a flourishing state once more' (Sabina, 1866, 681–683). Marini emphasizes freedom of trade and maintenance of the principle of morality and the necessity of proceeding according to *judgement*, i.e. subjecting all decisions to reason. Buyers are not to hold 'dead money', they should not have it in one place, but should put it into circulation, they are to keep their word and not trick business partners. He also formulates many of the king's obligations: To support trade and craft to the extent of assuming entrepreneurial risks, checking the correctness of measures, weights and currency, but also to support 'economic' education. The author himself promises to write books which would advise craftsmen on how to proceed in business issues, so that the king would not have to send 'to certain towns in Germany to teach his own people'(Ibid.).

Other authors of the 16th century emphasize the traditional 'Protestant' virtues as a way towards the growth of the prosperity of the nation. Referring to the Holy Scriptures and ancient thinkers, Jan Brtvin of Ploškovic, in 1535, distinguished between two levels of life: The Christian and the economic; he considers the second as a decent and useful economic order. He therefore criticizes the adornment of women, whose beauty should be shown in good acts; he entirely rejects secular beauty, above which there is the mercy of good; he attributes to the authorities the obligation to supervise the business activity of private businessmen (Chleborád, 1869, 94).

Daniel Adam of Veleslavín (1546-1599), a secret member of the protestant Unity of Brethren, originally a university professor and a publisher after his marriage to the daughter of publisher Jiří Melantrich of Aventin (c.1511–1580), wrote in 1584 the work *Politica Historica*, concerning how the establishment, town administration and sovereign should behave in order for the nation to live in welfare. He criticizes usury, in which he includes every loan for which interest is collected, and likewise, luxury in consumption. He is the first in the Czech environment to elevate the significance of industry and uses as an example the English, who 'raised for themselves the most comprehensive industry of all the nations in the world' (Ibid., 95). In his view, every nation should process its resources at home.

The manner of period economic thought reveals itself also in town rights which, first and foremost, solved the tension between the nobility and the towns. They bring valuable information on the organization of the markets, checks on prices and the quality of goods in them, but also on how certain theological maxims relating especially to issues of wealth had been broadly accepted by the public. For instance, the principle of the modesty of burghers as businessmen and artisans: 'No burgher should have a belt worth more than two talents and his wife a belt worth more than one' (Ibid., 91).

You will be like the angels

Comenius, the last representative of the specific Czech endeavour to surpass the Middle Ages by medieval means, attempts to find, methodologically and objectively, a harmonic fusion of a Christian-theological concept of the world with his constructive rationalism. His concept, which is the last fruit of Czech millenarianism, is primarily pedagogical and includes a reform of private, public, state and international affairs. Comenius's call for the democratization of upbringing and education has its consequences in the relativization of the estate arrangement of society, which with his demand that nobody be a non-philosopher, non-king and non-priest is an expression of the autonomy of every human being. The aim of his reform effort is to present instructions how to make people human, how to organize them into unified, general, harmonious work and activity in the entire sphere of their lives, including economic. Yet a human is neither a passive viewer of the theatre of the world nor a wandering pilgrim, as the title of his book says, but a being endowed with freedom: 'I assert that freedom is the most wonderful human good, created together with humans and inseparable from them' (Komenský, 1992/II, 323).

John Amos Comenius (Komenský) (1592–1670) was born in Moravia to a Protestant family. He was orphaned when he was ten, and with the help of the Unity of the Brethren he studied at the Universities of Herborn and Heidelberg. In 1616, he was ordained as a Unity priest. In 1628, he went into exile and worked in England, Sweden, Hungary and finally in Holland, where he also died. He became renowned not only through his pedagogical activities and reforms which he implemented in numerous European countries at the time, but also through his political and philosophical works.

Comenius's fundamental legacy is his life's work *Všeobecná porada o nápravě věcí lidských* [*General Advice in the Emendation of Human Matters*] (1662), one of the most comprehensive and intellectually deepest-grounded social projects in the 17th century. His economic views, however, can easily be identified also in his earlier texts, such as *Listové do nebe* [*Letters to Heaven*] (1619), *Labyrint světa ráj srdce [Labyrinth of the World and Paradise of the Heart]* (1623), and *Gentis felicitas [The Happiness of the Nation]* (1659). Methodologically, he adheres to comparison, analogy, and synthesis and analysis which are based on the assumption of the harmonious structure of the universe – God is the creator, and the substance is that particulars are gathered into a sum. He esteems the Scriptures as the highest authority, although he quotes Socrates (469–399 BC), Plato, Aristotle and the entire cream of period theology and pre-Cartesian philosophy. He frequently refers to Tommaso Campanella's (1568–1639) work *Universalis Philosophia Sue Metaphysica Rerum* (Paris, 1638) and emphasizes that the success of all human conduct is always in God's hands.

Comenius's concept of economics as the rational control of other people in the bounds of a certain society (Ibid. 1992/II, 225) is connected with his idea of the necessity of universalistic correction of reciprocally non-transferrable relationships of people with things, with other people and with what is above humanity.

These three types of relationships have been deeply disrupted by ages of misuse of human freedom, which is why it is necessary to return them to the 'golden age' of unity and integrity. The main attribute of this 'best possible world', *mundus angelicus*, is freedom and will. It is through the free decision to relinquish one's own will, overcoming nature and natural selfishness, work, social organization and the endeavour for eternity that humans should rectify the disharmony of the world and bring it to Truth and good. People thereby replace the role which was originally entrusted to the angels.

Although technology and the skills of humans are still understood by Comenius as an imitation of nature and service to things, humans form with their work the *mundus humani opificii* or *mundus artificialis*, the world of human work and new things, the purpose of which is to serve them. This thereby achieves harmony between people and things as well as harmony in their own needs. Work at the same time forms people as such, their individual lives and their relationships with others. These relationships are based on morality and their natural instinct for peace and harmony. The skill to arrange this peace for oneself and others is *prudentia*, which in the moral world has the same role that naturalness has in the material world (in nature) and that skill has in the world of human work.

Comenius places the demand of morality, frugality and utility on economic action, which he follows from the micro-level of family economic management to international organization. As attributes of economic action he formulates perfect competition and comparative advantages; as tools of its security and simplification he formulates standardization (hours, measures, weights, coins, but also roads) and universal language.

His interpretation begins from 'the most honest' exchange, which takes place in the open market into which anyone can enter as a seller and buyer. Traders approach with the best merchandise from their countries and exchange them with one another. The utility of such exchange is indubitable – without it countries would necessarily be unable to satisfy certain needs, 'for none of them are fortunate enough to be self-sufficient in everything' (Komenský 1992/I, 109). The way to simplify commercial relationships is to use the same language, and he sees the simplest way to achieve this in so-called 'unilingualism' – the implementation of a single language throughout the world – and proposes such a new, harmonic language. An open market implies by Comenius's rejection of monopolies and oligopolies, which he defines as profit for one and damage for many, including the state, that: 'The enlightened age should be ashamed that some people arrange . . . a monopoly, and thereby exclude others from trade, taking the bread out of their mouths' (Ibid., 408). He identifies a tendency towards tyranny, which hides behind a façade of order, in every monopoly – including that of the guilds.

Comenius respects the social stratification of society, private ownership and the free choice of every individual in every economic action. When considering the issue of inequality in society – which he analyzes as a relationship between the wealthy and the poor – he weighs out the same measure for both sides. On the one hand, he concedes that the unjust behaviour of the wealthy through taxes, fees and usury is the source of poverty. In this regard, Comenius observes not only the fact that the same tax or fee is more burdensome for the poor than for the wealthy, but also a fact which had been the order of the day in Bohemia since the second half of the 14th century: The wealthy often acquire their property and their rights to the poor by means of clientelism and corruption. On the other hand, he also sees the cause of poverty on the side of the poor – in their laziness – and vice versa, he considers wealth as God's reward for industriousness. Nevertheless, he exhorts the wealthy to be just towards subjects, whilst their instrument should always be Christian love for their neighbours and the performance of good deeds connected therewith (Komenský 1929). He differentiates good deeds from paying the state fees and taxes (which are obligatory), for the state has to receive constant revenues for the church, schools and the poor (Komenský 1992/II, 405).

To Comenius, education is a key instrument on the road to *mundus angelicus*. Although education is required especially by those designated to lead, teach and direct others, future philosophers, theologians, kings and officials, wisdom is necessary for all. *Pampedia* or pan- education is in this sense a 'universal ennoblement' of the entire humankind. It is education which is meant for all and is at the same time all-encompassing. Every person should be educated, but not only in one particular thing or in a few, but in all things. And not for ostentatiousness or mammon, but rather for Truth, so that everyone may be rendered as similar to God as possible: Truly wise, active, honest, pious and thereby so that they may live like the angels. Only then will they be able to organize society in such a way that no-one will be able to miss the meaning of their role in the world, not to be foolish to the world and to be wise for eternity, to understand the world, thought and words, goals and the action of oneself and others, and to distinguish between the important and the unimportant.

Although schools are intended for education, people should educate themselves throughout their lives and especially in the family – education by example and for practical skills is the best medicine for laziness. For the needs of such universal education there should be strict control over all published books – but only books approved by the state, only original and not copied, based not on disputation, but on mathematical method, i.e. proof. Every new invention should be presented to the public and all educated people should offer their services to the country, whether as a public official, a private businessman, artisan or farmer. He assigns to society seven main estates, among which the highest are the philosophers, theologians and teachers. But as a practical man who knows that the road to happiness and prosperity is highly economic, he places merchants just behind them.

All of them contribute to social bliss through both public and private service. Public service includes ensuring that no-one does anything irrationally ('using clocks should be standard everywhere' (Ibid., 412)) so that no-one can live idly, so that no part of the country may lie fallow, so that no-one can cause harm either publicly (judges) or privately, so that public buildings (schools) can be maintained, so that the food supply may be secured and the state may avoid hunger. Private services pertain to artisans, buyers and to other 'people in honourable professions, who earn their bread and abide by pertinent rules' (Ibid., 415). By contrast, no-one who does not contribute to social welfare with their work should suffer. Comenius even proposes enacting laws to remove the sorts of individuals who prevent the acquirement of social welfare: Sluggards and beggars, usurers, speculators, astrologers, magicians and comedians, tightrope walkers (and 'otherwise useless money-squanderers') and to forbid activities which are sources of temptation (immodest images, secular songs, fictions and secular books in general, taverns and card games).

These demands are given by Comenius's conviction that the welfare of the nation takes priority over the individual one, or better put, individual and social welfare are in a dialectical relationship. Welfare is the goal of human society and should be its highest law (Ibid., 406). In other words, the dialectical bond between the happiness of the individual and society lies in the Smithian-sounding maxim that everyone is born in order to act for the good of the whole, not only for themselves – with the exception of the depraved, adds Comenius. The endeavour for the common good is in fact the immanent attribute of every nation.

Among the 18 steps to the happiness of the nation he names theological, general and also purely economic steps: The numerousness of the nation, natural wealth ('God's gift'), good administration of public affairs (including the domestic king and just courts), freedom, an industrious people versed in crafts and enterprise, for it is the source of the bounty of things, so that nothing need be imported from anywhere, the signs of God's presence and the admiration of foreign countries. In this regard, Comenius's encouragement towards activities that secure one's happiness is noteworthy, which contains in itself the germ of the definition of *homo economicus* and the subjective theory of needs: So that the desire for happiness does not remain a mere wish, but becomes a reality, it is necessary to choose a goal well, find the means that lead to it and the correct manner to use them. In addition, luck also has its place. He also recommends keeping one's intentions secret for the longest possible time so that they are not thwarted by enemies (almost two hundred years later, another thinker, Bernard Bolzano would use the same argument when refusing to publish his book) and to contemplate one's intentions with the greatest care. In this regard, he uses the same example of the tower builder that would be used more than two hundred years later by Josef Kaizl to prove the necessity of the existence of a state budget for state economic activity. In Comenius, it is meant to support the idea that strength to the lazy and wealth to the miserly are useless (Komenský, 1901, 44).

Comenius's legacy is latently present in Czech economic thought. Two hundred years later, we find Comenius's search for the harmonious organization of the world society in the work of František L. Chleborád. In the later search for the difference between state and national economy, we find Comenius's analysis of the economic situation of the nation; with the emphasis on the influence of population growth, he demarcated the content of the first chapter of every economic textbook until the First Republic. Although Comenius's books were banned by the Habsburg monarchy when he was still alive (Bažantová, 2003, 260), only a few years later, Emperor Leopold I. (r. 1658–1705) would invite Johann J. Becher to advise him on what to do with the backward economy of his monarchy. And Becher's advice would follow the same logic: The happiness of the individual and the nation are harmonically connected. In the analysis of the economic situation of the land, he emphasized the same positive and negative aspects as Comenius, identified the same roots of poverty and barriers to the happiness of the nation and proposed instruments similar in content for their elimination. But his language would no longer be theological-philosophical, but rather philosophical-economic and practical.

2 Between occupation and mission

From Enlightenment to Institutionalization (1648–1882)

'Unexpectedly, I found the scholars in this place much disposed towards the Enlightenment and, in part, to possess good brains as well.'

G.Forster (Teich, 1981,141)

If someone who lived in Rudolphine Prague had visited Elizabethan London (1558–1603), they would clearly not have noticed any significant difference. The Thirty Years' War changed this situation dramatically. The power of the Bohemian estates had been broken after the Battle of White Mountain (1618). Bohemia remained a constituent part of the Habsburg monarchy. Bohemian and Moravian aristocrats pursued successful careers serving the Emperor, but the specific distinctness of the Bohemian Crownlands eroded. During Joseph I's reign (1705–1711) there were some changes in the mode in which the central authorities approached the estates, but it was under Maria Theresa (r.1740–1780) and her son Joseph II (r.1780–1790) that reforms were undertaken that increased the ties binding the Bohemian Crownlands directly to Vienna and continuous efforts began to forge a unified, centralized, bureaucratically administered realm.

As a result of war, and in view of the epidemics, hunger and emigration that followed, Bohemia's population decreased. There are various estimates but it has been accepted that the population in Bohemia diminished from about 1,750,000 to about 950,000. One-third of the land remained untilled (Teich, 1981, 145–146). One hundred years later, in the 1770s, the Bohemia Crownlands were struck by a famine to which about one tenth of the population fell victim. Together with new wars (with the Turks or on the Silesian inheritance) this all led to a decline in the economic efficiency of the Habsburg monarchy.

A direct by-product of the Thirty Years' War and the subsequent Counter-Reformation was the expansion of the manorial economy. A major role in its formation was played by the fact that by confiscating the property of the rebellious estates the Habsburg house paid for war expenditures. The Catholic nobility – native or foreign – profited enormously thereby, for they could purchase confiscated domains very cheaply. The large estates thus started gradually to represent a complex manorial system based on an extended and deepened demand for a work force, which fettered the peasants through the system of *robota* (the Czech word for forced labour) and led to the emergence of the so-called second serfdom. As a consequence, the peasants had no other possibility for subsistence than to serve on a large estate, and their economic and social situation was burdensome. The situation of the townspeople, masters and journeymen in the guilds and artisans was very similar.

However, the rulers attempted to alleviate this situation by the so-called *robota* patents (1680, 1717, 1738, 1775), in which they attempted to harmonize the financial interest of the state, protection of the feudal privileges of the lords and pacification of the rebellious serfs; the Bohemian aristocracy prevented effective changes in the system so stubborn that only a patent enacted in 1781 established a situation where the subjects no longer had to request from their lords permission to marry, move or study. From the second half of the 18th century, Enlightenment reforms are also associated with modernization – they have been called *enlightened absolutism* – such as the Toleration Patent (1781), the abolition of the Jesuit Order (1773) or the above mentioned *robota* patent which together with industrialization began slowly to change the social and economic structure of society. The real overture to this process was the possibility to employ in the monarchy non-Catholic artisans and professionals without special permission, implemented in the 1670s, i.e. at a time when allegiance to Protestantism was still punishable by death in the monarchy.

The burdensome economic situation after the war also changed the social context in which the sciences unfolded and new economic ideas were born. The role of education cannot be overlooked. It was Maria Theresa who in 1774 made the education of the entire population a state matter by implementing compulsory school attendance for children between 6 and 12 years of age. And it was again the economic interest of the nobility protected by the second serfdom that slowed the dissemination of new economic ideas, whether cameral or liberal, through Bohemian society, and it was at the same time the individual effort of the individual noble families (in the territorial sense, their origin could be Italian or French) who are merited the most with this dissemination. Besides the nobility, the second ambivalent factor of social-economic development and the development of economic thought was the pervasive influence of the Jesuits in intellectual life, including education and censorship, which resulted in religious teaching as the intellectual standard; even after the abolition of the Jesuit order when the Jesuits were removed from all levels and types of schools, the close connection between the sovereign and the church remained intact.

The genesis of economics as a field of scientific research in Bohemia and the Czech Lands was not the result of the efforts of one exceptional spirit, but of the spirit of the Enlightenment which spread through the intellectual stratum of society and that of the ruling structures. There were four sources of economic thought: Aristotelian science, explorations in the natural sciences, empirical knowledge of the Habsburg territory and the natural wealth thereof, but also the legacy of the Czech Reformation, the work of which was spread thanks to the invention of typography. In a unique syncretism, these were generated at a time that Czech historiography still has referred to as the *doba temna* (the age of darkness), the intellectual ferment from it bore fruits as varied as the polymath and passionate alchemist with a sense for economic considerations, about whom they would later joke that he would often burn his trap with the 'court' soup. Respected university professors, whose disputations would be visited by Empress Maria Theresa herself. The priest whose work is proof of the Catholic ethos in the Bohemian Enlightenment. The nobles who were the first to conceive of the mathematization of economics. But also the social reformers, the first statistician and utopist, the first propagator of Liberalism and cooperativism. Interdisciplinarity, the Catholic ethos, the Cameralistic order and critical reflection of the limits of the Enlightenment and the programme of the national revival will connect in the work of the last in this line of thinkers who are almost forgotten today, who searched for sources of well-being, progress and ordinary human happiness in the backward serf-born Bohemia, and who believed in the importance of both education and morality for economic development.

Interdisciplinary roots of economic thought in the Bohemian Crownlands

Between science and practice: Cameralism

It was Adam Smith (1723–1790), who in his *Wealth of the Nations* (1776) divided economic systems into mercantile and modern (or classic) ones and characterized Cameralism as a system of regulations and tariffs. Gradually, and especially thanks to Wilhelm Roscher (1817–1894), a pioneer in the field of the history of economic thought, Cameralism became the German variant of Mercantilism, characterized by regulations and state interventionism in opposition to the *laissez-faire* system. In his work *Geschichte der National-Oekonomik in Deutschland* [*The History of the National Economy in Germany*] (1874) – 3 years after the unification of Germany no less – Roscher in substance adapted Cameralism to Colbertism, the French version of Mercantilism. He used three criteria in his analysis of economic schools: The degree of development of theoretical and analytical tools, originality and nationalism. Cameralism could not meet any of these criteria, which is why Roscher deleted the 'ism' and left only the individual cameralists and cameral sciences of the 18th–19th centuries. In his overview the science of economic and state administration, however, is in fact the second phase in the development of this school in Austria, whereas the period of the second half of the 17th century forms the first phase. Even at that time, the cameralists were focused on consultancy in favour of the rulers of the Habsburg hereditary domains. At the same time, however, economics was in their hands a holistic science.

The following interpretation of Cameralism is based on two premises: First, Cameralism originated from the spirit of the rising rationality of the Central European Enlightenment and scientific research in the natural sciences. Second, Cameralism was a reaction to the need of rulers to increase their incomes after the turbulent time of the Thirty Years' War. This second premise, however, is at the same time the reason why precise contours between Cameralism and Mercantilism are lost at the turn of the 17th and 18th centuries. The study of Cameralism is in many cases possible only as a study of how the proposals and ideas of the cameralists worked in practice. For that matter, it was precisely these practical steps which gave Cameralism its name. The German *kammer*, Latin *camera*, was an authority whose area of competence was originally – from 1501, when the first authority of this sort was established – the administration and management of royal property. The ideal English term would therefore be chamber sciences, *chamberism*. Until the 17th century, the authority had an exclusively fiscal significance, and it was for this reason that keeping accounts, financial administration, allocation of taxes, economic and administrative supervision were among its activities. The continuing financial difficulties of the monarchy led Emperor Leopold I to invite to Vienna J.J. Becher to help to fill the state treasury.

Becher, however, was in substance not a state official, but a scientist. His advice to the Emperor was based on the elaboration of the functioning of the economic mechanism and the changes he proposed were meant not only to fill the state treasury, but also to lift the population from poverty. Not only he, but also other cameralists were even of the impression that it was the obligation of the state to ensure that all its citizens had work. It was Becher who formulated the idea to analyze the structure of society and the state economy, uncover its strong and weak sides and identify and propose (and bring to life) the instruments to suppress the former and strength the latter. The cameralists viewed society not as composed of separate economic subjects, but, as a mutually connected whole, which is why they sought the sources of prosperity and wealth of society as a whole. Their main hero was not, to put it into today's terminology, *homo economicus*, but rather *homo socio-economicus*.

The cameralists did not aim merely to theorize; their aims were also normative. They endeavoured to express the kind of economic policy which leads to the wealth of society – not of the ruler or one of the population groups, but also of the subjects thereof, or more precisely, of the inhabitants of the monarchy. Nevertheless, they did not make any distinction between both branches of today's economics – positive economics expressed by economic analysis and description and normative economics which approaches with economic-political recommendations. There was one kind of economics. For them, the word *economics* had ancient and medieval roots.

An important aspect of Cameralism is the fact that the cameralists operated in agriculturally backward countries based on estates, without the possibility of colonial expansion and participation in naval trade (Barak, 2015). This is why they emphasized the natural wealth. For instance, P.W. Hornigk points out that Boheima is teeming with necessary basic raw materials for the development of industry in such amounts that they even export them. Becher emphasized the amount of fertile soil in Bohemia suitable for cultivation of basic raw materials for industrial production. A hundred years later, J.I. Butschek used the comparison that, if the wealth of a state is not based on flourishing agriculture, that entire wealth is but borrowed. Agriculture remained for all cameralists the foundation stone of the economy, not only as a raw material base, and therefore the source of production and connected trade, but also as a source of subsistence for the population. We find similar theses in Czech economic texts as late as in the interwar period.

Despite vast natural wealth, the population of the monarchy was evidently poor. The cameralists saw the causes of this state in the poor management and organization of the economy and set new goals for this economically underdeveloped society, if rich in resources, and offered a new interpretation of state economy and its administration. Their proposals included a fair economic order, the abolishment of serfdom, the establishment of schools, innovations in the areas of individual and social prosperity, support of public healthcare or the construction of a social and health insurance system; but most fundamentally, they confronted the state of agriculture and proposed the division of estate land or the emergence of a state monopoly on trade with its most significant raw materials.

With a view to the society in which they operated, even the first cameralists repeatedly emphasized that it was not trade, but production and the advancement of domestic industry which has the power to bring money into the country. They therefore called for support of production based on domestic resources, the products of which would only then be exported. Conflict with businessmen who imported to the country otherwise unavailable goods – Hornigk referred to them as the greatest enemies of the development of a country – was unavoidable. For the cameralists, money and precious metals were only a medium of circulation among all economic subjects, and consumption was a mechanism bringing into movement all economic activity. Their consideration of the function of money went yet further, however: Becher was among the first who accepted the idea that money is a specific commodity: 'There is no commodity as expansive and necessary as money; and no commodity going out of the country should be charged with more duty than money because money is equally the nerve and soul of the country' (Teich, 1988, 154). This was repeated by Hornigk 15 years later – money is the nerve, and to gain and keep it should be the aim of all enactments and laws.

This was why the cameralists saw the value of money as being dependent on the amount thereof, the same as with any other commodity. The price of a commodity is given by agreement between the seller and the buyer; if the amount of money in circulation increases, the buying power thereof decreases, for prices also grow. The cameralists also became aware of the problem of lack of capital. They had but vague idea of the possibilities of its increase – if we leave aside Becher's alchemistic whims, state issues (in period terms 'incomes from the printing press' as a source of state finances) and a state-guaranteed low interest rate remain.

Whilst in Mercantilism (state) support of trade served the interests of specific – private – groups of businessmen, the cameralists thought about society, including its weaker segments such as the poor and unemployed, and hence about the state and its economic and political power. The first cameralists had already discovered that the division of labour is the fundamental condition of social wealth. According to them, division of labour was not the product of nature or divine organization of the world, but rather the piece of work of man implemented into the economy. They were therefore able to examine the limits for social welfare represented by the guild system and by the second serfdom.

To them, welfare was a social category based not on trade (and the active balance thereof), but rather on the effective connection of four elements: The wealth of the country, the wealth of the ruler, trade and production. It is also from this that a concept of the balance of trade other than that of the mercantilists stems. The relationship between export and import is the criterion of the economic independence of a country, but what is crucial for it is not so much the 'numerical' balance as the utility balance, which assesses the number of the population in connection with the pertinent production, which is the subject of trade and the foundation of balance of trade.

Many of the practical cameralists' proposals were unsuccessful. The error was not entirely on their side, however. The stubborn opposition of the Bohemian nobility and guilds, and to a certain extent the church, was a retarding factor for the progress of Cameralism, its specific concepts and thereby capitalism in Bohemia. The first of the cameralists who operated in Bohemia, Becher, spoke of the nobility with great contempt; he viewed the noble as a tyrant, an ignoramus who only drinks, gambles, dances and oppresses his subjects: 'Those who do not need them should keep away from them; those who have to live with them fear them, as for those who are subjected to them, it would be better for them to live in Turkey' (Klíma, 1965, 106). He therefore warned emphatically against state attempts to support the establishment of manufacturers by the domestic nobility. Hornigk even wrote that it would be not a blessing for business, but the destruction thereof. And history proved him right, at least in the way he estimated the reaction of the nobility – its representatives were willing to make concessions towards the Emperor's modernizing patents only at the price of yields from such activities or state subsidies for their own entrepreneurial activities, which was naturally in contrast to the intentions of the cameralists.

The great trio: Becher, Hornigk, Schröder

When Wilhelm Roscher labelled economists operating in the Habsburg monarchy as one of the streams of thought of German Mercantilism, he at the same time divided them into three groups: into the scientific, practical-conservative and practical-progressive streams of thought. All cameralists operating in the Bohemian Crownlands in the second half of the 17th century fell into the last group, and Becher is to this day labelled as the leading representative of German (Austrian) Mercantilism.

Johann Joachim Becher (1635 or 1625–1682) was born in Speyer, to a family of a Protestant pastor who later converted to Catholicism (Teich, 1988). After a several-year stay in Sweden, he was the personal doctor of the Archbishop and Elector of Mainz Johann Philip von Schönborn, in whose services he also began to focus on economy. In the services of Elector of Bavaria Ferdinand Maria he visited numerous Dutch factories, especially in silk farming. In 1666, he was invited to Vienna, appointed by the Commercial Council, and from that moment on, all economic innovations by the Viennese court are connected with his name. As early as in that same year, he gained from Emperor Leopold I an approval for economic activity in the territory of the Habsburg hereditary domains. When he fell out of favour in 1674, he left for Holland and then to London, where he died forgotten.

We can get an idea of Becher's economic thought especially by drawing from his *Politischer Discurs* [*Political Discourse*] (1688). In the theoretical part, Becher elaborates on civil society, on the form of government and those who rule, on those who are ruled, but especially on the mode in which society (also economically) runs. He attached to this numerous calculations, documents and agreements of his own proposals for establishing manufacturers or colonial businesses – whether Austrian or Bavarian – which proved his entrepreneurial activities.

In Becher's concept of society and its functioning, natural sciences are interwoven with economics in a unique way. According to Becher, the state is a community abounding in people and providing plentiful subsistence, and it is at the same time the highest employer. The first obligation of the state is to supervise that all are employed. Because all subjects are to work, albeit by force, there have to be factory houses, and work houses there as well as market halls and stores as a means towards maintaining cheap living expenses and facilitating exchange of goods; the bank has to specifically control commerce with money. The inhabitants are of two sorts. The larger group is the economically active one and comprises three estates: Peasant, artisans and merchants. The smaller group is here to serve the latter and includes, apart from the feudal authority, clergy, scholars, medics, apothecaries, barbers, bathhouse assistants and soldiers. Each of the named groups needs the others for their lives: Without peasants, the other inhabitants would have nothing to eat. A hundred peasants produce raw material from which one artisan manufactures a product. And in turn a hundred artisans are engaged in producing goods to be sold by one merchant. According to Becher, the merchant is decisive for the functioning of economic activities, although he has in mind small rather than large merchants. It is indeed merchants who ensure that goods go from one group to another. In this society divided by the division of labour it is consumption which holds all of the groups together.

Through these considerations, Becher demonstrates that he is aware of the changing social situation in Europe, where the old feudal forces give way to the incoming capitalist ones, and clearly expresses economic realities connected with the expanding number of things which undergo the process of purchase and sale, and the growth of the role of business capital. At the same time Becher demonstrates the extent to which his economic thought is interdisciplinary, based on his knowledge of the natural sciences and natural philosophy (Teich, 1988, 151). Becher's leading idea of circulation based on the underlying principle of the natural and economic order of things clearly springs from his metallurgical and chemical interests, which he shared with his English contemporaries Boyle, Locke and Newton (Teich, 2015, 115–117). In his theory of money he also adds alchemy to the natural sciences. In this question Becher emerges as someone who unquestionably believed that transmutation was possible.

Therefore, while his knowledge of the chemical properties of metals enabled him to understand the fact that money is a commodity, it was interdisciplinarity that enabled him to apply the concept of circulation on economic processes. His economic thought is cyclic and connected with the idea of *recurrence* and *continuity*. Precisely at that time when Becher considered how society functions on the principle of circulation (consumption), the Austrian Emperor began to take an interest in how to increase both the efficiency of his economy and the state revenues which were in constant financial difficulties. In February 1666, at Becher's behest, a Commercial Council was brought into being in Vienna as an institution supporting the development of domestic industry, monitoring the prices and level of consumption, but also monitoring cash flows and foreign trade of products and raw materials. The Council was therefore able to assist the establishment of factories for wool processing as close as possible to the sources of raw materials, i.e. in Bohemia.

Besides this Becher also established 'his' work houses and factories, submitted proposals for the elimination of the guilds and for the implementation of tariffs as a defence against import, the formation of the Austrian equivalent of the East India and West India Company, for a company for trade with Holland, and other institutions. In his suggestions, he reflects his concept of good government which does not suffer from harmful monopoly; production and trade lead to the prosperity of all and keep money in the country. In his suggestions – like in Comenius's – raw materials are processed domestically and are exported only once processed, are sold and bought abroad without intermediaries, and foreign inspiration and experience are utilized. The last-named principle appears to be an open door of sorts, so that the monarchy can, contrariwise, invite experts from abroad.

The institutions suggested by Becher did not last long, however. For instance, by establishing work houses Becher hoped to employ all who were able to work. We can fully appreciate the effort when we take into consideration the institution of second serfdom; outside the system only people on the periphery of society remained: Vagrants and thieves. According to Becher, a thief is evidence of poverty caused by feudal authorities. 'What' asks Becher, 'can the thief hung for fifty gold pieces contribute to whom he stolen from.

In contrast to this, in the work house he can be beneficial both to himself and society'. (Becher, 1688, 244) Becher actually wanted to teach vagrants, corrected thieves and children to work, and even considered the possibility of such people being brought in from abroad. This was by no means either charity or police supervision, but rather a search for labour forces for new factories. After Becher's departure from Austria, however, it became a real penitentiary.

In establishing a factory house in 1666, Becher pursued an intention to create an exemplary state industrial enterprise and at the same time a practical school and a type of experimental laboratory of new production. It was first an imperial, then a state and then a private business. The concept of a factory house contained clear elements of division of labour based on specialization; it had a chemical laboratory, an alchemistic laboratory, a pharmacy, there were even machines invented by Becher himself. Even this project suffered from little activity and lack of funds, and it eventually led to Becher's departure from Austria.

Twenty four years after the war, Philipp Wilhelm von Hornigk (1638–1712) saw only poverty in Austria. 'From head to heel, there is here no order in this matter' he wrote (Hornigk, 1753, 120). Hornigk was born in Mainz and studied law. He was Becher's brother-in-law and was also certainly inspired by him, although he sharply criticized him later. (Schindler, 1904, 510)

Hornigk's main work, *Oestereich ueber alles, wann es nur will* [*Make Austria Great Again*], the full title of which was *A Well-meaning Proposal How to Help by the Orderly Established Land Economy so that the Hereditary Land can in a Short Time be Elevated above All Other European States and Render it Independent to the Rest,* was first published in 1684. He here attempts to prove – in the footsteps of his brother-in-law – that by utilizing a suitable economic policy, Austria could surpass all other European countries. He himself says about his proposals that they are not the result of the work of a speculative spirit, but that the very nature of things dictates them and reason confirms them. The book was issued 11 times, for the last time in 1784, and was probably an immediate inspiration to Joseph II's Enlightened reforms.

According to Hornigk knowledge of the natural sciences and research of society leads to the recognition of the significance of technology and mathematics by connecting science with industrial development. This was reflected in his suggestions to establish a network of specialists from various disciplines on the principle of division of labour for creation of technological education and for free and independent circulation of results of science in public through scientific institutions and journals. The significance he attributed to natural research is also connected with the fact that he expressed the need for economic utilization of domestic resources, and even appealed for the adaptation of foreign plants and animals – usable in industry – to domestic conditions. At the same time, he focused intensively on tax issues and purposeful state expenditures. Inspired by Antoine de Montchrétien (1575 or 7 – 1621), he summarized his ideas into the parable of the rich man who has his wealth hidden in several pouches – when he takes from one and places into another he shall not consequently be poorer. It was his argument in favour of state expenditures into science, research and the implementation of its results into industrial production.

Nevertheless, it was the nine main principles for the country economy expressed here that had an influence on the steps of the imperial court. These partially repeat Becher's requirements for processing domestic raw materials by domestic industry, a ban on the export of raw materials, employment of all possible free manpower, and invitation of foreign experts; but they newly contain an appeal to giving preference to domestic over foreign goods, or giving preference to the barter in-kind exchange over payment in gold abroad. Hornigk expresses a mercantilistic principle that the power of the state is derived from the surplus of gold, silver and all necessary subsistence goods in the balance of payment.

The last of the trio of the first economists in Bohemia was Wilhelm von Schröder (d.1689). Becher labelled him as '*einem ignorante solcher Sachen*' at the moment when Schröder assumed after him the management of the factory house and the position of councillor of the Commercial Council (Schindler, 1904, 472). Schröder entered Austrian service in 1674, when the government sent him to study English economy. In his work he uses as a departure point the thesis that the sovereign is as powerful and wealthy as are his subjects. Although he places emphasis on balance of payment and elaborates on all its components, he tries to prove the incorrectness of the ban on exporting money using Thomas Mun's (1571–1641) parable that money is the crop that a peasant sows so as to harvest manifold in autumn. According to Schröder the state should actively aid the development of the fields of human activity that could bring greater welfare to its inhabitants. He uses the same inspiration from Montchrétien as Hornigk and says that if one resews some pearls from a jacket to a pair of trousers, their total amount does not change (Ibid., 421).

This is the moment at which one can see the difference in the thinking of the first Austrian cameralists and Mercantilism. While the mercantilist Montchrétien used the parable as a proof of the unproductiveness of internal trade, the cameralists use it as an argument in favour of support of certain components of the economy, although the individual authors may differ as to the means and extent of this support; while Becher proposed protecting emergent domestic manufacturers, Hornigk proposed placing a ban on the import of pertinent commodities prior to the start of their production in domestic factories to generate a demand for the commodities. Hornigk was closest to Mercantilism for his protectionist view that precious metals should remain at home even if the costs exceed the profits, and that it is more prosperous to buy more expensive domestic goods than cheaper foreign ones.

There were differences also in political views among the individual cameralists: While Becher was a democrat fulminating for a constitutional monarchy, Hornigk and Schröder countenanced absolutist monarchy. All the cameralists manifested participation with the people who suffered under the tax burden: 'I mean the tears and cries of the poor subjects who suffer unbearable taxes', writes Schröder (Ibid., 70) for instance, but neither he nor Hornigk in contrast to Becher, actively involved the new factories and institutions in work, but rather came forward with proposals as to how the state should intervene in the operation of the guilds and tax issues. Thus the implementation of a general tax on artisans' products, the reform of the guild code in 1689 or the repeated ban on the import of French goods is connected with their work.

Becher, Hornigk and Schröder emphasized that their proposals should be implemented in an environment which provides the best conditions for realization due to available resources; this is why Bohemia became for them an industrial laboratory and figure in the majority of their proposals. For instance, if the best wool in the monarchy is produced in Pilsen, it is not only a processing industry which should be built there, but sheep breeding should be spread throughout Bohemia to minimize the transportation costs for the import of this raw material.

Fruits of the Bohemian Enlightenment and National Revival

Cameral sciences

If Roscher pushed the cameralists to the periphery of the development of world economic thought, Albín Bráf, considered to be the founder of Czech economic thought, did so in the Czech environment (Bráf, 1923a, 5–26). Besides labelling the cameralists as mercantilists, he characterized Johann Gottlob von Justi (1705 or 1707–1771) as scribacious, but insufficiently thorough and structured and unstable in his views. He did not consider the work of Joseph von Sonnenfels as original and criticized him for what is at the very substance of all cameral books – copying from predecessors. Nevertheless, the named scientists have an entirely fundamental role in the development of economic thought in Bohemia. First, because von Justi played a major part in the systematization of Cameralism and *Polizeiwissenschaft* in monarchy (Tribe, 2006, 537–541), and Sonnenfels raised in Vienna the first generation of economists who could then occupy professorial chairs in economics at universities in the Bohemian Crownlands. Second, and more importantly, thanks to these cameralists, economics remained for another hundred years in the Becherian limits of 'controlling the state towards general welfare' and welfare itself was the main subject of all economic considerations in Bohemia. Thanks to the influence of the Enlightenment polymath Sonnenfels and his students, economics was a holistic system for getting familiarized with the functioning of the state, society and individual economic subjects. At the same time it opened up new questions on the techniques of administration, labelled as *menagieren* and objects of activity for state domains, a subordinate component of the discourse on government of states outlined by Schröder and Becher (Tribe, 1984, 269).

Joseph von Sonnenfels (1733–1817) was born in Mikulov in Moravia, as the son of a Jewish scholar and Berlin rabbi Lipmann Perlin, who resettled in Mikulov, accepted the Catholic faith in 1735, and had his son baptized. Sonnenfels studied law and Hebrew. In 1763 he was appointed professorial chair in cameral sciences at the Viennese university, where he was later voted rector twice. His first biographer, however, was far more enchanted by the fact that he was a lover and connoisseur of theatre and literature and does not pay much attention to his academic career (Bráf, 1923a, 6).

Despite this, his main economic work, the three-volume *Grundsätze der Polizey, Handlung und Finanz* [*The Principles of the State, Business, and Finance Administration*] (1765) was published in eight editions and was until the academic year 1846–1847 an officially prescribed textbook at universities and other higher education institutions throughout the monarchy. In the *Principles*, Sonnenfels conceives of all the domains of care of state welfare in the form of the science of administration, commerce and finance as practical applications of Christian Wolff's (1679–1754) natural-law theory of state (Tribe, 2009, 22). Without taking note of his contemporaries, the French physiocrats and Adam Smith (Smith's *Wealth of the Nations* had already been translated into German and published in 1776 and 1778), Sonnenfels draws his ideas from texts of old fashioned mercantilists and cameralists such as François Véron Duverger de Forbonnais (1722–1800), Jean-François Melon (1675–1738) and Justi, and was to the same extent under the influence of the *enlightened absolutism* of Joseph II with whom he is traditionally connected.

The content of the first part of Sonnenfels's book, political science, is the doctrine of how correctly to run a state, and its subject is derived from the needs of the state including economic ones. Von Sonnenfels conceived it primarily as an instrument for the advancement of a secure moral order – the task of promoting 'good' moral through religion, education and the sciences (Ibid., 23). The second part comprises commercial science, the content of which is the multiplication of the manner of subsistence, i.e. the study of the economic activity of economic agents (individuals and the state), where an individual may pursue his own interests, although these are always subordinate to the interest of the community. It includes both agriculture as a fundamental component of the economy, manufacturers and trade. Finally, financial science focuses on the study of the possibility of increasing state incomes from the royal estates, regalia and monopolies and gaining higher incomes from taxes. The reason for inclusion of financial science is clear – in order for the state to implement control of common good, it has to have the possibility to appropriate part of its citizens' incomes. According to Sonnenfels, the greater the prosperity of individuals is, the less the tax burden that shall fall on the individual. This part of the cameral sciences is thus the continuation of ancient and medieval care of husbandry; moreover, the German term *Haushaltung*, connects husbandry and its management according to a budget, and would be used in the Czechoslovakia as late as the 1920s to explain the content and function of the state budget.

Sonnenfels saw the aim of economic policy in the development of exchange and growth of wealth and as the means to achieve this goal he defined the growth of domestic production. He did not emphasize export but the development of the internal market and repeatedly turned attention to agriculture, the development of which was to be gained by technological innovations, cultivation of new crops and protectionist policy in favour of the peasantry. Instead of large estates, he propagated smaller ones so that maximum efficiency could be gained.

It was precisely agriculture that was the focus of Sonnenfels's student Joseph Ignatz Butschek, knight of Heraltice (1741 or 1745–1821). According to Bráf, his main work on economics constitutes two textbooks, *Versuch über die Absichten der Landesregierung bei Leitung der Landwirtschaft* [*Inquiry into the Purpose of the Government Management of Agriculture*] (1768) and *Abhandlung von der Polizey überhaupt, unwie die eigentlichen Polizeygeschäffte von gerichlichen und anderen öffentlichen Verrichtungen unterscheidensind* [*The Treatise on the State Administration*] (1778) (Bráf, 1923a, 9). Welfare is a key term for these works; in opposition to Sonnenfels, but in harmony with his colleague Leopold Ludwig Schulz von Strasznitzki (1743–1814), another of Sonnenfels's students, Butschek throws into contrast society in the natural (i.e. non-state) state and civil society. Indeed, according to them, the unification of citizens in the state enables the achievement of safety and welfare. While Schulz spoke of welfare as the 'ease of producing one's alimentation through one's work' (Krameš, 2012, 25), Butschek considers agriculture to be its foundation and continues in Comenius's way: Agriculture serves comfort and luxury, the state has to 'care' for as many citizens as grain and other sources of subsistence produce by its agriculture. *Economic trade* and manufactural production for foreigners depends only on the laziness of other nations, a nation which lives from such production lives at the cost of a borrowed and unstable income. These are also probably the sources of discussion which will flare up several decades later between members of the German historical school, on the agrarian and industrial state.

Butschek came forward with numerous proposals with which he wanted to improve the state of agriculture, including proposals for the research of an agricultural land and its cartographic processing. Under the influence of German cameralist Johann Petr Süssmilch (1707–1767), who was respected in this issue, he proposed the division of large estates into small farms insofar as a smaller area of land with several pieces of livestock would support one family as well as or better than an area ten times larger would; but he argues that the state cannot be indifferent as to how its landed property is divided and how it is managed as it is indeed the fundamental source of its prosperity. If we contextualize Butschek's argument – Austria had neither industry nor a working class, and the estates were the basis of the second serfdom – it emerges to be a periodically relevant argument for the solution of the social question. Although Butschek focused neither on the economic efficiency of agricultural production nor on the technical possibilities of implementing the necessary proprietary changes, he nevertheless considered whether such steps could lead to the removal of *robota*, a change of the structure of agricultural production and increase of taxes. His colleagues at renamed Charles-Ferdinand University (1638) in Prague, especially the natural scientists, criticized his thoughts as being unrealistic (Krameš, 1998, 27), and he thus focused more on the possibility of founding a 'learned' agricultural society which would familiarize farmers with the newest achievements of modern agricultural production.

Even if we take into consideration that Butschek was the author of the first German translation of Cesare Beccaria's (1738 –1794) volume *Dei delitti e delle pene* from 1764, Butschek's scientific work is modest given his 40-year tenure at the university. In several passages in his texts he cited Forbonnaise, Montesquieu (1689–1755) and Mirabeau (1715–1789), but there is no mention anywhere of Adam Smith, who had published his main work when Butschek was 35 years old and was at the time an active professor at two faculties of the university in Prague. But it is true that the same – the absence of mention of Smith – can be said of all economic texts which were published in Austria in 1776–1796; some professors had boasted that they had not written a single line – whether with Smith or without him (Gruber, 1924, 112), which is incidentally in sharp contrast with the general conviction that the cameralists were a group of writers (Wakefield, 2005).

A different image of Butschek as an economist emerges when we also attribute to him the anonymous work *Briefe zweener Boehmen über einige die Staatsverfassung ihres Vaterlands betrefende Gegenstände* [*The Letters to all the Bohemians about the Fatherland's Constitution*] from 1777, a small work written originally in the form of letters (Bráf, 1923a, 10), full of caustic tirades against Austrian economic conditions; an anonymous edition would be justifiable by Butschek's position at the university. Although the work has the form of a reflection of the era, more practical than theoretical, it enables an insight into the author's personal views: His ideal is a closed self-sufficient economy, the foundation of which is agriculture, and social inequality as a stumbling block to the growth of prosperity is a crucial problem in society. He places himself on the side of self-sufficiency against the deregulation of foreign trade and on the limitation of export of raw materials in favour of domestic industry. He criticizes the high tax burden and those who 'helped themselves' to a certain type of affluence, who only chase nobility and positions in the state service and label peasants as coarse, uneducated and stupid. He proposes monopolization of the grain trade by means of joint-stock banks (at the time, Austria suffered from changing periods of harsh winters, droughts and floods, which led to recurring famines) for the purpose of regulating its price, with the aim of preventing 'destructive reciprocal competition' among the peasants in years of good harvests.

Other works from this period which can still be categorized among 'economics' are of a purely descriptive character and in terms of the period were included under the area of statistical writings. Yet statistics were more a doctrine on *state landmarks* than an instrument of quantitative analysis. The first statistician of this type was Josef Antonín knight Riegger (1743–1795), who worked as a teacher of general state and international law, but the result of his scientific activities is the statistical *Materialien zur alten und neuen Statistik von Böhmen in*

12 parts (1787–1799) [*Working Papers about the Old and New Bohemian Statistics*], the *Archiv für Geschichte und Statistik von Böhmen* in three volumes (1792–1795) [*The Historical and Statical Archive of the Bohemia*] and unfinished *Skizze einer statist. Landeskunde Böhmens* [*The Outline of the Bohemian Statistics*] in three volumes (1796). All contain descriptions of natural wealth, the population, the state of education, industry and agriculture, but also public institutions. A hundred years later, these works would be a source of information for the first texts of Albín Bráf and his students (Bráf, 1923c, 7). Moreover, a student of the professor of statistics in Vienna at the time, Heinrich Joseph Wattenroth (1756–1819), brought a change to economic thought in Bohemia.

Václav Gustav Kopetz: break with tradition

The significance of Václav Gustav Kopetz (1781–1857), born in Planá in West Bohemia, lies in the critique of Sonnenfels's work and in the introduction of Smith's works and the German historical school to the Czech academic environment. He especially saw Karl Heinrich Rau (1792–1870) as an authority, but quoted also – besides Adam Smith – J.C.L. Simonde de Sismondi (1773–1842), Friedrich List (1789–1846), Henri de Saint-Simon (1760–1825), Charles Fourier (1772–1837) and Robert Owen (1771–1858); surprisingly, he does not mention David Ricardo (1772–1873) even when describing land rent. He assumes a markedly critical stance to everyone except the physiocrats, and labels many – especially the socialists – as economic dreamers (Bráf, 1923a, 15–16.) He dismisses Smith's theory as a mere synthesis of mercantilistic and physiocratic doctrine; Kopetz claimed that application of theory to practical policy is possible only given the use of relevant methods – appropriate to the given theory – but in Smith's work he did not see this logical instrument of economic analysis based on economic interest from which it would be possible to deduce certain regularities or even patterns of economic life. He only later admitted that Smith's industrial structures are irrefutable. He criticizes Friedrich List for the arrogance with which he presumes to offer his new system as against Smith's cosmopolitanism, when he in fact offers only a markedly 'tired' version of Mercantilism. Thus it is only with the physiocrats that he shares the 'old' Becherian conviction of the naturalness of economic life which stems from the same source as the laws of the natural sciences.

Practical interpretations dominate over the theoretical in Kopetz's own work, and his point of departure is cameralistic – the state and its needs – although he grounds the implementation of pertinent policies on new theory, the German historical school, as the *Österreische politische Gesetzkunde* [*Austrian Political Law*] (two volumes, 1807, 1819), a systematic interpretation of political administration in Austria and the Bohemian Crownlands and in Galicia, and the *Allgemeine oesterrichosche Gewerbegesetzkunde* [*General Austrian Trade*] (two volumes, 1829–1830), a careful interpretation of the current trade legislation and practice, show.

The mathematization of economics and its noble cultivators

Some of Kopetz's contemporaries had already embarked on the path of systematic interpretation of economics and its formalization and mathematization. Foremost, Georg Franz August Count Buquoy (1781–1851), a polymath and a representative of later Enlightenment, a philosophizing poet, mathematician, natural scientist, expert on technology, politics and economy, was the son of one of the first freemasons in Prague, Leopold Adalbert Count Longueval-Buquoy (1744–1795). His ancestor, emperor's general Charles Bonaventure, Count of Buquoy/Bucquoy, originally from the Spanish Netherlands, arrived in Bohemia with Catholic troops in 1618, and in 1620 he received the confiscated property belonging to the Czech nobleman Petr of Švamberk as a payment of the emperor's debt for unpaid soldiers' pay. Although W. Roscher in his *History* (1874, 664) values him more for his knowledge of natural sciences and does not credit him much in economic issues, Buquoy left fundamental texts proving the level of economic thought in Bohemia in the first half of the 19th century. He constructed his concept of economics on a critical reception of Smith, to whom he frequently refers, and considers Smith's interpretation of economic systems in the *Wealth of Nations* as the only correct one for its correspondence to the natural character of economic processes.

Buquoy understood Smith's methodological approach and was able to apply it to practical policy. He demonstrates this in his main work *Die Theorie der Nationalwirtschaft nach einem neuen Plane u. mehreren eigenen Ansichten* [*The Theory of National Economy*] (1815), which is, after the pattern of Becher's *Politischer Discurs*, divided into a theoretical part with technical supplements. Buquoy perceived economics as a theoretical and technical science. He fills the technological part with numerous technical diagrams, mathematical formulas and calculations, but also takes into account physiology and physics. He criticized antecedent economists for 'not using such important tool as mathematical analysis to the degree that would be suitable for an economics' (Bráf, 1923a, 17). At the same time, he is aware of the weaknesses of using mathematics in economics and expressly abandons it where 'psychological and physiological circumstances arise' (Ibid.). Despite the fact that his contemporaries labelled his *mathematical* economics as unclear and obscure, for the language of algebra, William Stanley Jevons (1835–1882) in his *Theory of Political Economy* (1871, 1888) states him as being among the first cultivators of the quantitative methods in economics and places him in the ranks of the greats of mathematico-economic analysis such as Leon Walras (1834–1919) or Alfred Marshall (1842–1924).

Indeed, thanks to the use of the quantitative method, Buquoy also sees the limits of Smith's abstractness – he rejects *laissez-faire* and the economic policy drawn from it, labelling it as the result of an unphilosophical, or better put, illogical concept of economic phenomena. Deductive method itself he sees as an expression of period tendencies to interpret economic phenomena only in the intentions of the assumed motives of the individual economic action summarized under the notion of interest. Yet mere knowledge of theory and its methods does not suffice for implementation of theory into practice, says Buquoy; it is also necessary to know under what conditions they apply. And this is not possible unless we take into account other factors than private interest. Buquoy here took as an aid the parable of the significance and role of algebraic functions: 'Whoever does not know how also to construct the formula he wishes to use, and does not even know its nature and limits of validity, becomes a mere artisan in the most ridiculous nonsense' (Bráf, 1923a, 18). It is precisely because he is aware of the interdependence of theorems, he asserts, that generally valid solutions do not exist in economic policy. Contrariwise, relative solutions are unavoidable, for which it is not particular theoretical rule, but rather certain economic-political conditions and socio-political goals that are decisive.

His further critique of Smith is based on the unjust division of incomes, which is the necessary consequence of the situation when the wealth of a nation is based on the surplus of annual production over annual consumption. This is why Buquoy adds to Smith's theory Becher's requirement of general welfare in all social classes: The highest goal, according to him, is not the greatest possible production, but the greatest and most lasting consumption 'divided to the very limits of civic welfare' (Ibid., 19). A hundred years later, Buquoy's sentence that the 'goal of economic policy is the ideal of self-sufficient national economy if it runs on the subjects of consumption of the broadest stratums' (Ibid.) will be almost literally adopted by Karel Engliš. But in Buquoy's concept, such self-sufficiency had its limits. On the one hand, in order to secure the consumption of its citizens through import without intermediaries, a country without access to the sea has to develop as many industrial fields as possible by using 'customs barriers'. On the other hand, these have to be removed after industry has been built because of the threat of price growth in the closed economic space.

Nevertheless, despite recognition of the significance of industrial production, agriculture and the preservation of 'a strong and healthy' rural population remained for him the foundation of individual and social welfare. Against the depopulation of the countryside he proposes the introduction of machines in agriculture and even to farming cattle which also deprive people of certain work. And finally, in his texts we hear a repetition of Becher's emphasis on the role of civic society and the significance of education: 'A productive worker [does not mean – AD] such workers who exert their strength to exhaustion like cattle, but the kind who attain their subsistence with moderate strain and find time to continue in the education of the soul in which everyone as a human should participate' (Ibid.).

If Buquoy was a representative of moderate criticism of Adam Smith, Alois Lexa, knight of Aehrenthal (1777–1843), who Roscher in his *History* renamed Ehrethal, was among the exponents of Smith and Frédéric Bastiat

(1801–1850). In his work, it is noteworthy not only that he endeavours wherever possible to insert a mathematical device, but also that instead of using foreign language terms, he creates his own economic terms in Czech. The breadth of Lexa's economic interests is demonstrated by his three-volume work *Staatswirtschaftliche Aufsätze in strenger Beziehung auf Zeitumstände und besonderer Rücksicht auf Böhmen* [*Essay on State Economy in its Relation to History with Special Attention on Bohemia*] (1801–1802), *Über das öffentliche Schuldenwesen* [*On Public Debt Policy*] *(1810)* and *Staatswirtschaft nach Naturgesetzen* [*State Economy According to the Natural Law*] *(1819)*. He there focuses on the relationship between the peasants and the authorities and the possibility of its reform, the position of the Jewish population in the Bohemian Crownlands, public finance and crediting, including instruments for strengthening the capital facilities of the Bohemian Crownlands. The axis of his considerations was the position of public power in the economy, including such categories as price and value, money and debts – private and state – and pertinent legislation, including tax or trade. He based his considerations on the premise that the only genuine and true economy (cleared from randomness and arbitrariness) is that that rests on natural laws. According to Lexa, the very existence of the naturalness of things is given by the fact that many events and facts in economic life are repeated in various countries and nations. The inspiration by Bastiat is demonstrated in Lexa's reasoning that every pressure which prevents the effect of natural laws causes a counter-pressure which not only thwarts all the original intentions, but elicits yet new, unintended problems.

This critic of modern Austrian economic (mercantilistic) measures labelled any state intervention as arbitrariness. The state should exclusively remove barriers to the development of the economy, not create them, and it should not even form any supportive measures for domestic industry: 'If the state economy is neither able to take the broad way of arbitrariness (i.e. state control) nor the natural path fully, and a path midway is adapted for it, it is a safe way for everything to go astray' (Ibid., 21). Lexa is thus the first critic of the third path so favoured in the Czech environment in the future.

Bernard Bolzano and the Catholic ethos of the Bohemian Enlightenment

A contemporary of Buquoy's and Lexa's, if an entirely different thinker, Bernard Bolzano, is proof of the Catholic ethos of the Enlightenment in the Bohemian Crownlands. This mathematician, logician, philosopher, but most importantly theologian, influenced an entire generation of students at Prague University – as a preacher at the university Church of St Salvador. In his sermons, he connected scriptural interpretation with an interpretation of the newest directions of social thought and his own original ideas that, for another hundred years, became an inspiration to every social thinker in the

Bohemian Crownlands. But he also markedly affected the broad spectrum of his contemporaries from other areas of social and scientific life, with whom he maintained friendly relations.

Bernard Bolzano (1781–1848) was born in Prague to a businessman's family. Italian on his father's side and German on his mother's, he professed throughout his life his Czech national feeling through territorial citizenship and cultural solidarity (Vozka, 1937, 5). He studied mathematics and philosophy at the Faculty of Arts at the Charles-Ferdinand University in Prague, eventually settling in theology, which he also lectured in at the university as of 1805. After the strengthening of the absolutist regime in the monarchy, he was deprived of his professorship in 1819, and his philosophical and theological texts were banned by the church. For the rest of his life, he lived in seclusion and only thanks to the support of his friends. His work endured in spite of this – in logic and philosophy of science he is evaluated especially for his *Wissenschaftslehre* [*Theory of Science*] (1837), which covers not only the philosophy of science, but also epistemology and pedagogy, and for his posthumously published *Paradoxien des Unendlichen* [*The Paradoxes of the Infinite*] (1851). His name is of fundamental significance in mathematics, for he was among the first who required precision in mathematic analysis, and he was the first who treated exactly the concept of the infinite; the first purely analytical proof of the intermediate value theorem – Bolzano's theorem – is named after him. His mathematical and philosophical work also influenced such figures in the history of mathematics, philosophy and philosophy of science as Georg Cantor (1845–1918), Richard Dedekind (1831–1916), Bertrand Russel (1872–1970), Rudolf Carnap (1891–1970), Willard Quine (1908–2000) and Edmund Husserl (1859–1938) (Víšek, 2013, 9). But his sermons were not forgotten either – in 1831, Bolzano himself reworked them into the *Das Büchlein vom besten Staate* (*On the Best State*), although he himself never published it in view of the conflict with state power. In the foreword of the work, however, he emphatically warns anyone into whose hands the text falls that he – Bolzano – would call them to account at the seat of God for the manner in which they handle it. He warns against its destruction, damage or suppression, for the ideas contained within it could bring good to people (Vozka, 1937, 8).

This book is – with the exception of the brochure published at the end of his life, *Praktische Vorschläge zur Behebung des einem beträchlichten Teile der Bewohner Prag's* [*Practical Proposals for the Life Conditions Improvement of the Prague's Citizens*], in which he describes the social situation of workers in Prague and suggests proposals on how to improve it – a text from which Bolzano's economic views address us. Better put, in which economics and the principles thereof are the fundamental elements of the interpretation of a just society, and its organization and functioning. Influenced by Becher, Cameralism and social aspects of church teaching, he plans society as it ought to be. In its form, the book is reminiscent of medieval theological works, in which the author composes a positive interpretation, objections against it and falsifications thereof. One cannot rule out that Bolzano was also influenced by period authors, but references to them are missing. Nor does he cite Saint-Simon, although the text is also in many places reminiscent of his *New Christianity* (1825, 1964).

Bolzano's new society is, first and foremost, to overcome backward feudalism, mutual intolerance – religious and national – and the unfair division of property. Women and illegitimate children are also to be emancipated, the possibility of divorce granted, the secession of the church from the state implemented and all feudal titles removed. Bolzano rejected the view that the current conditions were the result of God's will, and his enlightened character allowed him to grant that progress is possible. In his best state, society was to be reformed on the model of the first Christians: Not by revolution, but by slow reforms over a long stretch of time so that society as a whole could accept them. The functioning of society is based on an entirely economic category: Property.

Bolzano does not entirely reject private ownership, but insofar as he labels (after Jean-Jacques Rousseau, (1712–1778)) societal division as the source of all its injustices, he devotes an entirely insignificant amount of space to it: 'Let a thing therefore be declared a private property if it is more beneficial to the whole so as to grant rather than deny the individual ownership rights' (Bolzano 1937, 103). His concept of ownership stems from the idea that every individual's ownership is possible only thanks to the state, so it ought to cease after an owner's death and the property be transferred to the state. The examples he provides are truly peculiar – a blind man who will never again see cannot own paintings: These ought to be given up for the joy of everyone. He also provides an example for expropriation without compensation: If a sick man needs fruit from a neighbouring garden, the state can expropriate that fruit so that the sick man can eat it. The thoroughly considered principle of social contract and the critique of the period practice of *fideicommissum* lead him to a radical rejection of institution of inheritance; inheritance is a moral danger, for it leads to the young generation becoming lazy. We can hear in his words the later George Bernard Shaw (1856–1950) and other *Fabians* when he says that the young 'only kill their youth – a precious time for gaining useful knowledge – in idleness and inactivity' (Ibid., 117). There is also a moral aspect to Bolzano's statement that a wealthy man chooses whether to utilize his wealth for good or evil and at the same time misuses alms as a guarantee for eternal bliss.

Limiting the principle of private ownership leads to the fact that the state in Bolzano's best state has the monopoly on all publishing and scientific activity, all inventions, works of art and natural wealth. In this regard, he shared the cameralist conviction that the Bohemian Crownlands are abundant in wealth sufficient to support its entire population. He calls for state interventions in handling property, into purchases, sales and price-setting; he rules out private credit and reserves this activity for public institutions, in which a low interest rate (1/2 %) has to be paid on all deposits; he even forbids people from lending things, including books, to one another; in the same way as Buquoy, he proposes the usage of paper money for internal trade and leaves coins only for the needs of international trade. He proposes transferring land ownership, as well as the ownership of houses, flats and industrial plants, into the hands of the community of those who live and work in them.

But the obligation of the state is not only to secure for its citizens health and sufficient housing (whilst ruling out any kind of luxury), but also to enact by law owners' shares in production yields and even to cover accidental losses (e.g. as a result of climactic influences). Because he holds the view of 'to each according to his merits' in relation to work and remuneration, he proposes to implement the obligation to work and thus to force even idlers to work, and to exempt only children, the sick and the elderly from this obligation. The state should at the same time organize the labour market and thereby prevent lacks and surpluses of work and consequent unemployment, and it should also ban useless employment. The most useless work he sees in trade: Bolzano's cure is clear – to declare trade a state monopoly (trading house) and give employees a steady salary. In short, in his best state, work – under state supervision – becomes a source of joy. This is why he proposes that the state build so-called entertainment houses as an alternative to spending time in coffeehouses and taverns.

Bolzano was well aware of the impact of these steps on the growth of the redistributive function of the state; this is reflected in the space he devoted to the state budget. State revenues and expenditures should be balanced. In view of Bolzano's approach to hereditary law, the property of the deceased becomes, along with voluntary citizen contributions, the most significant source of state revenues. Besides this, Bolzano names highly progressive taxes: He differentiated between a taxpayer and those who bore the expenses thereof, and the utilization of state revenues to the benefit of the citizens justified the tax burden.

Among state expenditures, he placed foremost importance to care of the youth, including education, housing and alimentation, and this care was not to have a voluntary, charitable framework, but a legal foundation. According to Bolzano, education was the best way towards a new society – it was therefore not to be a privilege. The amount of state support for education, as expressed by Bolzano, corresponds to the notion of opportunity costs (Ibid., 126), with a moral postscript that the state thereby manifests its willingness to reward properly the services rendered to humankind and country. Moreover, an advantage for the state is that a studying youth adheres to the state and will work for its benefit during adulthood. Among the other tasks of state Bolzano included care of 'all who are unable to secure subsistence and other things necessary for their living'; this definition would be used by Czech economists for the next hundred years. But he adds that everyone has to contribute towards this care, for nobody knows whether or not they shall at some point find themselves in a situation when they too will need this care; this also concerns childless individuals contributing towards the education of children – it is precisely they who will need help from others, including educated children – or the unemployed. The state ought to be the guarantor of general insurance including reciprocal damage insurance. But he is aware in this regard of the problem of moral hazard; for such insurance could make people 'less careful' (Ibid., 211). This is again the purpose of education – to teach alertness. The state also ought to secure services which the individual cannot manage alone; a transport network or the construction of residential buildings are not surprising; perhaps the task of the state to cover transport of goods from places where it is in surplus to places where it is lacking is somewhat unorthodox. Bolzano, in a manner often reminiscent of Smith, labelled all state interventions as prudent.

Let us add that his theoretical views had their practical implications – when he published in book form his sermons on charity, the proceeds of the sales went to institutions which cared for the poor. As an enthusiastic supporter of the cooperative system, he wanted to establish the first worker savings bank in the Bohemian Crownlands in 1831, but his attempt failed. Likewise, he failed in his attempt to establish a school for the education of the working-class youth according to modern pedagogical principles or the proposal to eliminate intermediate trade from economic circulation. His other proposals, such as raising working-class wages and protective legislation for workers, had to wait several decades to be introduced.

František Ladislav Rieger: the liberal enthusiast

The revolutionary year of 1848 challenged the cameralist stereotype that agriculture is the basis of prosperity. But as is shown by the example of the national revivalist Rieger, what seemed to be a radical change in the texts of several authors was in practice only a very circumspect turn.

František Ladislav Rieger (1818–1903) studied law at Charles-Ferdinand University, where his teacher was Kopetz, but a subsequent 2-year study trip to France (where he was even received for an audience with Napoleon III) and England had a fundamental influence on his thinking. Influenced by Joseph Droz's (1733–1850) book *L'économie politique* [*Political Economy*] (1853), which he later translated into Czech, he wrote his habilitation work *O statcích hmotných a nehmotných* [*On Material and Immaterial Possessions*] (1850) in Czech when still in France. But his application for a professorship was rejected by the university professorial committee. The reason given being that none of its members understood Czech and therefore could not evaluate the text. The real reasons are clearly revealed by the response of the Minister of Education, Count Thun, to whom Rieger appealed: Such a professor would only incite the youth (Rieger 1910, 257). A disappointed Rieger left for England, where he wrote *Průmysl a postup výroby jeho v působení svém k blahobytu a svobodě lidu zvláště pracujícího.* [*Industry and Development of its Production in its Influence on Welfare and Freedom of the People, Namely the Working Class*] (1860). An almost 10-year negotiation with the publisher in Prague shows that not only in the academic environment, but also in the public sphere, liberal ideas had to fight hard for their space. Rieger compensated for these wrongs with activities in the context of *Jednoty pro povzbuzení průmyslu v Čechách* [*Union for Encouragement of Industry in Bohemia*] and by writing economic entries for the first Czech encyclopaedia, the publishing of which he managed and which carries his name. He thus had nonetheless a fundamental impact on the broad Czech public awareness of economics.

Rieger did not come up with any ground-breaking ideas, but it is interesting to observe how enthusiastically and originally he translated and interpreted English and French thinkers, especially Adam Smith, Jean-Baptiste Say (1767–1832), Frédéric Bastiat and Henry Charles Carey (1793–1879). Nevertheless, he did not always entirely agree with them. He divided economy according to two main figures – the individual and the government – into national and government (state) economy. These two areas are distinguished from one another by the role the state plays in them. The economy is based on Rieger's liberal conviction that all individuals take care of their needs as best they can themselves, and the government should therefore only enact laws adjusting individual economic activity and, as the case may be, protect its members: Rieger uses the term economic *care taking activity* of government, and considers it as a *negative*; in this regard, he explicitly mentions education, security and justice. At the same time, the government should act for the welfare of all by running its own business and act as an individual; this is a *positive* activity and includes state enterprises in the trades or schooling, providing credits and banking, and in transport and communications. A key Rieger category is welfare in a typical Becherian-Bolzanian concept; it enables the *civilizing of manners*, level of education, and likening for spiritual matters.

In one aspect, Rieger tries to surpass Smith's concept. He proves the contribution to welfare also through *non-productive* or *intellectual* work: Artists, teacher, inventors and doctors – all enrich the life of man and have a share in social welfare (Rieger, 1850, 62–63). But in substance, he is opposed to intellectual possession becoming the subject of political economy; this would be 'the creature blaspheming against its creator, a degradation and dishonouring of the entire intellectual sphere' (Ibid., 76). According to Rieger, all work – whether material or immaterial – which creates material (not immaterial) possession is productive. Among productive factors he also names ingenuity as the ability of improvement and discovering and defines it in conformity with today's concept of human capital (Rieger, 1860, 118). Immaterial possession is generated through education and science that bring new inventions, open new horizons to people and new possibilities and needs, and teach sensitivity for beauty and art; its consequence is the progress of humankind.

He identifies two problems connected with the growth of industrial consumption. Unemployment, which he defines as a short-term phenomenon and a result of the disharmony between the 'qualifying and geographic' structure of work. As a long-term problem he defines the moral consequences of industrial production stemming from the fact that people of different genders work together in factories that leads to the moral decline. Therefore, industrial production – in contrast to education – is not a problem-free road to welfare.

Yet despite these considerations on morality, there was critique of Rieger's views not only from the side of the nobility, but also from the church. Rieger rejected the critique being filled, thanks to his British experiences, with enthusiasm towards private ownership and the individualism and competition that stem from it. In later years and with the passage of time, he began to be evaluated as the founder of Czech economic literature and the author of Czech economic terminology; some also added him the hallmark of originality (Horáček, 1903).

František Ladislav Chleborád's inquiry into the nature of economics

In Chleborád's work all the fruits of the Enlightenment converge in a unique way: Becher's interdisciplinary roots, the Aristotelian philosophical tradition and the tradition of Cameralism as the science of leading the state towards general prosperity and the Catholic ethos. But in his time, Chleborád's work met with a mixed reception. With the exception of the socialists, for whom he became a leader for several years, his views were judged as being adapted from the German propagator of cooperative ideas, Franz Hermann Schulze-Delitzsch (1808–1883). Chleborád opposed such a connection and considered himself an original and creative thinker, which he confirmed in the introduction to his main work, *Soustava národního hospodářství politického* [*The System of National Political Economy*] (1869): 'In this book I present a structure which is thoroughly original – that is, not one of the compilations with multitudes of notes that have been growing in our neighbouring countries like forest mushrooms after the rain' (Ibid., II). Although he did not deny being inspired by American economist H.Ch. Carey, French economist Charles Coquelin (1802–1852) or German economists Friedrich List and Eugen K. Dühring (1833–1921) he built on their shoulders the original concept of what we can call *homo economicus ethicus learned*, based on the idea of the subjective theory of value and human capital. He works with the methodological distinction between what is and what ought to be and with the distinction between the micro-, macro- and supranational level of economic issues. He himself considered the theory of the limits of the division of labour, the theory of economic freedom, the theory of economic competition, the theory of commercial justice, the concept of social reforms and the way of solving the workers' question to be his contribution towards the development of economic theory.

František Ladislav Chleborád (1839–1911) studied at the Faculty of Law at the Charles-Ferdinand University in Prague. Immediately after his studies, he travelled through Great Britain, France and Belgium, where he was especially interested in the experience of the cooperative movement. After his return, besides his work as an educator in the titled Desfours Walderode family, he started to establish worker's associations, the main goal of which was to improve the social conditions of workers. He also established for workers the *Oul* [*Hive*] consumer cooperative, which grew into a network numbering 500 societies, and he stood at the birth of credit unions in Bohemia and the Slavia cooperative bank. When he had to step down from his position as the director of the bank due to property disputes, he withdrew from all public activities and focused on advocacy and scientific work. His application for habilitation in the field of economics was rejected, however. Primarily due to continuing financial difficulties, he moved to Russia in 1888, where he gradually worked his way up to the position of an advisor at the Ministry of Finance. He even prepared a project on social insurance, although this was rejected by the State Duma. He died in St Petersburg.

Chleborád's main scientific work, the above-mentioned *System*, is the first comprehensive interpretation of economics in Czech. In a noteworthy manner, he combines an economic analysis of social processes with natural sciences, ethics, legal science, the political sciences, philosophy, history, statistics and financial science, as well as technology, physiology and sociology; Chleborád labels them as 'auxiliary sciences' of economics, and explains their connections with economics: In his explanation of the significance of technology as a science of the future, one can notice the influence of the 50-years-older Count Buquoy; physiology helps to understand the influence that economic activities have on the strength and beauty of the body and its flexibility, and brightens the spirit; in philosophy he sees the Aristotelian-defined science of sciences.

The first part of the book contains the very first Czech interpretation of the history of world economic thought. Chleborád here demonstrates knowledge of the older and the latest world economic literature, including books on the history of economic thought written in French, English, German and Italian. Even despite the descriptive character, Chleborád thinks through many themes and offers an original interpretation of individual directions of thought. He rejects Communism and Socialism, for they threaten individualism and private competition, which are the content of the remaining two schools. He divides the industrial school into the Manchester and social schools which endeavour to remove the most flagrant consequences of *laissez-faire*. He further divides the Manchester School into old English (Smithian) and new English (Malthusian-Ricardian) and criticizes the latter in many ways. He considers himself to be the founder of the *školy národovců* [*Patriotic School*].

In the second part of the book, Chleborád offers his own proposal of economic structure in which private ownership and the freedom of individuals are harmonically connected with the interests of the whole. This part is infused with Chleborád's ardour for the solution of the workers' question and the cooperative system; but from the perspective of the history of economic thought, it is the interpretation of fundamental economic categories here given which is of importance. First, it is a concept of economics as a science. Chleborád rejects the idea of value neutral economics (he uses the term political economy); economics is for him an *aposteriori* and a synthetic, ethical and normative, but also theological, science. In this regard, he considers himself a continuator of Adam Smith, and contributes to the then current discussion, known as '*das Adam Smith Problem*' in the German historical school with the statement that economists threw themselves on Smith's individual dictums, 'the dictums of their master' (Ibid., 4) and did not at all see this ethical dimension anymore. According to him, all relations in society, including those of economics, are the work of Providence, and economic laws are unchangeable, for they have been embedded into society by God. But they are not natural in the same way as laws of nature; the laws of economics have to be in accord with the principles of morality. For him, the fundamental economic law is to 'love your neighbour as you love yourself'. The task of economics is to recognize these laws and express, on the basis thereof, what ought to be and also to find a way of achieving it.

According to Chleborád, the subject of economics is not the economy, but all economic activities in the sense of praxeology. He understands the methodology of economics ('instruction' in his terminology) as the construction of science according to principles well considered by reason. Labelling the Scots and Germans as the only theoretically deductive thinkers, he as a Slav including himself among the English and the French, who are by contrast able to think only inductively. He defines his method as genetically combining both methods – induction captures the breadth of the problem and its content, and deduction then finds the basic causes of the problems, systematic and reasonable (or critical). And finally, since the fundamental construction element of every scientific structure ought to be 'basic truth', the falsification of which results in the collapse of the entire structure, Chleborád expresses the fundamental truth of his system: Freedom is the basis of prosperity (Ibid., 165).

When he then expresses another truth deduced from it, it is as if Becher's spirit is speaking to us after centuries; so strong is the motive of cycle and circulation:

> Freedom is the mother of uniqueness; uniqueness is the source of trade; trade is the father of welfare; welfare is the seed of freedom [. . .] So flows in the eternal cycle the strength which is the lifeblood of human welfare. The more perfect each individual component of this resultant is, the more powerful is its effect.
>
> (Ibid., 170)

The cycle motif likewise appears when he interprets Smith's free play of individual interests in another passage: 'Freedom for individuality, individuality for trade, trade for affluence and affluence once again to freedom continue in an eternal circle' (Chleborád, 1884, 15).

A key analytical term in Chleborád's system is therefore *welfare* as a law of human nature, and economics as a science recognizes the laws according to which it is necessary to farm if we want to gain welfare. In its content and form Chleborád's welfare corresponds to Aristotle's eudaimonion: It is a state of well-being, which is not generally valid; it is rather the result of the historic process and the effort to achieve it that has accompanied man throughout his whole life; man is willing to undergo self-denial and sacrifice for it. This is precisely why the human spirit is, according to Chleborád, the starting mechanism of the entire economic cycle: It includes the moral and Enlightenment sides, which form the real economic man, not as per Smith 'some fictitious being', says Chleborád (1869, 171). Morality turns the mind towards ideals, and education and erudition help to spread the results of scientific effort to all layers of society.

Chleborád's theory of needs was constructed on his concept that could be characterized as *homo economicus ethicus learned*: In his effort to attain welfare, man pursues various purposes and satisfies various needs analogically in the instinct for regular organization and self-preservation observed throughout nature. In man, this instinct has two levels of *snažlivosti (assiduousness)* – *sensual assiduousness*, which elicits imaginations and needs, and *rational assiduosness*, which 'elevates' them to the level of will. Sensual assiduousness becomes rational when man recognizes the connection between his wishes, their fulfilment and the means which lead towards it. Satisfaction of needs which have become intellectual will bring man delight and pleasure, which together form man's bliss. A hundred years later, Marxist economist Ota Šik would make the same (rational) distinction between (economic) needs and (economic) interests.

Chleborád classifies needs according to six categories in which we once again see the cycle motif: According to the basic character, degree of urgency, degree of education, extent of needs, frequency of needs and the time of satisfaction; he also distinguishes objective and subjective needs, where objective needs represent a set of goods for the satisfaction of the subjective ones. In order to survive, man first has to satisfy his material needs. According to Chleborád, to fulfil material needs is possible only through work, which is why he sees work as the cost of welfare, and why for him 'economic activity is the activity that leads towards attaining material welfare' (Ibid., 2). He defines work as the material effect of manpower led by an immaterial force towards overcoming the resistance of nature. The basic incentive of work – historically and in every individual moment – is the need to change something; to do nothing works against it. Work, together with nature, are the two productive powers he recognizes; capital is only an instrument which increases the productivity of work. Chleborád rejects the thesis that capital is formed on the basis of restraint from consumption. On the contrary, he views consumption as the foundation of economic dynamics, and the reduction of consumption leads to *prázdnění (emptying):* To emptying capital, to emptying workers and to stagnation of the economy.

According to Chleborád, needs are not an appropriate analytical instrument of economics due to their all-encompassing breadth. Value is thus based on the concept of satisfaction. Satisfaction has a material and immaterial form, which he calls the *moral and Christian level* of welfare. Material satisfaction is naturally based on work, mainly in agriculture, which is the basis of all life, but the key role is played by level of education and *human capital*. Education supports freedom and serves to cultivate the human intellect. Education also plays an important role in Chleborád's system due to his denial of Thomas Robert Malthus's (1766–1834) Law of Population: Chleborád asserts that the number of inhabitants cannot exceed the sources of subsistence, for natality will decrease with the growth of the level of education. And contrariwise, if mankind does not educate itself, prosperity will not grow, nor will be there any resources for population growth (Ibid., 410).

Chleborád identifies in an entirely modern way a low level of education as an obstacle to the growth of welfare; among other such obstacles he names insufficient exchange of information, missing infrastructure, feudalism and serfdom, the system of privileges and guilds, the renewal of slavery and 'tricky bankers'.

Value is for him a subjective category defined as utility gained by certain expenditures (Ibid., 195). Besides this, there is also a value which people have set so as to compare all other values with it, and it has the form of currency (he also uses the terms precious metal and money). In all cases of the measurement of value, however, there is a limit beneath which value will never fall. It is the so-called *náklad obnovný* (*regenerative cost*) for which a thing can be renewed or replaced (Ibid., 187–198).

Freedom, which in Chleborád's concept of the economic cycle is the prerequisite of welfare, is not freedom in the political or material sense, but freedom as a certain principle of liberty enabling the individual to decide – even between satisfaction of material and immaterial needs; real free competition has to respect not only individual differences, but also national particularity. Because welfare is a historical term and value is a subjective category, Chleborád here extends his concept to *homo economics ethicus learned socialised*, and allows the state to enter the game as an active economic agent. By implementing reforms of the economic and political system, state has to help natural laws to harmonize the interests of the individual and society. In this regard, Chleborád criticizes Adam Smith for not understanding the role of the state. By contrast, it is clear how he has been inspired in this consideration by the younger German historical school, especially Adolf Wagner (1835–1917), whose idea that the state is a moral being of the unified will of the nation towards the common good is repeated in several places (Chleborád, 1884, 57–58).

At the same time, such a state has the right to an independent life and logically also to secure the funds for it in the form of state revenues; the state is thus authorized to distribute the yields, the *fruits*, says Chleborád, of labour. In this connection, he speaks of fair taxation and implementation of both a tax-free minimum and a certain degree of limitation of free competition, and also of the fact that the state ought to behave like a *private* businessman, paying attention to the balance of revenues and expenditures and using expenditures only for purposes which support the generation of capital. But while private accumulation of capital leads to the accumulation of property for a limited social group, the state gathers funds in order to dispense it for the benefit of all. This is why the state also has to invite the unpropertied citizens to the performance of state duties; this in fact meant the task of abolition of the existing voting census.

According to Chleborád, the entry of the state into the economic system makes the relationship between the individual and the state dialectic: If the foremost duty of the state is care of the flowering of national welfare, the highest duty of every citizen is to contribute towards this; the expression of this dialectic is Chleborád's concept of community: Community becomes society only once it guarantees freedom for all of its members, and as an economic system it is based on the principle of division of labour which enables specialization and higher efficiency (Chleborád, 1869, 172). In an anti-Rousseau sense, he sees all economic subjects as mutually connected to one whole: In the same way that it is impossible to divide the material and intellectual side in man, no-one can realize their welfare on their own (except by deciding voluntarily to live in poverty). Community is 'one organic whole', and has two dimensions: Voluntary private associational activities and state activities paid by taxes in the social area and in education, for it is there where the prerequisites of the freedom of every individual member of society lie.

Two degrees of economy correspond to this: Civil (private) and state. The first is related to the economic activities of citizens as state members, the second to economic activities of the state itself, including financial science. In Chleborád's view thus the financial science shifted from the position of 'auxiliary' economic science to the position of a part of political economy as a normative science. Chleborád's explanation for it is clearly under the influence of Cameralism: Because the life of the state is personified will of the nation, the subject of activity of such a will has to be the development of all of the community's forces. And financial science secures funds for state expenditures which are to facilitate this. Yet he refers to Plato's thesis that the perfect state has to be similar to the perfect man, and explicitly mentions that the first who understood the relationship of the financial sciences to their 'more general relative', political economy, were Justi and Sonnenfels (Ibid., 28). Let us add that Chleborád is aware of the principle difference between economic processes taking place on a micro-, macro- and supranational level. This is why he divides his economic structure into two levels: Patriotic and universal ('cosmic'), and divided his book into the same two parts. He did not, however, finish the part on universal economics, the content of which was meant to be the relationships between the states.

When interpreting macro-economic connections, Chleborád pauses over two issues: The relevance of Liberalism for the establishment of a just organization of economic relationships and the relationship between civic and economic activities. He shows the issue of the relevance of Liberalism for the welfare of the state in a light different from that of Rieger before him. Chleborád asks whether this world based on Liberalism will be socially fair and whether it will include all social classes and whether, for instance, contract with a businessman is voluntary and free for a worker. His answer is negative. The worker has only two alternatives: To prefer free time and starve or accept the capitalist's conditions and work, but scrape along anyway (Ibid., 394). The relationship between work and capital is thus unequal, and the worker is not free; Chleborád uses the term *nevolnost pracovní* (*labour serfdom*) which in Czech even carries an implication of disease. But he does not agree with the proposals of the socialists that establishment of the domination of work over capital is the solution. He sees the solution in balancing the position of work and capital so that both sides can truly decide freely. Chleborád was convinced that social justice is part of social welfare, and that social welfare takes priority over individual welfare.

And because the driving force of the economic dynamic is the capitalist, the workers must become the businessmen; Chleborád uses the term *podnikatelský tovaryš* (*entrepreneurial journeyman*) and private companies must be transformed into *ztovaryšněné podniky* (*journeymanized companies*) with the employees having a share in the profits and management. But this was not a purposeless transformation: The aim was to establish harmony between the workers and the capitalists, development of the creative power of the entire nation, the growth of a middle class and the growth of intelligentsia.

In the second issue, Chleborád asks for legitimacy of the term *national economy* that, at that time, under the influence of Friedrich List and the German historical school, had settled in Central Europe. Chleborád rejects opinion that the national economy is the set of all economic activities of persons affiliated to the state, and that it is more than only many private economies standing next to one another. He demonstrates (inductively) that no economy besides private and state exists: Every economic activity is either private or state. The *national economy* does not exist, for the nation does have any specific economic mechanism for its economic activity; the mechanism of the economic activity of the nation is either private or state. A *national economy* could exist, but only in the sense of *patriotic economy*. Nevertheless, the science of such a national economy still does not exist, for its content would have to be the analysis of the economic activity of one nation in the context of a state with domination of another state. The direction of Chleborád's considerations is clear: Such a nation has to farm nationally, through both private and state activities (Ibid., 167–169). Precisely these thoughts led him to label his whole system as *the system of the national political economy*. It is understandable that the enthusiastic Chleborád applied his normative considerations on how to improve society to Czech conditions at the time. And even if the struggle of the nation for greater freedom in the bounds of the Habsburg monarchy was, in his intentions, more economic than political, some of the instruments he proposed to implement included the extension of political rights, the right to strike, a law-guaranteed minimal wage, collective negotiation on wages, workers' share in political power and company management. It is therefore not surprising that the state, instead of considering his recommendations and proposals, assigned to him the Imperial-Royal Police Councillor Dedera – the same secret agent who, 10 years previously around the revolution of 1848, had inspected Karel Havlíček Borovský and other politically suspicious Czech national revivalists.

Although later Marxist historiography rendered Chleborád as a 'servant' of the bourgeoisie who led the working class astray and his original economic ideas are not connected with his name today, he remained an important part of the story of Czech economic thought for his reflections on how to help workers through the cooperative system; after the Great War he was followed by the branch of Czech economists connected with the transformation of cooperative ideas into the form of cooperative Socialism. But most importantly, Chleborád himself asserted that the greatest reward for his work would be another wave of *political-economic literature*. And he was successful in eliciting this: 10 years after the publication of his book, at the time when he had withdrawn into seclusion, he could watch how ambitious lawyers born in the fifties – Josef Kaizl and Albín Bráf – entered the scene.

Teaching economics in the Bohemian Crownlands

Becher, Hornigk and Schröder were already well aware that advising the Emperor was not the only way of advancing their ideas in society. Part of their proposals as to how to spread 'useful knowledge' and to improve well-being were educational institutions which were aimed at a broad spectrum of the population, in many cases even at socially excluded groups, when they proposed the establishment of practical schools as a part of factories.

As late as a hundred years later, between 1771 and 1774, Ferdinand Kindermann (1740–1801), town priest of Kaplice in Southern Bohemia, led the foundations of what became known as *průmyslové školy* (*industrial schooling*). Concerned with integration of the lower classes into the labour process, Kindermann encouraged pupils to acquire one rather than many skills. While actually attending school they were expected to spend some time, possibly in association with a local factory, in gainful occupations such as spinning or in various agricultural activities. Although the children's earnings paid for school fees and contributed to the home budget, it was not a type of child factory that supposedly allowed some time for education. Rather it constituted a form of elementary schooling combined with training for industry and industriousness. In his view, the more enlightened the nation is, the more industrious it is. In contrast, laziness and indolence are always a consequences of stupidity (Teich, 1981, 252). Taking the name 'von Schulstein' Kindermann became a school reformer of Maria Theresa, under whose influence education became a political matter in the Habsburg hereditary domain; and it was under Kindermann's direction that industrial schooling for both sexes became its distinctive feature (Ibid., 160).

The leaders of the Czech National Revival endeavoured to propagate education as a means for supporting modern economic development. Although the traditional path to enterprise or trade was still through an apprenticeship, interest in expanding formal education appeared in the 19th century. The proposals included steps that went from increasing the range of practical subjects at primary schools and improving the syllabuses of grammar schools and academies, through to the establishment of higher education. The first concrete steps were taken by Antonín Skřivan (1818–1887), who opened a small private *commercial academy* and wrote the first trade textbook in Czech. When the German community established the *Prager Handelsakademie* in 1856, the Czech entrepreneurial community reacted by establishing the *Československé akademie obchodní* [*Czechoslavonic Commercial Academia*] in 1872. Part of its syllabus included foreign languages, law, accounting and teaching about goods, a course on determining the quality and origin of products and on technology of production (Albrecht, 2011). The second *Academia* was established in Chrudim 10 years later – in the same year that the university in Prague was divided into Czech and German sections with tuition of economics in Czech in the Czech section.

But the start of university economics education preceded the emergence of *industrial schooling* by two decades and were motivated by two circumstances: First, in the middle of the 18th century the nobility had become dissatisfied with Jesuit education and at the same time saw the limits of private education through private tutors. This was why increasing numbers of young noblemen were sent to Protestant universities in Germany, because these universities offered more appropriate and modern education. Second, they were motivated by the establishment of the first departments of Cameralism in Prussia and Sweden in the 1720s and 1730s. In 1752, Maria Theresa decided to establish the Theresian Academy, *Theresianum*, in Vienna.

In the beginning, the school (where economist Joseph Schumpeter (1883–1950), but also art historian Ernst H. Gombrich (1909–2001) and Oscar-winning actor Christoph Waltz (b.1956) would study in the 20th century) had the form of a higher school. But there emerged within that setting a department of Cameralism, and the then-renowned economist J.H. G. von Justi acceded to its helm. Although Justi, according to some sources, did not begin by teaching whatsoever, for he did not want to convert to Catholicism from Calvinism, he built over several years the foundations of the system of state sciences and is considered the founder of Cameralism in the monarchy. According to his concept, the tuition of cameral sciences included basic insights from various fields which were in some way related to state economic activities. One part consisted of general political economy and political science, to which economics, administrative sciences, trade and finance belonged, and the second part was specific and included agricultural science, mining science, teaching on manufacturing and factory production, craft and trade.

But because the education within the *Theresianum* did not fulfil expectations, the Empress established the department of cameral sciences at the Faculty of Law at the Viennese University and entrusted its management to the lawyer Joseph von Sonnenfels. Thanks to him, the systematization of economic education was completed in the form of political sciences, comprising administrative, business and financial sciences. Sonnenfels's task was to build the school in such a way that its graduates could enter the newly emerging university departments throughout the monarchy. He was truly successful in this. As early as in 1766, three of his students, Butschek, Schulz and Carl Geist (b.1732) occupied the professorial chair of political sciences in Bohemian Crownlands - in Prague, Olomouc and Opava.

By court decrees from 1770 and 1771, the cameral sciences were implemented as compulsory for all future state officials at all levels of the state administration and were part of the tuition at the faculties of arts at all universities in the monarchy. Statistics was added to them in 1774. When new study rules for the university were issued 10 years later, all lectures had prescribed textbooks, and the cameral sciences were transferred to the faculty of law. Although the implementation of cameral science tuition was from the beginning connected with the need to centralize state administration and the functioning of all of its institutions, including the economic ones, narrowing it to the education of loyal state officials would be limiting. Graduates had to understand not only the functioning of the state, but also the functioning of economic mechanism generally.

Although Cameralism had by the 1790s entered terminal decline at German universities (Tribe, 2009, 25), this does not apply for the Austrian environment. The courses based on Sonnefels's textbooks continued to be the basis of economic education not only at universities, but also at all educational institutions throughout the monarchy. Reference to Sonnefels's textbook is missing in the university curricula only in the 1848/1849 academic year. This was thanks to Kopetz, who replaced Butschek at the professorial chair there. Thanks to Kopetz's student, F.L. Rieger, the standard textbook for university courses became *Politické hospodářství* [*Political Economy*] (1853) written by French economist J. Droz and translated by Rieger.

But economic education underwent further formal adjustments thanks to the so-called *Thun school reform* (1849). The Department of Economics remained a part of the faculties of law and political sciences were mandatorily lectured, but in the syllabuses of political sciences, economics was driven out by ever-newer subjects focused on the problem of administration. This was clearly a manifestation of desperate defence by the state against Liberalism. Under the influence of the older generation of the German historical school and Friedrich List, the term *national economy* (*Volkswirtschaft, Volkswirtschaftslehre, Nationalökonomie*), which included economic theory, economic policy and financial science, became common at the time.

In 1850–1853 at the university and then from 1868 at the Polytechnic in Prague, statistics and economics were lectured in Czech by Eberhard Antonín Jonák (1820–1879), who acquired a special professorship in 1849 for his loyalty in the revolutionary year of 1848. Jonák came from a Czech landlord's family, studied law in Prague and in Vienna, where he was a supply teacher in political sciences from 1846. In 1860, he received a full-time professorship. He never wrote a textbook of his own for students, apparently because no fixed Czech economic terminology existed. But it is possible that his intellectual horizon did not enable this; furthermore, one of his students, Albín Bráf, doubted his professional level and refused an offer to write such a textbook with him. In his lectures, Jonák used the term *economics* instead of *national economy* or *political economy*; economics was for him a science on laws which regulate economic life of the whole created by individual economies. He published only the popularizing book *Základové hospodářství* [*The Fundamentals of Economy*] (1871), written in the form of a dialogue with a peasant, whom he instructs on basic economic terms. His point of departure was classical political economy, he rather unwittingly accepted Adam Smith, but he was especially inspired by J.B. Say and F. Bastiat. He saw the way to prosperity of the individual in the improvement of one's position on the labour market, which could be positively influenced by education. But such interpretation was at the same time in accordance with the development of economic thought in the Bohemian Crownlands since Becher.

At the beginning of the 1850s, students began gradually to divide into Czech and German with the latter concentrated around Karl Thomas Richter (1837–1878), who had been appointed professor of political economy at the university. This process was completed in 1882, when the university was divided into I.R. Czech Charles-Ferdinand University and I.R. German Charles-Ferdinand University. Although division of the university became a political issue, the last stone paving the way upon which economic thought in the Bohemian Crownlands would be set in motion in the next decade was thereby laid. Nevertheless, this would not have been possible without the implementation of cameral science a hundred years previously.

The significance of these first teachers of economics in the Bohemian Crownlands is fundamental for two reasons. First, it was precisely they who underwent the 'struggle' with Jesuits over the place of teaching economics and its form. Yet they entered into a complex problem for which they were not responsible: There was only one lay professorship in Austria at the time – that of political sciences; it was established by the Empress who also appointed professors and bore its costs including professors' salaries. The Jesuits occupied all the others. The significance of the first teachers of economics was therefore not the originality of their thoughts or ability to reflect new currents of economic thought, but inasmuch as they were able to elicit from their students an interest in science, which in the Jesuit-guaranteed education system did not gain the necessary space.

Aside from this, conflicts with Jesuits were not avoided even by Sonnenfels in Vienna, where cardinals, the archbishop, and in exceptional cases even the Empress, participated in doctoral disputations. During a disputation in 1776, for instance, the archbishop contested the fact that a science could have an aim other than the realization of Christian principles. J.I. Butschek in Prague was not even allocated a seminar room and had to teach in his flat. The Jesuits criticized the fact that he taught in German, not Latin, that he did not dictate lectures, as was customary at Jesuits' lectures, but spoke freely according to a textbook (Sonnefels's), and that he also published, along with his lectures, a form of shortened excerpts which served as theses defended at the end of studies. The Rector of the university in Olomouc commissioned the Jesuits to add into economic textbooks short insertions from the Bible. Local professor L.L. Schulz was prevented from involvement in university life; his disputation themes – despite literally keeping with Sonnenfels's textbook which had been approved by the Empress – were rejected; he received the worst rooms for his lectures, which were also disturbed by deliberate noise from adjacent rooms. In the end, Schulz, like Butschek, taught in his flat. Surprisingly, the pressure by the Jesuits did not abate even after the abolition of their order in 1773 (Olomouc was the seat of the Archbishopric of Moravia), which was why the university and Schulz's department were transferred from Olomouc to Brno in 1778. Schulz found strong support there in Count Johann Nepomuk von Mittrowsky (1757–1799).

Second, the significance of these first teachers of economics in the Bohemian Crownlands (as in the whole of Austria) is given by their unprecedented influence on the whole of society; to characterize the social prestige of the university professors, the term *Mandarins* was used (Ringer, 1969). Their social prestige was based on two pillars: Their exceptional scientific significance, since universities were the only centres of scientific research, and their role in examining all future civil servants. The first pillar, moreover, is connected with the fact that the existing professors decided about all new professorial chairs and thereby influenced who would teach at the university and what they would research. As regards salary, the professors were categorized in the same class as the heads of ministerial departments, with a higher salary than army officers received (Havránek, 1998, 217). The second pillar is demonstrated by the fact that passing the state examinations was included in the qualifications for all state officials; while passing the doctoral examination laid the foundation for the career of lawyer – state as well as private. So the professors opened or closed the doors for a career in both the state institutions and the private ones and often took into account not only their knowledge of students, but also their family backgrounds. The son of F.L. Rieger, Bohuš Rieger (1857–1907), was very nervous about the professors who were political opponents of his father (Ibid., 221).

The emphasis on creating a loyal meritocracy in a monarchy is often connected with the famous sentence from the speech of Emperor Franz I (r. 1792–1835) in the 1820s: 'I do not need scholars, I need obedient state officials' (Ibid., 226), but it is clear from the fact that the government established an extensive scholarship programme for talented but needy students. The application of this programme proved to be a successful class-inclusion strategy. The result was that the basic reform values of the administration were successfully transmitted to new generations of professional and loyal officials (Khavanova, 2017).

In this regard, the academic longevity of the Prague professors is admirable – Butschek taught for more than 40 years (1766–1807). Kopetz, who replaced him, even taught a year longer (1807–1849). Jonák, who acceded in the revolution period, held his post for more than 30 years (1849–1882). After 1882, when the university was divided into Czech and German parts the development of Czech thought was the result of their work. Aside from this, Albín Bráf, who acceded in 1882, retained his influence until his death in 1912. Almost all of the First Czechoslovak Republic economists, whether theoretical or practical, were his students.

Enlightenment's economic sentiment in the Bohemian Crownlands

The encouragement of economics

University education remained an elitist matter and the number of students in the whole university was only in the hundreds. This led to the fact that, despite the undeniable scientific talent and unflagging effort of several generations of Czech pioneers of economic thought, their insights remained for a long time without broader social response. This is why in the Bohemian Crownlands *učené společnosti* (*learned societies*) in the spirit of the best Enlightenment traditions endeavoured to acquaint the broadest public with the results of contemporary science. Two types of institutions emerged from their ethos: Scientific institutions built on a professional basis and institutions supporting the spirit of capitalism – societies, cooperatives, libraries and newspapers.

The family roots of Czech economic thought

Family roots of Czech economic thought are already apparent in relations between the first cameralists –Becher was a brother-in-law of P.W. Hornigk They criticized each other, although the latter was undoubtedly inspired by the first one. Another example is illustrated in the fact of how important it can be when you married well, i.e. the relationship between František Ladislav Rieger and Albín Bráf 200 years later. Bráf married into a family at whose start there is a Czech historian and politician associated with the revolution of 1848, František Palacký (1798–1876). It was his daughter, Maria, who married Rieger, and Bráf married Rieger's daughter Libuše. In addition to that, Bráf inherited an economic library from his father-in-law that was been 'lost' after the *Velvet Revolution*.

Thanks to Becher, the first systematic scientific effort in the Bohemian Crownlands was connected with understanding natural wealth – but the need for this research was substantiated by the economic needs of the state, not only by intellectual effort. It was first emphasized by Becher's successor von Hornigk as early as in 1684. But another hundred years were needed for the advancement of his ideas, for it was first Maria Theresa who began to support the research of natural resources in the Bohemian Crownlands in the 1750s and 1760s – no doubt under the influence of her husband, Francis of Lotharingia (1708–1765), a leading entrepreneur in Austria. She charged with this task Jan Křtitel Boháč (1724–68), a professor of the Prague medical faculty and a commercial councillor to the Bohemian *Gubernium* (Teich, 2015, 70–71). Boháč did not doubt that the development of industry is possible only through development of the natural sciences. He argued that the systemization and classification of natural objects could be of aid in their usage in industrial production. But because he undertook his research himself and died relatively young, his work did not have the economic effect he himself expected.

That came only with the establishment of *learned societies*. The first centre within the Habsburg monarchy in which West and Central European notions of Enlightenment were cultivated and from which were they disseminated through different ways was the *Societas incognitarum auditorum in terris Austriacis*, founded in 1746 in Olomouc through the initiative of two aristocrats – Count Franz G. Giannini and Baron Joseph von Petrarch (1714–1772); the latter was a former *aide-de-camp* of Eugene de Savoy (1663–1736), and he therefore enjoyed the support of Maria Theresa. Among the further members were aristocratic *curieux,* state officials and clerical historians. From the very beginning the *Societas incognitarum* propagated various streams of contemporary thought including the philosophical rationalism of Christian Wolff, who influenced Sonnenfels.

Two other societies, which had a narrow connection to economic themes, were also the same type of *learned societies*: The *Commitee of Société patriotique* [*Patriotic Society*] and the *Agriculture Sozietät* [*Agricultural Society*]. The latter was established in 1770 with the support of Maria Theresa. Three decades later, the *Society* became one of the scientific centres of the Bohemian Crownlands and initiated the establishment of the first museum in the Habsburg monarchy; it encouraged a new spirit in the humanities and sciences and even became the place where early Liberalism penetrated the Central European space. The *Commitee* was established by Count Maxmilian von Lamberg (1729–1792) in Brno in 1780. The notion of patriotism was explained by Lamberg as a sentiment based on cosmopolitan ethic and a civic-minded mentality. A patriot was one who strives for general well-being, actively supports the advancement of science, gives his fellow-citizens advice in practical life issues and strives for happiness.

At the turn of the 18th and 19th centuries, the *Geheimorden der Illuminaten* [*The Secret Order of the Illuminati*] played its far- reaching role. In Brno, Praha a Opava *Iluminati* organized a number of lectures and discussions dealing with such themes as education, popular Enlightenment, morality and virtue, academic institutions and patriotism. The ideals of *Iluminati* included above all diligence, thrift, a simple lifestyle, genuine religiosity and love of education as the means to attaining well-being and happiness (Kroupa, 1998, 170). One cannot overlook the extent to which their thoughts matched the concept of Protestant ethics, which is why it is not surprising that we find numerous Protestants among the members of the *Illuminati,* especially in Brno, where a great deal of manufacturing had since the Josephine period been in the hands of Protestants, who were respected burghers.

Soukromá vědecká a patriotistická společnost [*The Private Scientific and Patriotic Society*] in Moravia was established thanks to the efforts of young aristocrat Count Johann Nepomuk von Mittrowsky (1757–1799) in 1794. This society focused on mineralogy, medicine, topography and a broad spectrum of education, including an economic one. Mittrowsky linked its activities with those of the *Královská česká společnost nauk* [*Royal Bohemian Society of Sciences*] in Prague, whose leading members were *Illuminati.* Mittrowsky himself became a member of a number of Enlightenment societies; for example though his participation in the Berlin Academy of Sciences he became familiar with the works of the French *idéologues,* typical Late Enlightenment thought. Due to Mittrowsky's premature death, many of his project, such as establishment of a Moravian state museum, were not realized. But his last years may serve as an example of a gradual transition from French encyclopaedism to early English Liberalism.

Twenty years earlier, Ignaz von Born (1737–1791) founded the *Soukromá učená společnost* [*Private Learned Society*] in Prague (1774) and became a leading figure of the Enlightenment in the monarchy; he was accepted as a member by the Royal Society in London on account of his merits in the field of mineralogy. Born criticized the aristocracy for its lack of comprehension of the utility of natural wealth and emphasized the usefulness of science to the economy and the state (Teich, 1976). His conviction about the necessity of open scientific communication led him to reorganize public scientific life. His supporters in these efforts were Count Franz Joseph Kinsky (1739–1805), a member of the ancient Czech aristocratic house and Prince Karl Egon Fürstenberg (1796–1854), the head of the *Gubernium* in Prague. Count Kinsky shared Born's concern that the aristocracy needed to know the fundamentals of the natural and agricultural sciences. The *Private Learned Society*'s transformation into a public body occurred when it became the *Česká společnost nauk* [*Bohemian Society* of Sciences] in 1784 and the *Královská česká společnost nauk* [*Royal Bohemian Society of Sciences*] in 1790 (Teich, 1981, 152–153).

The main legacy of all of these Enlightenment societies was the connection of the old and new aristocracy, officials and entrepreneurs, their religious tolerance and patriotism. Yet patriotism was based on the current endeavour towards individual private happiness and on the happiness and welfare of the whole of society and even mankind. Nevertheless, although certain nobles settled in the Bohemian Crownlands were enthusiastic propagators of Enlightenment ideas and concepts, the majority of the nobility assumed a defensive attitude. The case of the second serfdom has shown clearly how long the journey was from the discussion of Enlightenment ideas in aristocratic salons to implementing them in practice. The introduction of modern entrepreneurial modes and technological improvements was another case. The enlightened attempt to open scientific knowledge to the broader public found its platform both in popular scientific institutions and in the newly emerging magazines, newspapers and in numerous popular publications.

While the purpose of the *C. k. vlastenecko-hospodářské společnosti v království Českém* [the *I.R. Bohemian Patriotic-Economic Society*] (1788–1872) was consultancy in practical economic questions, especially in agriculture, the *Jednota ku povzbuzení průmyslu v Čechách* [*the Union for Encouragement of Industry in Bohemia*] which was established in 1833 set broader goals. The *Industrial Union* was established as a private society at the time when the Austrian state was not liberal, but rather strived towards centralization. Due to two reasons, its founders and first leaders were representatives of the Bohemian nobility: First, the nobility still represented the most educated stratum of society with foreign experience; and second, most factories in the Bohemian Crownlands then were established as a part of the manorial estate; the nobility had financial resources at their disposal. Moreover, the nobles saw themselves as a mediating link between the manufacturers, who think in the framework of protectionism, and the traders who want freedom: The old feudal class puts itself into the position of the socially most progressive force.

In the activities of the *Union* we can distinguish three stages which both reflect the broad range of their activities and the attitude of the Austrian state towards such institutions, as well as the social processes which liberated the now considerably impatient capitalist spirit in the Bohemian Crownlands. Since the municipal exhibitions at the turn of the 1820s and 1830s were the inspiration for the establishment of the *Union* their first goal, besides work on various testimonials on economic questions for the government, was primarily to awaken the spirit of enterprise and industrialization in Czech society. This was especially in the form of examples from abroad which were meant to show the way for domestic industry by spreading technological innovation and the support of the Austrian consulates towards promoting Czech products abroad. But as of the 1860s, the *Union* could not compete with the *Obchodní a živnostenskou komora* [the *Chambers of Commerce and Trade*], as they were established by the state for consultant and promotional activities. This is why in the second stage, the *Union* focused its activities on building a network of industrial schools, where Czech intellectuals taught in Czech and educated the first generation of Czech entrepreneurs. The interest of the nobility in the activities of the *Union* markedly weakened during this period. The baton was taken up by the new economic elite which had emerged from the bourgeois environment. It was for this reason that public collections formed the economic foundation for the newly established commercial academies. Likewise, at the beginning of the 1880s this activity of the *Union* also came under public administration. The attention of the *Union* turned to political work, support of emerging laws (the Trade Code in 1883) and the popularization of economic issues on a broader social scale by publishing magazines and building libraries.

The popularization of economics

Karel Havlíček Borovský (1821–1856) is interpreted in Czech historiography as a critic and later a victim of Bachian neoabsolutism in 1850s and even as a national martyr. Nevertheless, his 'amateur' economic considerations were as sharp as they were precise and devoted; but most importantly, they reached an extremely broad and new spectrum of readers.

Havlíček Borovský studied at the Faculty of Arts in Prague and then entered the Prague Archbishop's Seminary, from which he was expelled after a year. Two years later, he worked as an educator in Moscow, and clearly thanks to this experience he lost all illusions on the idea of Slavic patriotism; he cast a very critical light on Russian political and economic conditions. In 1846 he embarked on a journalistic career as a reporter for the government newspaper *Pražské noviny* [*The Prague News*] and later on as a founder of *Národní noviny* [*The National News*] and the weekly magazine *Slovan* [*the Slav*]. The publication of both was soon halted by the Imperial and Royal Censorship, Havlíček Borovský was investigated in court, subjected to repeated confiscation of property and finally, in 1851–1855, he was interned in Brixen.

Havlíček Borovský's economic background was formed by university courses in cameral sciences, and in accordance with them, he was of the impression that the Emperor should justly rule the nation and nurture its well-being. At the same time, thanks to F.L. Rieger, he was acquainted with the teaching of the English philosopher John Locke (1632–1704), that all of the ruler's power originates from the people and is based on a contract between the ruler and the subjects. Besides common sense, it is indeed these two premises which lie in the background of all of his texts that we could label as economic. But we must always take into account that Havlíček Borovský was first and foremost a political journalist; almost every mention of economic questions stems from his critique of period conditions. He criticized Viennese centralization, political conditions and ignorance, and in the scope of this criticism he used either as an example or as a context economic issues such as the state budget, taxes, money, inflation, bankruptcy or ownership; he always labelled such economic problems as 'political limbo'.

For instance, his defence of the principle of private ownership has its roots in essential rejection of limitation of personal freedom, so he focuses on this economic theme in the text on the democratic organization of society (Havlíček Borovský, 1903/II, 116–117). In another interpretation on the nature of democracy, he criticizes in a Bastiatan manner (he wrote the text in 1851, a few months after Bastiat's death) the opponents of machine production as he does the proponents of protectionist measures for their inability to see the other side of the same coin: Reduction of goods on the market. He contrasts the benefit of a small number of workers or producers and a large number of consumers (Ibid., 682–697). His interpretation of taxes – rejection of intervention into the rights and property of others – has the same roots. This interpretation is part of the text on Communism (Havlíček Borovský, 1903/I, 100–108), which he labelled as erratic and fallacious teaching born of the heads of two insane people. He identifies the absolutist government as the first and greatest communist, for it gives some – in the form of all sorts of privileges and subsidies – what it took from others in all sorts of ways – through confiscation or taxation. His calculation of tax quotas should, for instance, prove the harmful and undemocratic nature of the existing property census in elections (Ibid., 289–301). In the treatise on money, he blames the government for disturbing the currency (he did not use the term *inflation*) and for state bankruptcies (Ibid., 538–550). He did not consider paper money to be mere pieces of paper. He explained that there was concrete material value and work behind them.

From his texts it is clear that Havlíček Borovský understood two things well: First, how fundamental is the role that economic questions play (and will play) in the everyday life of every individual and entire nation, and second, what an impeding role the aristocracy play in the development of capitalism in the Bohemian Crownlands. But for him the term aristocracy did not only include the noble entrepreneurs whom he criticized for acting dishonestly and misusing the state to their benefits; after the abolishment of the second serfdom, he also added to them the bankers, factory owners and wholesalers, who he called the 'monetary aristocracy'. According to him, they all create 'unnatural' industry living with protective duties and prohibitions, 'suck the blood of the rest of mankind like a vampire', and are therefore the true enemies of 'honest democracy' (Havlíček Borovský, 1903/II, 683).

After Bolzano, who popularized economic and social issues from the pulpit at the academic church, it is thanks to Havlíček Borovský that topics which were until then discussed in the academic environment and in the learned societies were spread among a large number of readers. His impact on the economic uneducated public was quite fundamental at the time: Havlíček Borovský was not only a national martyr and hero, but as has been asserted by some of his biographers, he was also the darling of the nation; his portrait hung in almost every Czech household in the second half of the 19th century (Traub, 1925). Although the visionary Havlíček Borovský was fatally mistaken in some of his thoughts, such as the question of the acceptance of Communism in Czech society, which he considered entirely unthinkable, even foolish, his key economic statement that 'only hard work and effort helps towards progress' became within two decades a publicly accepted motto of the national revival, in which economic questions increasingly became the agenda of the day.

The beginning of cooperative theories

Cooperative ideas became to permeate the Czech environment in the first half of the 19th century. And they here fell on relatively fertile soil, for the majority of economic activities was in the hands of tradesmen, artisans and small businessmen. With only one exception, the cooperative movement did not offer any fundamentally new ideas from the perspective of the history of economic thought, however, it did form economic awareness in the Bohemian Crownlands in a noteworthy way. Yet the sources of information were the activities of the *Industrial Union*, the texts of Bolzano, the newspaper articles of Havlíček Borovský, worker newspapers (the first began to be published in 1848) and lectures which were held at the university by Anton Heinrich Springer (1825–1891) in the autumn of 1848. The enactment of the Act on Voluntary Associations in 1852 and the Cooperative Act in 1873 contributed to the significant boom of the cooperative movement, which was formed either as a part of association life or as a financial institution.

The first stream had the form of educational and cultural associations, the aim of which was the general elevation of inhabitants, especially the poor social classes by awakening 'slumbering entrepreneurial spirit' through self-help activities. Their ideas had mostly national and patriotic foundations and concerned the length of working hours, work safety, progressive taxation and – generally – associations and their positive effects. Rieger and especially Chleborád were among the main propagators and also the implementers of these types of associations – whether industrial or in the social area. Chleborád summarized his recommendations for work in production and consumer societies into 13 rules concerning trade management and administration, division of profits, keeping accounts and business policy (Chleborád, 1869, 440–444).

The second stream of cooperative movement took the form of savings banks and credit self-help cooperatives, the establishment of which was based on the non-existence of banks which would be able to provide credit to small and medium enterprises – whether in industry or agriculture. The first chronologically were the so-called self-help *Občanské záložny* [*Civic credit unions*], established in the 1850s and 1860s and inspired by the activity of Prussian liberal Schulze-Delitzsch, who was propagated in the Czech environment by entrepreneur and journalist František Šimáček (1834–1885). And although these institutions had the name Schulze-Delitzsch, they were not a copy of the German institutions; they had a broader member base which comprised of small tradesmen and artisans. In 1865, there were already 130 such credit unions in existence. Several years later, *Hospodářské záložny* [*Homestead credit unions*] began to be established in rural parts as a tool for solving the situation in agriculture after the abolishment of the second serfdom in 1848.

An original Czech contribution to the cooperative movement is represented by the concept of the doctor and journalist František Cyril Kampelík (1805–1872), who in the 1860s proposed and propagated the establishment of small rural credit unions that would provide cheap credit to peasants and rural artisans. Kampelík entered public life in the ground-breaking period around 1848, he became friends with Rieger and Havlíček Borovský, and as a journalist he expressed himself on current political, cultural and economic issues; it was he who began, in 1848, to publish *Hlasník* [*Announcer*], the first Czech magazine for workers.

His work *Průmyslné návrhy* [*Industrial Proposals*] (1859) was published with the motto 'What is impossible for the individual is possible for many allied in unity', and Kampelík propagated in it self-help as a means to prosperity. The full title of the work details at great length – in Hornigk's 200-year-old style – Kampelík's way of economic thought: *Industrial Proposals on how Wealthy and Poor Citizens from Bohemia, Moravia, Silesia and Slovakia, Being Perfect Craftsmen and Reasonable Farmers, – Instead of Expensive and Dangerous Emigration to Far America – Model, Industrial and Nice, by Cultivation Renowned Towns or New Villages in Sparsely Populated Fertile Areas of the Austrian Empire Under the Protection of the Imperial and Royal Government Should Established, so that Before Becoming Horrible Poor and Getting into the Trouble, They and Their Descendants Have a Good Life. Given by Frant. Cyril Kampelík to All Citizens for Thinking and Working, As Well As Having Several Sons, to Each of Whom They Cannot Give an Estate or a Large Craft Trade.*

Kampelík here – as he does in his other books – proposed the self-help system of saving and credit associations suitable for the small rural regions – three to four neighbouring parishes at most. His practical proposals, elaborated many a time in the finest detail, including internal organization, statutes, ledger forms, a cash book and documents on deposit and administration, ensued from reliable economic analysis and calculations. His proposals disappeared entirely and were replaced by the similar proposals of Friedrich Wilhelm

Raiffeisen (1818–1888), which were published as late as 1866. A consolation to Kampelík, albeit posthumously, is that countryside saving and credit cooperatives, that were established in the Bohemian Crownlands from the 1890s precisely according to Raiffesen's model, carry his name – *Kampeličky*; and the same name was also given to the re-established cooperative savings bank in Czechoslovakia after 1989.

3 Between economics and politics

From the glorious beginnings to the bitter ends (1882–1948)

'The nation may be politically awakened through words, but economically its independence can only be attained through deeds.'

Albín Bráf (Gruber, 1921, 506)

This chapter covers the most turbulent time in Czech history. The political regime changed four times, four dozen governments changed, two war conflicts scarred the country and two totalitarian ideologies afflicted it. In the second half of the 19th century, the Habsburg monarchy was the second-largest European country in terms of territory (without colonies) and the third largest in population. In terms of industrial advancement, however, it remained seriously underdeveloped, without compensation in agricultural production. The reasons behind this were the slow accumulation of capital and extensive farming, but most importantly the hindering influence of the absolutist regime prior to 1848. The accession of *laissez-faire* was missed.

The development of capitalism was hampered primarily by the passing of the Commerce and Trades Licensing Acts of 1862 and 1859. Through them the state declared almost absolute freedom of trade and thus opened the doors to unprecedented level of new business applications. Between April 1867 and April 1873, Austria approved 1,005 applications to establish joint-stock companies; a third of them were operating in the Bohemian Crownlands (Urban, 2003, 73). However, the stock market crash in Vienna in 1873 brought an end to this liberal period and the ensuing depression impeded industrialization at a point when small-scale production predominated over mass production. Small businesses and home enterprises with up to five employees accounted for 93% of all companies and 41% of all industrial workers. Conversely, only 0.01% of companies in the Bohemian Crownlands had more than 1,000 employees, and they employed 6% of all industrial workers (Ibid., 86–87).

When discussing the economy of Bohemia, the nationality composition of the population cannot be ignored. In 1900, the Czechs formed 13% of the monarchy's total population and 22% of those employed in its industry, whereas the figures for the Germans were 25% and 41%, respectively (Ibid., 62). The economic foundation of the Czechs within the Bohemian Crownlands continued to consist of agriculture, handicrafts, retailing, the sugar-beet and sugar industries, beer and malt production and the distillery industry. They tended to be medium-sized enterprises. It is estimated that only about 20–30% of the capital value of the industry in Bohemia was in the hands of Czech entrepreneurs, and they did not dominate in any branch of industry, with the exception of sugar manufacture. The Czech banks had a significant position thanks to the export of their capital further to the East – first to the less developed parts of the monarchy, and then to Russia and the Balkans.

At the beginning of the 20th century Czech entrepreneurs began to engage in branches of industry that had been almost exclusively the domain of German capital – the textile, chemical and ceramic industries. In the last decade before the Great War, industrial production was developing much faster in the Bohemian Crownlands than in the rest of the monarchy; the per capita national income of the Bohemian Crownlands was 118% of the European average (Lacina and Hájek, 2002). The Bohemian Crownlands, however, were no leaders of technical progress; the enormous duty-free space of the monarchy did not inspire the growth of labour productivity.

The Great War and the Treaty of Versailles changed Europe. Austria-Hungary's 'marriage of wheat and textile' fell into pieces. Six new countries were formed and every one of them tried in their own way to cope with its heritage that was suddenly labelled as inauspicious and monarchy itself was branded as a 'jail of nations'. Czechoslovakia was built upon this ruins on 28 October 1918 encompassing the territories of Bohemia, Moravia and southern Silesia, Slovakia, and Ruthenia. Czechoslovakia carried over the Monarchy's inheritance for the entire 20 years of its interwar existence: It inherited almost 70% of the entire Monarchy's industry, hence why it was necessary to realize up to 30% of the entire production through foreign trade; it inherited imbalanced economic development of western and eastern part of the Monarchy (the Czech Lands had 72% of the whole population of the country, but 92% of the industrial production (Ibid.)); it inherited monarchy's multinational structure (the minorities share on the entire population was 33% and the German minority accounted for 25%). As compared with the year 1913, Czechoslovakia recorded above-average economic growth in the 1920 in relation to all countries of Europe, in particular in comparison with Germany, Austria and Hungary (Ibid.). But the economic crisis of the 1930s was deeper and of longer duration in Czechoslovakia than in most European countries, which resulted in far-reaching social, political and nationalistic consequences.

All of Czechoslovak 18 governments agreed on relatively extensive state interventions in the economy that manifested themselves by nationalization, monetary and land reform and so-called *nostrifikace* (domestification) of industry. Nationalization affected sources of (strategic) materials and some industrial fields and gave birth to state-owned enterprises. The monetary reform created an individual currency and was followed by a strongly progressive property tax. The *nostrifikace* transformed the ownership structure and executive and administrative functions in favour of Czechoslovak citizens in those companies that had their headquarters in Austria (or Hungary) but their operational premises in Czechoslovakia (Doležalová, 2013b). Under the banner of 'revenge for White Mountain' and in the context of land reform the forests and large estates with acreage larger than 150 ha were sequestrated and subsequently expropriated (Doležalová, 2018a). In addition, nobility titles were abolished.

Twenty years after its establishment, the Munich decision by the great powers changed Czechoslovakia – its political system, international standing and economic situation – and started a half-year episode of the existence of a territorially and institutionally curtailed state, with reduced raw material resources and industry. In March 1939, Czechoslovakia was divided into the Protectorate of Bohemia and Moravia and the Slovak State. Prior to this the Czech government had implemented certain elements of a controlled economy, for instance, mandatory organization of business and financial centralization. In October 1940, the Protectorate became part of the German economic space, with consequences in all spheres of social life. The economy was affected by state control of industrial production, by a system of mandatory supplies in agriculture and by a compulsory association of entrepreneurs. The market was replaced with a voucher system. The state controlled prices, wages and distribution of the labour force by means of Labour Offices, as well as foreign trade, and a payment system was introduced. Besides this, a process of changes was also taking place in ownership relationships in favour of the German population, represented by Germanization and Aryanization (Teichová, 1998).

After its liberation in May 1945 Czechoslovakia embarked on its way to socialism. The legal system, political elites and parameters of economic development were transformed. The national composition of the population was dramatically changed due to the expulsion of 2.5 million Germans and the loss of Carpathian Ruthenia. In three years Czechoslovakia had to deal with two key issues: nationalization and planning. In October 1945, president Edvard Beneš signed a decree on nationalization of mines, selected industrial companies, banks and insurance companies; as a result, the state took over the most important industrial and financial subjects. This decree had considerable support among the public. From this point on, 60% of all employees worked in the nationalized sector. All nationalized companies were to be managed in accordance with a two-year plan of reconstruction proposed by the Communist Party. In May 1946, the plan became an integral part of the program declaration of the Czechoslovak government and, on the 28 October of the same year, on the anniversary of the establishment of independent Czechoslovakia in 1918, was symbolically put into force. Within three years, Czechoslovakia abandoned its own way towards Socialism and the Communist Party became the only leader of the people.

The main hero of this chapter is evident from the start. The founder of Czech economics, who persistently sought solace in his work after the loss of his only son, and opened the doors to the world to his students. But there are also others. An original thinker, one of the closest friends of the future Czechoslovak president Tomáš Garrigue Masaryk, who exchanged science for the Viennese Parliament. A shy young man akin to the one from Kafka's *Castle*, something of an unacknowledged genius. He almost went insane from desperation that his work as an official was depriving him of valuable time for science. An ambitious and extremely conscientious career official fighting on many fronts for acknowledgement, which would be granted to him in full measure 30 years after he died. A Don Quixote struggling with the new political and economic elites of the First Republic, who would find peace to work only in exile. And dozens of Bráf's students. All of them together would push economics in the Bohemian Crownlands to the very summit of social prestige, yet many of them would later only watch powerlessly their path into the slavery of ideological clichés and also their bitter fall into obscurity.

Economics institutionalized: main figures and topics

Albín Bráf: the founding father

Albín Bráf fundamentally influenced not only the time in which he lived but also that which followed. He was not only a scientist who laid the foundations for the methodology of economics and significantly helped to complete Czech economic terminology. He was also the first teacher who lectured in economics in Czech at the undivided Charles-Ferdinand University and was later on the first professor in the Czech part of the divided Charles-Ferdinand University (1882). Besides this, Bráf is also considered one of the founders of economic history during the ground-breaking period at the end of the 19th century, when many disciplines of social sciences were still searching for their subject and method and were writing the first chapters of their histories (Doležalová and Holec, 2016). Finally, Bráf was able to connect economics with the practical problems of the nascent Czech entrepreneurial stratum and Czech civic society generally.

Albín Bráf (1851–1912) was born in Třebič in Moravia, to an agricultural official's family. After completing legal studies (1874), he undertook a brief legal practice in court, but in the same year he accepted the post of Professor of National Economy at the *Czechoslavonic Commercial Academia* in Prague. Besides this, he also taught at the school of *Ženského výrobního spolku* [*Women Production Association*], which was the first girl's school to teach economics in Austria at the time. In 1877, he was habilitated as a private associate professor of political economy both at the Faculty of Law at Charles-Ferdinand University and at the Czech Polytechnic. He later resigned his post at the Czech Polytechnic in favour of Josef Kaizl, and in 1882 he became a part-time and in 1890 a full-time professor of political economy at the Faculty of Law at university, which had by then divided into the Czech and German part. Thanks to his father-in-law, František L. Rieger, he was politically active in the *Staročeská strana* [*Old Czech Party*]. In 1883–1895, he was a deputy of the Czech Diet, a member of the Bohemian Council and a lifetime member of the Imperial Diet. In 1909 and in 1911–1912, he was the Austro-Hungarian Minister of Agriculture.

Bráf's scientific work cannot be overlooked even in terms of its broad thematic sweep, which ranged from theoretical economic issues to purely practical ones. A key area of Bráf's interest was, without doubt, the practical nexus of social issues. It could even be said that it was as though every theme on which he focused did not interest him on its own, but with regard to the way in which it contributed to the solution of the social question. This is connected with his political and public engagement: In practical politics, he successfully advanced many issues to which he devoted attention in his texts. The range of his interest included themes from economic policy and administration and the tuition of economic education. His texts often overlap one another thematically; so, for instance, certain pedagogical texts could also be included under the theme of the social question – especially texts on the need for tuition of economics at theological faculties and with it the connected social role of the clergy.

Bráf's theoretical-methodological demarcation of economics has far-reaching consequences for the further development of both his and, general, Czech economic thought. According to Bráf, economics without a theoretical background (and economic history) becomes but 'a pack of empty generalizations or the instrument of the interests of the privileged' (Bráf, 1923c, 12). In another passage, he says that, 'anyone who does not know method will remain a dilettante until death' (Bráf, 1923a, 66). In his search for a 'suitable' methodology for economics, Bráf's work becomes an example *par excellence* when researching the evolution of economic thought in the Bohemian Crownlands. As he wrote: 'This time of my searching and wandering, frequent disappointments and occasional total decline of self-confidence encompasses more than 10 years of my life' (Bráf, 1922, 224). In his work, this 'methodological wandering' can be observed very clearly in a wavering between the deductive and inductive method, and likewise in an endeavour to find a specific method which draws, on the one hand from the German, and on the other hand from the Austrian school. As a university student, Bráf was influenced by classical Liberalism.

Since A. Smith, D. Ricardo, John Stuart Mill (1806–1873) and other liberal theorists were not included in the curriculum of the Law Faculty in Prague in the early 1870s Bráf studied these authors on his own, with little guidance from his professors (Albrecht, 2013, 13). The first book he studied was Mill's *Principles of Political Economy* (1848). Subsequent reading of H. Ch. Carey did not make much of an impression on him. By that time he had already become absorbed with another economist – Albert E. Schäffle (1831–1903), thanks to the media interest which accompanied his brief tenure at the cabinet of Count Karl Sigmund von Hohenwart; Schäffle resigned from his professorial post at the University in Vienna in order to become the Minister of Commerce, and from this post he actively involved himself in negotiations on so-called fundamental articles – vital issues for the Czechs. Schäffle's steps made such an impression on Bráf that he set about studying his writings and those of other representatives of the German historical school. This somewhat 'corrected' his liberalistic enthusiasm; the study of Roscher and List and especially Karl Kniese's (1821–1898) *Politische Oekonomie vom geschichtlichen Standpunkte* [*Political Economy from the Historical Perspective*] (1930) shifted his further work to the direct influence of the German historical school; in his own words, when writing his habilitation work, *Papiergeldentwertung und Agio* [*The Banknote Depreciation and Agio*] (1877), he was influenced by Mill and Kniese. Additionally, Eugen Böhm-Bawerk (1851–1914) and Friedrich von Wieser (1840–1921), successors of Carl Menger (1840–1921), also studied under Kniese, and Bráf would quite frequently meet them in Prague, where they worked. He later labelled Böhm-Bawerk as the only debater on a par with Karl Marx (1818–1883).

Although he criticized Marx's texts, he considered him to be a 'strong soul' and a 'superb mind' and was able to capture the substance of his theoretical approach: 'A relentless evolutionary law is unfolded in Marx's teaching, that is, the product of a theory, something far stronger than the older socialist concepts. Anyone who wishes to refute it has to conquer Marx on his theoretical ground' (Bráf, 1923a, 79, 116). It is also his placement of the theoretical sciences outside of ethics, and thereby also the class position, which is a clear polemic with Marx.

Dissatisfaction with the theoretical embedding of the German school led to the fact that it was Menger's *Untersuchungen über die Methode der Sozialwissenschaften* [*Investigations into the Method of the Social Sciences*] (1883, 1985) and subsequently the broad spectrum of literature which Bráf studied when following the dispute on method that brought him to a certain methodological clarification. In practice this meant that Bráf retained a liberalistic trust in the strength of individual initiative and self-help, what he called the 'optimism of labour' and sought a balance between it and social needs. In his other texts, this is manifested by the endeavour to 'add' a certain theoretical framework to the German school; in other words, to delineate a space for theory and history. Using Gustav von Schmoller's (1838–1917) sentence that 'as the right and left leg are a part of walking, so is induction and deduction a part of scientific thought' (Bráf, 1923a, 89) he reminds us that not even the Austrians, as much as they support the use of deduction, are not opposed to the use of induction.

When delimiting the methodology of economics, Bráf introduces three terms: the *foundation-forming abstraction*, by which economics delimits itself from other social sciences; the *isolative abstraction*, by the aid of which economics expresses its laws; and the term of *type*. His concept of methodology is founded upon the assumption that man is able gradually to develop a suitable conceptual apparatus which correctly classifies both really existing objects and phenomena and the relationships between them. The conceptual basis, including laws, is built in the framework of the inductive phase, and the logical derivation within models (i.e. systems of terms and their connections) continues in the framework of the deductive phase. Not only is the validity of laws proved thereby, but they can also be reapplied to reality. This notion is later adopted literally by Bráf's most gifted student, František Čuhel, when he launches into an analysis and elaboration of the economic conceptual apparatus, which had hitherto used the words of 'normal' language, which he considers to be a mistake.

With the exception of three aspects, Bráf's methodology is clearly inspired by Menger (Jonáš, 2013). Nevertheless, in many passages he not only connects the German and Austrian approach to scientific knowledge, but also develops it innovatively. He delimits himself against Menger and the Austrians in the concept of the exactness and universal validity of economic laws. First, Bráf asserts that the immutability of laws in the social sciences is disturbed by the effect of human will, and social laws are always only historically relative and subjective. Second, subjective inducements to acting cannot be quantified; and third, the consumer is not the only economic subject and the purpose of business activity is not only the satisfaction of human bodily needs, but also moral and intellectual needs, as Bráf says, perfect human development.

By contrast, Bráf follows Menger when he first emphasizes the necessity of distinguishing individual economic sciences – history, statistics, theory and practical sciences. History and statistics are, together with life experience, the departure of theory, but are not able to understand individual reality or decision-making. One cannot overlook how the same notion, growing from the same intellectual substrate, also guided Schumpeter dozens of years later when he conceived his *Analysis* (1954). While for Menger, the reason for distinguishing is that our knowledge has a different character and other criteria of truthfulness in each of these areas, Bráf innovatively emphasizes the complexity of social reality, especially in contrast to nature as the subject of the natural sciences (Bráf, 1923c, 147). According to Bráf, social reality is the subject of research in numerous social sciences, economics is but one of them. For this reason it is not within the means of one discipline to grasp social reality as a whole at once. This is why every social science has to choose only a certain part from the entirety of social reality. This act of original delimitation of a subject is referred to by Bráf as *foundation-forming abstraction*, where we 'abstract from the series of realities' (Bráf, 1923a, 84–85). This step, however, is crucial for the subsequent form of science as a whole; it is precisely its incorrect execution that he sees as the main error of the classical school of political economy and its subsequent necessary failure. At the same time, Bráf is aware that foundation-forming abstraction perpetrates 'violence' on reality inasmuch as it leads to a narrowing of the subject of a specific science to only one side of reality which nevertheless remains united with others and is thus influenced by them. The point is that a specific historical experience includes many factors – political, economic, but also customs formed by historical development and social organization; Bráf speaks of the establishment of economic life in institutions and, under the influence of Kniese, considers the legal code to be of paramount importance.

Second, in contrast to the German school and in accordance with Menger, science is for Bráf not only an accumulation of insights on individual phenomena, but has as its goal the knowledge of the general. He labels scientists in a John Hus manner, as spirits bent on the truth. Where Menger speaks of morphological and theoretical science, Bráf distinguishes science into concerning what is and concerning what is typical (generic, regular, logical), and calls this task theoretical (Bráf, 1922, 71). At the same time he distinguishes two types of regularity: empirical and exact. The first group concerns, in particular, statistical methods and the search for regularities in mass observation. These are not real scientific laws, for they express simple factual regularities derived from experience; Bráf here uses the concept of *isolative abstraction*. Although this insight never entirely corresponds with truth, it is not an obstacle to its exactness if we are aware of the logical nature of this insight. It is exact laws that are in fact true laws. Theory here wishes to know the simplest, irresolvable parts of bodies, elements, and the regularities between them. After the model of natural sciences, he labels some of these exact laws as *elementary* and the rest as *derived, causal* (Bráf, 1923a, 71). Bráf ranks economic laws among the *empirical*, for they have been *derived* on the basis of experience, and he criticizes 'deductive comfort' (Bráf, 1923c, 21), i.e. the mere memorizing of principles as opposed to the solution of problems, theoretical inconsistency and the inability to be aware of unintended collateral consequences. Bráf thus distinguishes between three basic methods of research: description by observing specific phenomena and connections, building abstract theory by researching typical phenomena and connections, and building practical sciences through practical application of knowledge in practice. The relationships between individual methods of research are dialectic; theory evolves from historical inputs, statistics and other sciences; and they, on the other hand, cannot exist without a theoretical foundation which enables them a better classification of specific phenomena.

And finally, *type* is a crucial category in Bráf's methodology, clearly inspired by Menger and then made famous by Max Weber (1864–1920) (Havelka, 2013). According to Bráf, theory searches for what is typical in the diversity of phenomena and events, it ascertains typical phenomena, typical connections. According to Bráf, to understand the *type* means to sort facts according to relative signs, form higher concepts and uncover regular connections (Bráf, 1923c, 144). But the Schmollerian emphasis on statistical completeness of experience and its inductive *totalization* (exhaustion of their connections) appears in the majority of Bráf's texts in arguing against Menger's *standardization*.

Defining the subject of economics follows after defining the methodology thereof. According to Bráf, this was the economic side of human society, i.e. the economy, which he defines as human activity, the goal of which is to secure the satisfaction of needs by external means (i.e. goods) whilst people try to progress purposefully so as to achieve successes (utility) to the highest relative degree with the lowest relative sacrifices, which he referred to as the *principle of efficiency*. Yet he distinguishes between technical and economic efficiency; the first becoming economic only with its relationship to the purposes of a certain economic subject. Referring to A. Smith, he considered ethics to be an integral dimension of economics. In this regard he distinguished between two branches of economics – the theoretical and the practical (Bráf, 1923a, 38); the ethical aspect can be required only after practical science, theory is ethically neutral. Theoretical economics is focused on the analysis of economic phenomena, seeks the interpretation thereof as well as the *forces* which influence them; Bráf spoke of the healthy core of practical sciences which are influenced by factors other than economic – the philosophical and social 'view' of the individual. He considered practical science to be the domain of policy, which concerns the improvement of social conditions and the elevation of the population to a higher degree of welfare. This is a thought which would resonate also with Bráf's students.

Distinguishing economics into theoretical and practical led Bráf to express the content of the terms *national economy* and *state economy*. He defines national economy, as had Chleborád before him, as the set of all individual public and private economies on state territory (i.e. the nation in the political, not ethnic sense); it is not a unified economic subject, but the sum of a large number of diverse independent economies which are connected in a higher unity, that is comprised of mutually conditioning and supplementary parts. The state economy differs from the national economy insofar as it has its own certain directive subject (the government) which also needs various goods according to its needs and manages its special economy – financial economy. As a maxim for every public economy, he expressed the thesis that there has to be a qualitative, quantitative and time concordance between revenues and expenditures (Bráf, 1915, 38–60). This notion is later fully assumed by his student Karel Engliš: Bráf inspired him to formulate a concept of *solidaristic economy* by the idea that change to a truly unified economy would occur only by realizing radical socialist ideals that would, as a result of common ownership of means of production, be the direction of production and distribution of revenue in the hands of a single common authority.

In Bráf's concept, economics does not limit itself only to events in individual economies; rather, its subject is all phenomena, relationships, connections between economies – price formation, the origin and function of money, credits, but also legislation and state administration (Menšík, 2013). Bráf accepted the subjective theory of value and rejected its working theory: Labour is but a source of utility, not value, for value always depends on human judgements (Bráf, 1913, 143). In this regard, he also criticized Marx for the disparity between the first and third parts of *Capital* (1913), a view which he shared with other Austrians, but also with so-called revisionist currents in Marxism itself. Bráf did not accept rent as the economic realization of land ownership, and he distinguished income only to entrepreneurial (profit) and non-entrepreneurial (interest and salary). Inspired by Schäffle, he considered profit to be the payment for entrepreneurs' labour, their social function and the risk they take. In substance, he copied Böhm-Bawerk in the concept of interest, although one can also find traces of the views of J.B. Say, K. Kniese and C. Menger, and he considered interest to be the result of the time factor, stemming from the difference of the value of present and future goods.

Most of Bráf's texts on practical issues can be characterized by the fact that they are always elicited by the current economic-social problems with which he was confronted. If Menger was for him an authority in the theory and methodology of economics, it here transpires which elements he assumed from the German school: historicism, descriptiveness and use of statistics, but also the concept of the state and the role of a legal order in social development. Bráf contextualizes social phenomena into relevant period contexts, although he avoids a mere transferal of notions from older traditions and naive ahistoric critique; he is under all circumstances a cautious interpreter. According to him, every reform or economic instrument has its time and every period has its valid legal code. No change in the principles of human endeavour and feeling occur through change of the social establishment. This is typically shown in his texts devoted to the social question, which in content copy relevant period streams – he focused on the question of the poor and the workers, but also on an entire broad scale of the nascent social insurance; he devoted space to a critique of the existing adjustments of each of these areas and to overviews on social welfare in various European countries.

Bráf's concept of the social question can be characterized by the fact that, first, social issues arise when a disturbance of the fundamental characteristic of society occurs – among these he ranked monogamous marriage, the private-entrepreneurial structure, individual ownership of means of production, the freedom of contracts and the legal equality of all people. Second, for them the content of the social question is the search for a certain form of social reconciliation that would include all social classes, and emphasized the private nature of the instruments used. Only if these instruments do not fulfil their functions adequately can state intervention follow – but first in the form of enacting pertinent legislation and only the next step can be the establishment of certain institutions by the state. In this regard, Bráf used the same distinction between the negative and positive function of the government, as did his father-in-law, F.L. Rieger. The first means the prevention of breaching the freedom of the employment contract, and second the initiative, organizational or forceful activity of the state. Bráf clearly leaned towards the first role of the state. But he rejected Liberalism for its negative social consequences – likewise, he rejected Socialism for its requirement to abolish individual ownership. According to him, the solution which eliminated the negative consequences of both was social insurance with only legislative support of the state. Thence stems Bráf's own definition of social policy as the operation of public legislation and administration in the favour of individuals whose living conditions are under threat and in respecting the effort to improve the living conditions of society as a whole (Bráf, 1923b, 148).

The substance of Bráf's consideration of the social question demonstrates illustratively his approach to the social situation of workers, the period worker issue that he understood as improvement of the living situation of workers. Workers were to receive their entire wage, which should reach such a level that it would ensure an adequate supply of labour and at the same time satisfaction of the necessities of workers and their families, even at a time when a worker could not work, for instance, due to illness, invalidity or accidental unemployment. State aid was not to limit the workers' endeavour to solve their situation by their own means 'without revolution' (Ibid., 196). He also expressed the risk of state intervention in the form of increased costs on the entrepreneurs' side (Ibid., 158) and from here resulting pressure to dismiss workers from employment; Bráf thought over the protection of entrepreneurs in the event that an agreement was breached from the workers' side. Although he placed emphasis on the accidental social causes of the poor social situation of workers and admitted that private ownership is divided unequally, he nevertheless also calculated the causes on the workers' side – dishonesty, lack of conscientiousness at work, unwillingness towards education, inadequate childcare, wastefulness, carefreeness, and frivolous and premature marriages (Bráf, 1913, 338). There is here clear inspiration from the teaching of Thomas R. Malthus. In Bráf's concept, the worker question is more a social and cultural question than an economic one, for it is in the interest of society that each of its classes can develop. And its content has to be the social elevation of workers by perfecting family life and the upbringing of children, the improvement of their economic and social welfare. Defining welfare, Bráf anticipated the fulfilment of certain material conditions, although he saw the substance of welfare in interaction with other individuals. Material welfare is not a goal, but rather a means, wrote Bráf, as did Chleborád, Rieger and Bolzano before him.

It is clear from Bráf's texts that he was an economist who did not lose sight of the whole when focusing on a detailed analysis of particulars. If his varied and broadly diversified operation in many areas of social life could be condensed into one sentence, it might be: Bráf was a politician who argued economically and an economist who argued socially. In the Czech environment, he opened up many economic issues with urgent necessity, he called for critical thought and deplored any personal prejudice; without doubt, his most important legacy is that he was able to awaken an ardour for economics in dozens of his students – whom he did not, however, hinder with any ideological borders. But it is true that their future careers were to a large extent predetermined by the apportionment of the seminar topics that he himself considered necessary to cover. Although he himself had minimal foreign experience, he opened doors for his students to economists both in Germany and in Austria with whom he maintained – sometimes very lively – written correspondence. Thereafter, his students felt great gratitude towards him throughout their lives; one of them, Cyril Horáček (1862–1943) proclaimed at his funeral that Czech science and the entire Czech nation will keep him in glorious and undying memory. Despite the fact that when studying interwar texts written by Czech economists, we find that Bráf had already addressed the topic, Horáček's words were nevertheless not fulfilled. Bráf's political influence was overshadowed during the interwar era, partly owing to the fact that he was almost too deeply rooted in the Habsburg monarchy and his ideal was the political arrangement of Austria in the spirit of Palácký's programme related to constitutional law from 1848 and partly due to long-term personal disputes with T.G. Masaryk. His remembrance underwent further blows during the forty years of Socialism when the professional public labelled him as an 'exponent' of the Czech bourgeoisie and he was practically forgotten in the public sphere.

Josef Kaizl: between economics and politics

Although Josef Kaizl underwent a similar methodological search as Bráf, he oriented himself very quickly thanks to his studies abroad. He even received the Strasbourg University award for his doctoral work *Der Kampf um Gewerbereform und Gewerbefreiheit in Bayern von 1799–1868, nebst einem einleitenden Ueberblick über die Entwicklung des Zunftwesens und der Gewebefreiheit in Deutschland* [*The Fight for Trade Reform and Trade Freedom in Bavaria*] (1879) written under the supervision of Gustav von Schmoller. But immediately afterwards, he criticized the German school for its resignation of any kind of theory; he even complained about Schmoller's lectures, that by halfway through the semester, Schmoller was still in the Stone Age: 'People were still climbing trees' (Kaizl, 1909, 332). While he was still studying he came to know the Marx's work and was fascinated by it. He simply considered it important to study everything – he knew and quoted Aristotle, Plato and Auguste Comte (1798–1857) as well as German, Austrian, Italian, French and Russian economists. He particularly evaluated the last of these and was often inspired by them in the context of his research in financial science. Although his work is relatively limited in its scope, we find in it a formulation of opportunity costs and the problem of rent-seeking, the application of the theory of marginal utility on state economic activity, the concept of fiscalism and fiscal illusions and the definition of public good.

Josef Kaizl (1854–1901) was born in Volyň in South Bohemia to an official's family. At the same time as Bráf, from 1871–1875, he studied at the Faculty of Law in Prague, where he received a doctorate in 1876 and continued in studies of economics under Schmoller's and and Georg Fridrich Knapp's (1842–1926) supervision abroad. On the basis of the above-mentioned book, he was habilitated in the field of political economy – positive references were then written not only by Schmoller, but also by Wagner and Schäffle – and he began to teach at the Polytechnic and at the Charles-Ferdinand University in Prague. In 1883 he became a part-time and from 1885 a full-time professor at the university. From 1885–1887, he was representing Old Czech Party in the Imperial Diet, and from 1891 until his death the *Mladočeská strana* [*Young Czech Party*], when his views approached those of Masaryk. From 1898–1899, he became the Austrian Minister of Finance and was then awarded the Imperial Order of the Iron Crown of Emperor Franz Josef.

According to Kaizl, economics is a theoretical (generalizing, not historical), normative and social science; he used the term *political economy*. Although he accepts that without history it would not be possible to understand 'what is' and delimits himself against those 'who replace new learning by expressive declamations or descriptions of social evil' as he does against a mathematizing concept of economics. Referring to Herbert Spencer's (1820–1903) *Principles of Sociology* (1882), he asserts that the goal of political economy is to interpret the economic organization of human society, whereas political science focuses on political organization. He defines economics in the same way as Bráf, as the 'elaborated activity of man for permanent, most plentiful satisfaction of all needs at the smallest cost' (Kaizl, 1883, 6). Political economy, as the science of human action, has get to know 'what should be and become a guide to practical policy'; to study economic relationships, however, is possible only if they are not entered into by the state which changes the purposes and possibilities of individuals: 'In the same moment when politics enters the field of economics, science escapes from it' (Kaizl, 1892, 30–31). But most of all, he criticizes the substitution of theory by policy, when political economy becomes an administrative science, 'a *vademecum* for officials', and this suppresses the development of theory and undermines the foundations on which only efficiency, utility, but also justifiability of practical sciences stand.

Like Bráf, Kaizl was so captivated by Schäffle, the politician, that he started to study his texts and let them influence his work. This concerns especially the textbook *Národní hospodářství* [*National Economy*] (1883), the first, and for many decades the only, Czech textbook on political economy. He thereby surpassed Bráf, who resolved never to write a textbook, although he had been exhorted to do so by his teacher E. Jonák as early as the 1870s. In his textbook Kaizl follows Schäffle's interpretation, including his variants of the subjective theory of value with one exception: He interprets the social question in accordance with Schmoller's programme for the Association for Social Policy, founded in 1873. But Kaizl soon formulates his own considerations.

The formulation of opportunity costs is part of Kaizl's theory of value. According to him, value is the validity which one attributes to a certain item (Kaizl used the term *good*). It is known by reason, which also calculates the costs required for the acquisition thereof. Whilst feeling decides what is pleasant or unpleasant for one and what purposes will be chosen, reason gives arguments as to what expenses have to be spent for the acquisition of the contemplated utility. But in the end, it is the will that decides, so economic value is the result of choice which pursues the greatest utility at the smallest cost. This choice, subjective and psychological activity is, according to Kaizl, the point of departure for all economic activities. And he adds a complicated overview of factors on the side of utility and costs on which value depends. On the side of utility it is the usefulness which a good has or which human ingenuity attributes to it, the urgency of personal need and the quantity thereof, but also the quantity of a certain good and the ability of a person to secure it. In this connection, he speaks of the so-called *effective value* that expresses that one values only those goods that can be attained. On the side of costs, value is influenced both by the amount of objective costs and by the amount of *labour sacrifices* required to obtain a certain good, but also the value of goods which for the same reason cannot be gained, i.e. opportunity costs.

Kaizl argues with the existence of free goods and asserts that utility itself cannot be the basis of value and he also denies the possibility of the objectification thereof. Both sides of value change according to person, time, place and circumstances. But he admits substitution, in consequence of which a previously valued good is valued less or even loses value. He criticizes the working theory of value insofar as it overlooks the fact that the same amount of labour leads to goods which are valued differently. Like Chleborád, he considers the capitalist to be the motor of production, for he determines the direction and manner of production, searches for useful value about which he judges it will be demanded, takes entrepreneurial risk and is the first to be affected by wrong choose. This is why he is entitled to capitalist profit. Nevertheless, he rejects the *Robbinsonnade* of the Austrian school with the argument on the advantages of a society of numerous economic active people.

Already in his *National Economy* (1883), there are clear elements of the theory of marginal costs and marginal utility in the interpretation of the category of price. According to Kaizl, price is always the expression of the exchange value of a good and its utmost maximum is always the highest utility which is felt on the side of demand; analogically, the lowest costs are the lowest costs on the side of supply. Equilibrium price is then the price, or more precisely, the exchange value, by which an equilibrium occurs between 'the relatively highest utility in demand and the relatively lowest costs in supply' (Kaizl, 1883, 171). The market is the place where decision occurs. Three conditions have to be fulfilled in order for an equilibrium price to form on the market: All participants calculate (they act according to the market); there has to be competition both on the sides of demand and supply; and free market access has to be enabled. The price of credit and wage run according to the same rules as any other price. Following a pattern of Schäffle, he rejected the conception of rent as land ownership; rent is any excess of any income over average level.

In the interpretation of money he refers to Schäffle, Wagner, Kniese and Knapp's theory of state money. Money is to him the measure of values, a means of exchange and the preserver of values having emerged from the needs of trade and is a phenomenon recognized by general practice. As an advocate of the gold reserve of money, he rejects state-issued notes as a consequence of the state monetary policy, for it leads to inflation (he calls it *revolution in prices*), although he admits, that inflation has certain positive aspects, such as acceleration of payments or limiting fluctuation in the value of money. The latter depends on the relationship between supply and demand, when supply is formed by a money supply and demand depends on the range of services for which it is used. That depends on the amount of exchanges, on the speed of money return and on the scale of exchanges.

A year before *National Economy*, Kaizl published his first work from the field of financial science, *Die Lehre von der Überwalzung der Steuren* [*The Teachings on Overruling the Taxes*] (1882), which together with *Finanční vědou* [*Financial Science*] (1892) secured for him the reputation of an expert in this particular field. Kaizl here attempted to apply consistently the theory of marginal utility on state economic activity and to analyze the state needs; the main idea of the book is that also in public economy there has to be the rule of the greatest prosperity at the lowest costs. Kaizl does not hide scientific ambitions to present the theoretical foundations of every other financial science, i.e. its methodology, systematic interpretation and history; history both in the sense of the history of financial science and practical financial policy. Indeed, the distinction between theory and policy is what delimits his work from other titles in the field, as does the effort to define precisely every term with which he wishes to work. Kaizl considers himself to be an original thinker in this 'tracing economic categories', for nowhere in the literature is it executed in as much details as it is in his work. He grants only Emil Sax (1845–1927), the professor of economics at the German part of the University in Prague, who does not, however, describe the content thereof as thoroughly (Kaizl 1892, 58, f. 35).

In contrast to period conventions to explain financial science as a subset of political economy, he considers it to be a theoretical discipline standing astride over economics and political sciences. The subject of financial science is not the economic activity of the state itself, but the manner in which the state acquires funds for the fulfilment of its needs; this is not necessarily only money, but it could be goods, services and performances. The originality of Kaizl's concept of public finances stems from the concept of the organic composition of the state economy and lies in the formal and content analysis of the state needs and costs necessary for its satisfaction. Kaizl is thereby truly different from his contemporaries and economists who focused on this area after him, with the exception of Karel Engliš, who takes over the structure of Kaizl's interpretation, although he does not cite him.

To a certain extent, one can observe in Kaizl's concept conciliation with the German school when he says that the state as an organic whole has to reflect also the composition of political power and not to try to fulfil the norms of absolute or historical justice. He also adds the notion which we noted already in Comenius's text that the state 'imposes through secular law the fulfilment of the moral law of love and participates in the development of its population and the welfare thereof' (Ibid., 9). Nor does he deny the influence of Cameralism when he names all performance of state tasks as administration and state itself as a great bailiff. He criticizes the approaches of other economists and their superficial analysis, as a consequence of which financial science necessarily becomes utopian and under the concept of financial science one finds hidden only advice on how the state should manage its husbandry, how it should adjust authorities collecting taxes and what expenditures the state should have. The examples which he gives for the mistaking of science with a historicizing description seem to be a criticism of Chleborád; but he particularly criticizes Wagner and his *Grundlagen der Volkswirtschaft* [*The Basics of the Economic Teachings*] (1876, 1892), although in many passages he labels him as an 'excellent' writer and copies some of his interpretations. Kaizl's inspiration is Henry Sidgwick's (1838–1900) *The Principle of Political Economy* (1883), but especially the works of Russian economist Vladimir Pavlovich Bezobrazov (1828–1889), *Gosudarstvennyie dochody Rossii* [*Russian State Revenues*](1866–1872). And although another of Bráf's students, František Čuhel, needles him for being too accommodating to Russian authors and manifests 'a sort of personal repugnance towards German literature', Kaizl retorts that Čuhel, on the contrary, acts as the historical school is the only one (Ibid., 122). In 10 years, Čuhel would prove to him the degree to which that estimate of his (Čuhel's) intellectual insight was mistaken.

In his concept of financial science, Kaizl emphasizes two aspects: First, the structure and economic substance of the categories of public finances is the same as in private economy. Second, there are no state needs different from the needs of individual citizens; it is always the needs of individuals that are at issue, albeit not necessarily of all of them. The entire state is as its members are – not only in the sense of various needs, but also in the sense of the realization thereof connected with the enforcement of political and private interests through the state. It is not possible to lay down a binding list of needs and tasks of state, except at their minimal scale. The institution which can fill this list with specific needs is for him the Parliament, as we will see later, when approving the state budget. The state in the sense of the government is unable to do this; it balances, according to power conditions, between 'niggardly philistinism and wasting' (Ibid., 18–19) to the detriment of all. Not even individuals are able to do this, for they will never relinquish their private interests in the favour of society, whether they enter economic relationships for themselves or as representatives of political power. This thesis can certainly be considered as an early expression of the problem of rent-seeking. Kaizl deduces also the specific group of needs in which the part pertaining to one or another individual cannot be ascertained – he here names lighting, sewerage, health facilities – and on the basis of considering the possibility of satisfying such needs by public or private means, he arrives at the definition of a public good: One cannot exclude anyone from consumption in this group of needs.

Kaizl expresses three differences between public and private economy: First, consumption among the private is governed by income, which is possible in the public sphere only to the extent until public consumption reaches the maximum elasticity of public income. This occurs in a situation when 'the immovable milestone under which the sources of all new public income dry up is reached' (Ibid., 17). Second, it is the difference between private profit and public welfare (he does not agree with this, but declares that the more proportionate division of property also begins to be relevant here under the influence of political changes and the influence of Socialism); but this difference passes away the moment the state itself begins to be an entrepreneur. He expresses the varying durations thereof as the third difference.

Public and private economic activities do not differ in any other regards, although they use different terms in certain cases. As in private economy, state possession is divided according to whether it is used (income) or postponed for later use (capital). Capital is divided into production capital, which in connection with labour is the source of production income, and consumable capital which is the base of *income for use*. Further, all income is either *original*, i.e. earned in the context of economic activity, or *derived*, when it is transferred to an economic subject from another person without economic merit (by donation, loan, inheritance, winning). In public economy, possession is usually called *public domain*. Further, the state treasury pertains to public consumable capital. State production capital (he uses the term *financial dominion*, and refers to the French and Italian inspiration of the terms *domain privé de l'etat* and *dominio fiscale*) is concentrated in so-called *public firms*, the purpose of which is not profit, but the fulfilment of the needs of society.

Original state incomes are formed by utility incomes stemming from consumable capital, production or domain revenues and tax revenues, and have from the beginning been determined for the covering of administrative costs. The source of tax revenues is the private possession of individual economic subjects in society as a whole, in the first place citizens' incomes. The reason for these lies only in the fact that a certain part of needs can be satisfied only through the *union of citizens*. But no economic values are formed by these activities, the army, judicature, administration, education, etc. This has clear implications for his concept of taxes, that stands on an *a priori* financial-economic imperative that every tax as a payment by payers is justified only when payers receive for it the same value in a service provided by the state (Ibid., 19).

Derived state revenues stem from the existence of consumable capital, and are generated by yield from state production activities, from the services provided by them and from inhabitants' contributions in the monetary, natural and performance form. Kaizl ranks among them also escheat condemned by John Hus 500 years previously. The source of productive income is the productive activity of the municipalities, based on its financial dominion, which is in substance the productive capital of the municipality. The municipality 'earns' these revenues in their businesses, which could have a so-called private-commercial character if they are in competition with other private businesses in a given sector. Or they can stem from a specific form of financial dominion which is a public dominion when the state itself sets payment for its activities, for it pursues goals other than profit. The state wants this activity to be accessible for citizens and does not take profit into account (Kaizl mentions model factories, but also services which the state provides entirely free of charge such as roads, bridges and mints) or wishes to multiply its capital (forests). And in this regard he points out the problem of *fiscalism* and the *crowding out effect* and the *fiscal illusions* connected therewith.

According to Kaizl, the problem of *fiscalism* arises when the state attempts to gain financial revenues regardless of the administrative and economic-political circumstances. He identifies the *crowding out effect* at the moment when the state, through its business activities that are not subject to profit criteria, worsens the position of private competitors to the extent that the real monopoly of the community becomes legal 'silently and suddenly' without any compensation for liquidated private competitors. The state can also build its production entirely outside of private competition and fix prices entirely arbitrarily in the same manner as would a monopolist. Nevertheless, while the 'arbitrariness' of the private monopolist is always conditioned by an effort to make sales and profits, the state does not have these limitations. If the state sets a price higher than that which would be stabilized on the market, the state revenues from it become similar to tax, for it forces the inhabitants to pay more than the usual price; this is the case for all financial monopolies. If state sets a lower or even zero price, it is an administrative monopoly. And he emphasizes that no state service is free of charge; it always has to be paid for. But these are places where margins are blurred between various types of state revenues and *fiscal illusions* occur. He also identifies *fiscal illusion* in the manner in which taxes and fees are paid. Fees are citizen contributions to state administration costs for tasks which the state provides for them. Taxes are contributions in general, collected when state production and fee revenues do not suffice to cover its costs. Yet a part of production revenues is similar to fees and blends together from the average point of view.

The state is not *a priori* entitled to any of its revenue. With reference to his *organic concept of the state*, he draws attention to the fact that people satisfy a large part of their needs individually and only a small part collectively insofar as they surrender, year after year, part of their income not for the benefit of the state, but to satisfy those needs which the state has obliged itself to fulfil. The highest principle of financial science (in harmony with Sax and criticizing Schäffle) is, according to Kaizl, the harmonic composition of the needs of the state and its private members. In this *harmonious whole*, the state ought to work, with its administration, towards certain ideals and at the same time ensure that its intentions are fulfilled.

The state budget is the instrument which enables this; he significantly refers to the pertinent chapter of his *Financial Science* as *Economic Prudence*. The state, says Kaizl whilst citing the parable of the tower builder from the Gospel of Luke (14, 28–30), has to compile in the same way as any private economic subject a 'preliminary' comparing its income and consumption (revenue and expenditures); Kaizl speaks of a numerical plan for the future economic period (Kaizl, 1892, 58). He describes how the budget is compiled according to administrative departments and ministries and how every revenue is firmly allocated to its purpose. He refers to this as *the principle of coarseness* – the budget has to be so detailed so that the government cannot shift any items later (a ban on virement). And when the Minister of Finance prepares the state budget, it is of interest to the entire government which requests the approval thereof by the Parliament. This is the crucial point of his interpretation of the state budget. Parliament gives the budget the form of an act which the government has to respect as the firm limit of its economic activities, and the state budget is for him the *Tocquevillian* cornerstone of parliamentarism as a whole (Ibid., 70). After he has made a strict distinction between the sources of state revenues and defined the substance thereof, he thereby also determined a clear limit to the expansiveness of the state: Parliament and the willingness of the citizens to support the state. Hence it logically follows that state must not have any surpluses for the satisfaction of some other state needs; this would be like supplying the king, he adds (Ibid., 50–51).

Division of revenue and expenditures, including mandatory and extraordinary, is then but a technical matter, pertaining not to financial, but to political science. With his financial theory, Kaizl showed that the distinction between various types of state revenues is based on the varying origins thereof and the varying character of needs which they satisfy and not on how they are sorted and classified; i.e. on their internal nature, not on secondary signs. These are historical, set by the inductive method, not absolute and logical, and they do not necessarily stem from the concept of the state – any kind of combination of individual sources can occur.

Josef Kaizl, a gifted economist who during a 10-year academic career published two fundamental books and several innovative studies which were focused on practical economic issues and were published in German and Italian, began intensely to focus on politics and journalism as of the 1880s and almost faded away from scientific life, as did the awareness of his theoretical ideas. Those which concerned public finances, which were based on the critique of

Wagner and delimiting himself against him, and on which other works would be based in the field over the next 50 years, would later be passed by Czech economists as the theses of Wagner himself.

František Čuhel: the unacknowledged genius

In his study on the history of Austrian school Ludwig von Mises (1881–1973) writes, that 'among the students of Menger, Böhm-Bawerk, and Wieser there were also non-German Austrians. Two of them have distinguished themselves by eminent contributions, the Czechs Franz Čuhel and Karel Englis' (Mises, 2003, 19). Čuhel was one of the first of Bráf's university students, and Bráf very soon perceived in him a theoretical spirit and even saw his successor in him. But Čuhel's life developed entirely differently and is more than anything reminiscent of the race for authorship of the invention in which he lost.

František Čuhel (1862–1914) was born into a Protestant family in Olešnice near Blansko in Moravia. He studied law in Vienna and Prague and gained a doctoral title in Prague in 1886. After an unsuccessful attempt – albeit on Bráf's recommendation – to gain a professorial post at the *Czechoslavonic Commercial Academia* in Prague, he worked as an official at the *Chamber of Commerce* for the next 5 years. Due to lengthy psychological problems, he went into premature retirement in 1903 and focused once again on scientific work; the result was the book *Zur Lehre von den Bedürfnissen: Theoretische Untersuchungen über das Grenzgebiet der Ökonomik und der Psychologie* [*The Teachings on the Needs: Theoretical Research on where Economics and Psychology Meet*] (1907) and up to 60 paragraphs in an abridged Czech version (Čuhel, 1907b). In 1908, he became an official of the General Pension Insurance Company for Private Officials in Vienna. He made an intense effort to pursue an academic career but was unsuccessful yet again. Likewise, none of his technical inventions which he had patented were successful, not even a counting machine from 1890 (Gruber, 1914, 426).

Like Bráf's other students, Čuhel first worked on historical studies of the recent past. Bráf's openness towards differences in opinion is attested to by vigorous mutual correspondence and his support even after their opinions diverged. While Bráf and Kaizl sought for a way between the German and Austrian school and the inductive and deductive methods, Čuhel entirely rejected history. He understood the *Methodenstreit* as a dispute about whether a science which describes human action other than history can exist. Čuhel clearly resonated with the Austrian school insofar as there are generally valid rules for human action. With his efforts, he thus relates, in the Czech environment, more to Chleborád than Bráf and to Chleborád's search for a way to generalize economic phenomena regardless of place and time, the national and race characteristics of agents and their religious, philosophical or ethical ideologies.

Yet Čuhel's search had a semantic and linguistic nature and is best characterized by an endeavour for conceptual clarity. He did not understand his theory only as a new version of a theory of value, but as an entirely new approach to the study of human behaviour generally; his book on needs was meant to be only an introduction to the new theory of human action. Its level of discovery is entirely exceptional: Besides the ordinal theory of utility, he balances on the boundary of psychology and economics in an entirely original manner and clearly delimits the boundaries between economics and other fields, including mathematics; he works with the notion of externality and time preferences. As a point of departure in his considerations, Čuhel focused on the notion of need, for he became aware that this concept – although considered a fundamental notion of economic science – is very rarely analyzed and is used without reflection, and economists behave as though it is sufficient to analyze general ideas about a phenomenon to know its substance. He finds 12 such various meanings of the term *need* on which he proves this. He himself wants, according to natural sciences, to analyze the phenomenon itself and discovers *needs* as they truly are (and ignores general language). This is why he undertakes a path – sometimes stressful for readers – for the clarification thereof, distinguishing itself by 'going to impossible degrees of dividing and schematizing, which transforms economics into complete scholasticism' (Ibid., 424).

In Čuhel's concept economics is neutral in value, focuses on phenomena the content of which is a certain type of human action and the result thereof and is able to express generally valid laws. *Desire* is the reason why a subject acts and can be compiled into a scale which expresses the degree of their satisfaction and its share in a subject's well-being. The subject becomes aware of the extent to which its desires are satisfied and the state in which it finds itself as a result of feelings; *feelings* are the regulators of *desire* and the subjective feeling of well-being. A conscious effort to maintain or improve this state enters on the basis of these feelings. But Čuhel is in no way a hedonist, he does not think that the true goal of all human desire and actions is well-being, i.e. the sum of such states of consciousness which are connected with pleasant feelings and free of unpleasant ones. These *desires* are only a mechanism with the help of which 'either the Creator or nature' wishes to accomplish an improvement of the situation, 'so that those animals that are lower on an objective scale of well-being were brought up to higher position; in other words, so that they can do what benefits the preservation and the development of their life as individuals and species' (Čuhel, 1907b, 4). A certain change of the state of consciousness of a subject and, as a rule, also a certain change in the external world is necessary to change this state and to assuage every *desire*: The subject has to find and use the material carrier of the feeling of well-being, a *means of satisfaction*, thanks to which *desire* for well-being becomes *use desire*. And for this reason, it needs to own this *means of satisfaction* in order to satisfy *desire*. This is why *possession desire* enters the game. In order for it to arise, it is necessary either to have a specific *desire*, the *means of satisfaction*, or the notion that this *need* will arise. In any event, the subject begins to act at this moment.

And economics is focused precisely on this action: Action aiming to acquire and maintain possession of certain *means of satisfaction* that the individuals subjectively consider necessary for the satisfaction of their *use desire*. Economics, however, cannot be satisfied only with ascertaining, describing and classifying this action and its results. According to Čuhel, its role is to interpret them; i.e. investigate its causes, reduce them to the smallest possible number of notions and formulate the laws. The demand which Čuhel thus places on economics is far-reaching: If economics is a theoretical science, it also has to answer questions as to why people behave so differently towards various world phenomena that surround them; why they endeavour to acquire and possess certain things and not others; why this endeavour varies according to place and time and why this endeavour is of different intensity in different subjects. Yet this does not mean to research *use desire* itself. That belongs to the area of other sciences (psychology), for knowing the world breaks down into a number of individual disciplines, among which a sort of a division of work exists. And he formulates a sentence which is to become the mantra of every future economic treatise: The rationality of the acting subject is the rationality of the choice of means, not goals. For economics, these goals are given facts. Čuhel describes this poetically: 'The border station, in which the economic science adopts the vehicle of research work from the neighbouring sciences, is a use desire' (Ibid., 8).

The transformation of *desires* into *needs* is carried out by Čuhel in another thought construction when he also includes in the analysis the situation where the subject feels *desire* but does not know how to satisfy it, and he introduces the notion of *disposition to desire*. The concept of *need* as the first and fundamental concept of economics – *use need* – emerges through the connection of *desire* and the disposition to it, that is, the disposition to action leading to the satisfaction of desire. *Economic use needs* are the type whose immediate goal is the consumption of economic goods. *Economic possession needs* are the type whose direct goal is the acquisition or maintenance of possession. All other needs are considered by Čuhel to be non-economic and economics should not focus on them. To this he proposes – in view of the capacity of various meanings of words in regular language – that economics relinquish entirely the word *need* and use the Greek word *chrenomos*. This would express precisely the substance of economics as a science; Čuhel is of the impression that research on needs should become an independent science and proposes for it the title *chrenomy* (Ibid., §17). In following he then presents dozens of new terms which are meant to be those terminological replacements of the word *need* in economics; he says this list can further be extended *ad infinitum*. In what follows I attempt to briefly characterize them by their division according to three categories: The relationships between desires and dispositions to them (the individual needs, others regarding needs, their mutual combinations); the nature of subjects (the needs of individuals, collectives or their combinations,); time (the needs of past, present and future); and measure (latent and effective).

The definition of certain new terms is entirely original, for Čuhel simply disperses between the lines considerations which will be revolutionary in economics (and other social sciences) only after several decades. First, he introduces the term *externality* and expands economic analysis also to the relationships between parents and children. He does so whilst dividing according to the relationship between desires and the dispositions to them, when he distinguishes between *ipsile*, *alterile* and *mutual needs* (self, others regarding, and mutual). He avoids the terms *egoistic* and *altruistic* for their moral tone (Ibid., §20–24). The former are sensed by subjects for themselves, the latter for others, and the third are mutual combinations of several *ipsile* needs. As an example of others regarding needs (*alterile*), he introduces the stepmother caring for a child (Ibid., §35) and the harmonization of *ipsile* and *mutual* needs is demonstrated with today's classic textbook example of a water polluter (Ibid., §38).

Second, he introduces the term *time preference* when interpreting the process of satisfying economic needs (Ibid., 22). He is aware that satisfaction does not occur at once, but gradually, in several stages; he speaks of the *economic possession needs of more distant orders* and speaks of future, but also past needs. The time factor is also related to his conclusion that under otherwise identical conditions desire, which aims to realize the increase of longer-lasting well-being, takes priority.

Third, when explaining the notion of individual and collective needs he expresses a primordialist theory of the nation and the national movement, but speaks of the *collectivity*. The action of the collectivity can be subjected to economic analysis, for it can have *ipsile*, *alterile* and *mutual* needs. According to Čuhel, the collectivity is not an independently acting entity, but the connection of individuals who for some reason act together; the task of economics, however, is not to explore how such groups arise. But the fact is that, like an individual, the collectivity too has a teleological determination: To distinguish states of well-being and find activities leading to it so that states of lesser well-being are replaced by higher ones (Ibid., §27). But it is not necessary for all members of a collectivity to have *feelings* and *desires* corresponding to a given *collectivity*. It is enough when it is shared by those members whose will represents it (Ibid., §31), and the rest can be forced or convinced to follow. And indeed, feelings which draw the individual to collectivities result in the fact that: Collectivities such as the state, municipality, church, nation, etc.

> are not just logical notions of species, mere abstracts, but real phenomena, a kind of super-individual organisms, towards which singular members are in a similar relation as a singular cells towards the entire individual's organism.
>
> (Ibid., 15)

The division of needs into individual and collective also has an impact on his concept of public finance. Čuhel is an advocate of the priority of individual, private action to state intervention. State needs – be they *collective use needs* or *collective possession needs* – are realized through the direct individual activity of the state through public businesses or public institutions; the former concerns *possession needs*, the latter *use needs* (Ibid., §41).

And finally, Čuhel's expression of the ordinal theory of utility: Instead of the term *utility*, he introduces the term *egency* which can be positive or negative (*disegency*) and asserts that, when satisfying *needs*, it is not the intensity of *feelings* that accompanies them that is of crucial significance, but rather the strength of their *egencies*. The strength of *egencies* cannot be measured, for people are able only to determine the order of their preferences (Ibid., §48). He then also builds, on the impossibility of measuring utility, a critique of Hermann Heinrich Gossen (1810–1858). Nevertheless, if *egencies* cannot be measured, this does not mean an absolute rejection of measurement and mathematics in economics. Čuhel proposes – analogically to the natural sciences – to compile a *scale of egencies* and investigate to which step of this scale this or the other *egency* is equal. He then subjects this compilation of scales to multiplication through all hitherto used criteria and rejects the interpersonal comparison thereof (Ibid., §54). As regards time comparisons, he allows them only in *ipsile needs*, and simple ones moreover, which do not change in the process of the act of satisfaction, although in connection with the critique of Gossen, he rejects the possibility of their assuming the form of a law. Nevertheless he admits a 'modest seed of truth' in 'discounting the future' which is hidden in the so-called *abstinence* or *waiting theory of capital interest* (Ibid., 32).

According to the proverb 'no one is a prophet at home' and despite the fact that Josef Gruber (1865–1925) spoke of Čuhel's book in his obituary as one of the most elaborated and deepest works ever to be written in the Bohemian Crownlands from time immemorial (Gruber, 1914), Čuhel was saved from complete oblivion only by a mention in Jan Koloušek's (1859–1921) textbook (Koloušek, 1918). Although Čuhel surely inspired Karel Engliš in his concept of profit tax principles as in the use of the term *teleology*, Engliš does not mention him as his inspiration. But it is possible that these were thoughts circulating in the context of Bráf's seminars at Charles-Ferdinand University, which both of them attended. And although Gruber writes in the same obituary that Čuhel's book on needs was difficult to read even for Germans, who are used to the stylistic tediousness of Marx, Sax or Schäffle, Austrians understood him – in German. Böhm-Bawerk answered Čuhel's critique of his cardinal theory with a broad polemic (Böhm-Bawerk, 1959, 124–136). Immediately after its publication, Čuhel's book lived to see favourable reviews in the *Economic Journal* and in *Political Science Quarterly*. Mises thanked him for his ordinal concept of utility when writing his *Theory of Money and Credit* (1934). Lionel Robbins (1898–1984) cited him in his famous essay from 1932, and Čuhel probably influenced him in the issue of the interpersonal comparison of utility (Hudík, 2007).

Nevertheless, the assertion of Čuhel and his concept on academic ground was ultimately prevented by circumstances entirely different from scientific disputes. The official post he held gave him little room for systematic scientific work which was purely theoretical and time-consuming even in the sense of travelling to Menger for consultations in Vienna or to Böhm-Bawerk in Innsbruck. Yet both were very interested in Čuhel's work; and they supported Bráf's exhortation to apply for a professorial post. Čuhel was still not satisfied with his work. So he was outrun by Bráf's other students, Horáček, Gruber and Koloušek.

Unfortunately, in 1903, he had to face a public 'scandal' of Prague proportions. As an official of the Chamber of Commerce, he filed at the Prague military headquarters a denunciation on Technical Sergeant Růžička to the effect that he was harassing the Chamber's clerk. Růžička did not hesitate and filed a lawsuit against Čuhel for slander (Krameš, 2016, 57). Čuhel's and Bráf's Czech opponents from the *Youth Czech Party* had the upper hand and Prague was entertained. Čuhel psychologically collapsed and left his work, moved to Vienna and assailed scientific work once again. He finished and published his theory of needs and wanted to apply for a professorial position at the University of Vienna. Initially, Menger, Böhm-Bawerk and also Wieser and Eugen von Philippovich (1858–1917) wrote positive assessments. But Wieser eventually discouraged Čuhel from applying for the post – first in view of the fact that it was not customary for Czechs to get a professorship in Vienna and second in view of the previous 'scandal'. Čuhel thus fell prey to the old Austrian approach to universities, insofar as professors were still viewed as state officials. It was therefore useful when they complied with political assignments but inopportune when they were connected with a scandal.

All of these circumstances led not only to Čuhel's bitter disappointment. They also led to the fact that economics does not derive the ordinal concept of utility from Čuhel, but from Vilfredo Pareto (1848–1923) and then from John Hicks (1904–1989) and Roy George D. Allen (1906–1983). But there is a possibility that they may have been familiar with Čuhel's work when writing their ground-breaking work. At the LSE at that time, Hicks was a member of the *Robbins Circle*, and Robbins certainly knew Čuhel. Moreover, Friedrich August von Hayek (1899–1992), who was familiar with the entire discussion in Austria also worked there. Almost forgotten in the Czech Republic today, in the history of the Austrian School he gave his name, thanks to Murray Rothbard (1926–1995), to the Čuhel-Mises theory of ordinal utility (Rothbard, 2009, 5).

Karel Engliš: the logic of human action

Engliš's work is the continuation of the effort of Czech economists to create a self-contained economic system. Like Kaizl, he succumbed to the temptation of political power, but similarly to Čuhel, he never abandoned thinking about economic issues; his scope spanned from philosophy through noetics to practical economic issues. He endeavoured to find a general and unified systemic foundation for the formation of economic theory which could be related to the behaviour of all economic subjects. Noetics became this for him, and he applied the logical rules of the theory of knowledge to economics. An historic accident crossed his life's path – he was 38 when Czechoslovakia was established and unexpected new possibilities were opened for him.

Karel Engliš (1880–1961) was born in Hrabyně, in Silesia, and studied law at Charles-Ferdinand University in Prague, where he was a student of Albín Bráf; he spent part of his studies in Munich in 1904, where he attended Ludwig Brentano's (1844–1931) seminars. Bráf, who recognized in him an exceptional student, supported and helped him to gain his first employment experiences – in the Municipal Statistical Office in Brno and at the Ministry of Commerce in Vienna. In 1911, Engliš was appointed Professor of National Economy at the Czech Technical University in Brno and then in 1919, at Masaryk University in Brno, the establishment of which he initiated, and the first Rector of which he became. In 1939 he began to teach at the Faculty of Law at Charles University, where he also became rector for a brief period in 1947. Apart from his academic career he also built a political career – he was a member of the rightist National Democracy, MP, Minister of Finance in six Czechoslovak governments, and in the 1930s he was also the governor of the Czechoslovak National Bank.

According to Engliš, the point of departure for research in economics as well as for the formulation of its rules is the behaviour of an economic subject. But neither the solution of the Austrian school, represented by Menger, nor the solution that Walras and Jevons offered through mathematic modelling satisfied Engliš. He was very familiar with the German and Austrian schools and kept personal contacts with the representatives thereof; he also knew the Stockholm school represented by Knut Wicksell (1851–1926) and Eric Lindhal (1891–1960) but in his texts he considered none of them to be a source of inspiration. This he found especially in Immanuel Kant's (1724–1804) noetic philosophy and in his distinction of the world as it is and as it should be. If Kant overcomes the causal view of natural sciences with the normative question of 'what should be', Engliš expands this dualism to a trialism with the question 'why it should be'.

He referred to the legal theory of Hans Kelsen (1881–1973) as his second source of inspiration, especially his normative noetics in contrast to the causal understanding of the natural sciences. This is certainly connected with the establishment of Masaryk University, which enabled him to gather around him at the Faculty of Law a unique and inspiring team of young lawyers with a sense for economics, such as Jan Loewenstein (1886–1932), Miloš Horna (1897–1958), Vladimír Vybral (1902–1980) and Alois Král (1902–1991), with whose help he built a workplace which was referred to as the Brno School of Economics in the interwar period. But his closest colleague was the Professor of Constitutional Law František Weyr (1879–1951). In their search for philosophical foundations for human behaviour exploration, they abstracted from the dispute between materialism and idealism and from the question as to whether the world can be known. Their foundation was both the assumption of the existence of the knowing subject on one hand and known objects and events on the other, and also the premise that various forms of noetics and interpretation are necessary to us in order for various objects and events to be known.

According to Engliš, the logical basis of all sciences lies not only in respecting the general logical laws, but also in a logically correct epistemological approach to learning and understanding the researched subject. Every reality is learned and understood in terms and inter-term's relationships which the human intellect has formed intentionally so as to capture the phenomena it observes and so that it can then process them further. According to Engliš, whilst the forms of quantitative thought have been thoroughly differentiated by mathematics and brought to exactness, this is not so in qualitative thought. This is why he approaches with a concept of three forms of qualitative thought in which qualitative notions and their relationships were developed. The sets of these notions form three logical orders: The *causal-ontological* order of the natural sciences; the *normological* order in which the organizing principles are logic and the search for an answer to the question of what should or should not be; and finally, the *final-teleological* order, based on *finality*, the purpose which the acting subject endeavours to fulfil – teleology seeks an answer to the question of what the purpose of action is, or more precisely, why something is wanted (Engliš, 1930, 28).

Teleology is the only possible form which can be used when expressing the regularity of economics; neither causal nor normative principles are adequate. Economics is based on the relationships between wanted goals (*telos*) and the means appropriate for the achievement thereof whilst the free will of acting subjects who choose between various alternatives exists. He almost literally assumes Čuhel's sentence that the content of purposeful action assumes a subject's deliberate action, 'whether we call it Nature, God or otherwise,' (Engliš, 1946, 3) but in contrast to Čuhel, he explains the process of decision-making through *teleological qualities*. The subject uses *criterial polarization* when evaluating the surrounding world: The object which can serve to fulfil a goal is useful; the others are harmful. Individual subjects acquire the character of goods during this process. If the purposes change, so can the teleological quality of these goods intended for the fulfilment thereof. This is why Engliš speaks of various forms of utilization (*direct, indirect, specific, abstract*) and various types of goods (*material and ideal, representable and non-representable*, etc.) (Daněček, 1991, 548).

In his interpretation of purpose Engliš started from the specific person: Each person follows a certain set of purposes which can be unified by a person not only as a subject of desire, but also as a subject of purposefulness. All purposes and means aiming towards care for human beings can be drawn together by constructing a common, central *purpose of all purposes* (this seems to be a variation of Menger's *goods of the first and highest orders*): 'The ideal of human is abstract of the care for person, and if this care is related to the entire nation, then (it is) the ideal of the nation. This ideal contains all the desired layers in a harmonic proportion' (Engliš, 1932a, 59). He first expresses this ideal as early as in 1916 in *Sociální politika* [*Social Policy*], where he contained all the desirable qualities of the person and nation in a harmonious mutual proportion: A healthy, educated, moral, safe and affluent person and nation. In *Teorie státního hospodářství* [*The Theory of State Economy*] (1932) he almost literally repeated the hundred-year old thesis by Buquoy, that 'to realize the ideal of the nation entails proceeding inside the nation according to the law of love for one's neighbour' (Engliš, 1932a, 149) and he added that the purpose is not education, morality, safety and affluence itself; this is a thought construction. Utility is only the realization of purpose (and damage is teleological harm). But the contents of the highest purpose, according to Engliš, are given by the interventions of the 'agents of power' and to a certain extent also by the difference of people and the prevailing material and cultural conditions. Engliš indeed granted that every state intervention is necessarily disturbing and destructive, for it changes original private purposes according to itself, and if state was to proceed thoroughly according to its purposes, it would liquidate the private economy (Engliš, 1932b, 52). Nevertheless, in the context of the highest purpose concept, the fight of political parties for power is for him (especially) the fight for the rectification of ideal of person and nation and for the achievement of public welfare (Engliš, 1938, 179).

The teleological method became for Engliš the starting point for the formulation of logical rules of the behaviour of economic subjects and, in connection with this, of all parts of his economic theory – theory of value, the theory of exchange and price, the theory of economic orders and the theory of state economy. In his theory of value, Engliš is clearly inspired by two of Gossen's laws – by the law of diminishing marginal utility and by the law of marginal utilities equilibrium although he criticizes H.H. Gossen insofar as he does not implement utility into the unit of goods and does not search for a proportion between the marginal utility of various goods. And this was precisely the issue for Engliš. His theory of value stands on two premises: First, when evaluating items, the subject evaluates their utility for achieving the intended purpose; and second, the subject evaluates the degree of this utility. To Engliš, therefore, value is the quantity of teleological quality. In other words, objects and events do not have value because labour is contained in them, but because they can serve more or less to fulfil a required purpose. Expended labour is only a secondary determinant of the rational securing of individual goods. It is not labour that determines value, but it is the value the subject attributes to a specific good which consequently conditions the amount of labour. The creation of values (goods) identifies this with the expended labour (costs) only in a marginal point in which motivation for other economic activity ends. Czechoslovak Marxists would later reproach him for he entirely overlooked the material area in which value is formed and he entirely ignored production and production relationships (Šmejkal *et al.*, 1962, 150).

From there Engliš proceeded further and attempted to deduce what logical rules are valid when subjects make decisions and act to pursue the maximum fulfilment of a pursued purpose. Yet he emphasized that there is always one highest purpose towards which all others stand in a certain hierarchy corresponding to diminishing utility. But hierarchy itself is a purely individual matter, for the same goods have for individual economic subjects a varying *utility gradient* or, more precisely, the securing thereof is connected with the varying growth of costs. This has its consequences when explaining the reaction of the market, the behaviour of the supply and demand side and price-setting. Every subject is aimed in the process of evaluation at achieving the maximum utility at minimal costs (maximum profitability), which is the first of two rules of the behaviour of every subject: *Frugality*. The second rule is *marginal rationality*, which is determined by the boundary on which the diminishing utility achieved during gradual satisfaction of every need is entirely annulled by rising costs. Marginal utility (value) is thus the lowest rationally feasible utility.

The last step of Engliš's theory of value is the relativization of the evaluation just described with regard to what relation individual purposes are pursued by one subject. This is why he attempts to transfer utility to a comparable foundation – to convert absolute utility to the relative utility which pertains to every material or monetary unit. But optimal satisfaction is achieved by a subject when the relative utilities of individual goods become equal. For the equalizing of marginal relative utilities, Engliš introduces the term *objective solidarity*, which then has a fundamental place in his *theory of economic orders*. Besides the term *subjective value*, he also used the term *objective value*; the latter was meant to express that it is not valid only for the subject that created it but for everyone.

Engliš's theory of exchange, the *teleological theory of natural exchange*, stands on three premises. First, exchange takes place when it is revealed to be useful for both exchanging subjects. Second, the impetus to exchange does not exist if there exists in the good designated for exchange the same relation between their marginal utilities. And third, by exchange, continuous adjustment of marginal utilities to existing exchange relations occurs until the impetus to exchange disappears.

From there, Engliš proceeded to the creation of his theory of price, where he consistently distinguished between price level and price ratio. The degree of price level is determined by the same factors as the purchasing power of a monetary unit. Price is the result of price ratio. In this issue, Engliš criticized Smith's classic theory, for production costs are no more than prices; and furthermore, prices are not a determined quantity, according to Engliš. In this sense he viewed Marx's theory as progressive as compared to Smith's, for Marx attempted to explain price by a category outside of the price structure (labour). But the concept of abstract labour, or more precisely, socially necessary labour, by which Marx attempted to solve the need to compare various types of labour, was considered vague by Engliš. Furthermore, objects Engliš, Marx's attempt suffers by the same imperfection as Smith's, i.e. insofar as he considers price to be a determined quantity.

Because Engliš thinks of his teleological theory as a general theory, usable not only for the individual, but also for firms and states, he applies it also to the state economy. His own *theory of economic orders* serves him as an instrument of application. Economics is thus ultimately, according to Engliš, a theory of order in which individual people and entire nations care to maintain and improve their lives (Engliš, 1938, 3). According to him, every economic and social order had two fundamental thoughts: First, how much and what should be produced, and second, how the costs and processes of social labour should be divided. He constructs three types of social orders, on the basis of which the economic orders are constituted: *Individualistic, solidaristic and cooperative*. The *individualistic order* is based on free private economies, the reciprocal relationships of which are governed by subjective utilities and subjective costs, and they are realized exclusively by means of the market, without intentional and systematic organization; the state has only the function of the legal state, i.e. it protects contracts, ownership rights, personal integrity and freedom, and it pursues no other goal different from the purposes (interests) of participant individual economies.

The *solidaristic order* is planned, with common ownership of means of production; in contrast to the first, it is formed by one entire economy governed by the unified purpose defined above – the ideal of the person and nation. Because it could cross the subjective interests of its own members, it has to be realized by force.

And finally, the *cooperative order* is also characterized by plan and common ownership of means of production. There exist, however, independent and free individualistic economies that acquire all their needs in a common establishment, and division occurs according to a previously given key, on the basis of which every member should receive a certain amount of cooperative money as freely disposable income. Engliš understood state economy as a field on which *solidarism* is cultivated, and only when solidarism is unable to achieve the interest of objective well-being is it in the line of the objective *ideal of the nation* to preserve a certain necessary degree of individual production. In *Social Policy* (1916) he referred to social policy as its 'cultivator'. In *The Theory of State Economy* (1932a), he did not understand economy as unified, but rather as an agglomerate of the solidaristic and cooperative activities of the state and state firms, and the above-mentioned highest purpose is at its helm.

Engliš's teleological system of economic orders offers analytical instruments for both researching Socialism and Communism and for a diagnosis of modern capitalism. Engliš never doubted that capitalism has a future, and he did not see a danger in cyclically repeating crises; this is why he often overlooked, for instance, the problem of unemployment, but expressed his fears about securing the revenues of an expanding state whilst preserving through a tax burden a balanced degree of satisfaction of all inhabitant groups. He therefore expected that capitalism would remain the most effective economic system, but certain rules of the game would be adjusted by a greater involvement of elements of the cooperative and solidaristic order. Engliš's assessment of solidarism was clear: It simply does not correspond to human nature and has to – on its own at best – be transformed into a form of *cooperativism* or capitalistic *individualism*. But as he added, history has hitherto known neither an example of conversion nor a truly real *solidarism*.

Noteworthy in this regard are his conclusions about democracy, which he contemplated still prior to the emergence of any international discussion on the economic efficiency of the socialist system. Engliš asserted that while the relationship between capitalism and democracy is binding, countries built on a purely *solidaristic order* are unable to adopt even minimal democratic government processes. Despite his critique of the *solidaristic order*, he did not focus on the problems of directive economy and the command plan. The reason apparently lies insofar as his conclusions on the issue of the *solidaristic order* are the peak of construction based purely on intellectual abstract performances; Engliš's writing appears to confirm this.

As a consequence of the application of the teleological method Engliš differed from his contemporaries also in the interpretation of financial science. Although he adhered to the period concept that the subject of financial science is the acquisition of funds for the state economy, he focused almost exclusively on tax policy. And it was precisely in the evaluation and interpretation thereof that he distinguished himself from his contemporaries. According to him, taxes were a solidaristic element in the state economy: 'The strong help the weak; that is solidarism' (1932b, 106), whereas fees were a cooperative element. The above-mentioned differences are twofold.

First, following Čuhel and his theory of individual and collective needs, he referred to the only tax principle as the so-called principle of the relative objective burden of the tax unit, or more precisely the burden (Engliš, 1932a, 141–142 and Engliš, 1938, 102,) when he compared the utility of a particular tax with the minimal costs connected with the acquisition thereof. According to Engliš, a tax-free minimum outside of this principle cannot be fixed, and at the same time there hence stems his respected progressive construction of the tax rate. He admitted that tax is a forced contribution and that the state reduces yields and incomes by its interventions and inhibits individual interest. Nevertheless, he added that it is necessary to confront these material losses, the decline of productivity, with the growth of the quality of the nation; the endeavour to achieve the purpose – *the ideal of the nation* – was thus to him an adequate justification for the tax burden and the limitation of the *individualistic order.*

Second, in his interpretation of taxes Engliš attempted to capture the common substance of national income and yields of *national labour*, which is why he proposed a tax structure intended to reflect the fact that various production and consumer acts are taxed differently. Therefore, property stood at the forefront of his tax structure, although he considered property tax to be entirely exceptional, for it has the form of confiscation that threatens the economic activity of the individualistic structure. According to whether the property arose as yield or income, he distinguished between taxes that affect revenues according to *personal capacity*, the yield of *national labour* or those that are connected with *individual private acts*. In another interpretation he does not deny inspiration by Kaizl – he does not cite him, but uses Kaizl's content for his own concepts. Engliš did not consider state expenditures and the division thereof to be so important inasmuch as it is difficult to fix a boundary between personal and real costs, and further, because it can only be a state motion, not the state expenditure as such that can be productive or unproductive, for the purpose of the state is not the increase of productivity, i.e. profit, but care for the nation and public well-being. He admitted profit only when it does not occur at the expense of public well-being and asserted that when the sum of contributions of a particular public item exceeds the sum of costs and becomes profitable, it ceases to be a part of the public administration and begins to be a business (Engliš, 1932b, 97). Literally assuming Bráf's thesis (Bráf 1915, 38–60) (but without stating it), he determines as the maxim of public economy the fact that there has to be a qualitative, quantitative and time concord between revenues and expenditures (Engliš 1932b, 224).

In the concept of the state budget, Engliš was influenced by his experience as a minister, and he always placed his interpretation at the end of his treatise on financial science – for in his view the form ought to be adjusted to the content. He defined the state budget as an economic plan that prevents chaos in the state economy, which has to be modified by the construction of this economy – *individualistic* or *solidaristic* – and has to observe the differences between them; this is why the expenditure of state mines and the administrative expenditures of schools, for instance, cannot be counted. It was indeed his ministerial experience that commanded him to place on the state budget a demand of such detail (*roughness*) that would prevent anyone from changing particular budget items. According to Engliš, it is the composition of the government (not the Parliament as in Kaizl) that gives the state budget its character and thereby prosperity for all.

Engliš considered his teleological method and its details in two decades of discussions with Brno colleagues and students, with other Czechoslovak economists, but especially with representatives of the Austrian School. Although he maintained personal relations with many of its members, such as J. Schumpeter, E. von Böhm-Bawerk and L. von Mises, he tried as much as possible to distinguish himself from the Austrian School by introducing his own concepts and by expressing his own teleological theory of utility, value, exchange and prices. He criticizes the Austrians especially due to the fact that their concept of individual economy lacks a purpose and that needs are mere psychological facts. When he criticized Oskar Morgenstern (1902–1977), he could not even resist a sarcastic remark – albeit only in a footnote – that a school that stands on the notion of utility has no concept of what utility is (Engliš, 1933, 361). On the other hand, F.A. von Hayek rejected Engliš's teleology; in a footnote as well: 'Others, like K. Engliš, have used it in an unobjectionable manner and sharply distinguished between "teleological" and "normative" sciences. . . . But the term remains nevertheless misleading. If a name is needed the term "praxeological" sciences . . . would appear to be the most appropriate' (Hayek, 1942, 278, f.1). Mises in his book *Human Action* (1949) refers to Engliš's *Begründung der Teleologie als Form des empirischen Erkennens* [*Teleology as a Form of Empirical Knowledge*] (1930) when explaining intentional human action (Bažantová, 2016).

But in real life, harder adversaries than his opponents in opinion awaited Engliš. Two totalitarian regimes – the Nazi and the communist – entered into his life. Immediately after the occupation of Czechoslovakia in 1939, he withdrew into seclusion and only returned to academia writing after the war;

in 1947, he became the Rector of Charles University. But being associated with the First Republic economic elites which were subjected to defamation, he was dismissed from his post soon after the 'victorious communist February 1948'. His Brno School was destroyed. Years of personal persecution followed. His books disappeared from libraries, his name from tuition syllabuses; he himself withdrew once again into privacy which he never left. In his hometown, and in abject poverty, he devoted himself to his theoretical considerations, which were meant to be forgotten, and to writing books which would never see publication during his life. On his death certificate it is written: 'Expect no reward you who serve your country'.

Josef Macek: non-conventional liberalist and socialist

Josef Macek belonged to the last generation of Bráf's students. Macek's first professional text emerged in the framework of Bráf's seminar and was published on the pages of the then prestigious *Obzor národohospodářský* [*Economic Horizon*] co-formed by Bráf, in 1912, in the same issue that Bráf's obituary was printed. Probably no student was associated with Bráf with as many common themes as Macek: Whether in terms of the methodological clarification of economics or the thematization thereof such as social sciences, the social question or economic education. And if Bráf attempted to pacify the German and Austrian school, Macek attempted to pacify Liberalism with Socialism. His social-liberal interpretation of Adam Smith, published at his own cost, was of entirely exceptional significance in the Czech environment (Macek, 1915); Austro-Hungarian censorship apparently confiscated several pages of the book (Habr, Jankovský, 1990, 527). Macek saw the cause of unjustly discredited Liberalism in the Czech Lands in ignorance and in its mistaken identification with capitalism.

Josef Macek (1887–1972) was born in Krumpach near Zábřeh in Moravia. He studied law and philosophy in Prague and Berlin. In 1912–1918 he taught at the *Czechoslavonic Commercial Academy* in Prague. After the Great War, he worked at the Ministry of Agriculture and at the Land Office. In 1919, he was a member of the Czechoslovak delegation at the Paris Peace Conference. In 1921, he was appointed as an associate and in 1926 as a full-time professor of national economy at the Commercial College in Prague, where he worked until 1949. That year, he emigrated to the USA, where he received a professorship at the University of Pittsburgh in 1953.

In the interwar period, Macek visited the world's most prestigious economic workplaces, studied French, American, English, German and Soviet economists, with many of whom he maintained personal friendly relationships. At a perfunctory glance at Macek's work, one could mark John Maynard Keynes (1883–1946) as his main inspiration. Macek no doubt knew Keynes from as early as the Paris Peace Conference and considered him to be the greatest economist of his time; he reviewed some of his texts and printed several of them in the journal *Naše doba* [*Our Era*], which he managed. As similar or entirely identical that certain specific approaches of Keynes's and Macek's were, they were guided by different intentions. While Keynes wanted to preserve capitalism in a certain form, Macek wanted gradually to eliminate capitalism and replace it with Socialism. But most importantly, when Keynes expressed views that suited Macek, he (Macek) was already holding similar views (Polášek, 2010).

Inspiration may have been played by Macek's close personal connection to representatives of the Stockholm school, especially to Bertil Ohlin (1899–1979), who had lectured in Prague on Macek's invitation in the 1930s. But Franz Oppenheimer (1864–1943), with his concept of liberal socialism, was a fundamental source of inspiration to him. He was a student of his during his studies in Berlin, although there is no hint in his memoirs that Oppenheimer particularly interested him at the time (Macek,1943). But he later explicitly espoused his assertion that Liberalism and Socialism are identical in their consequences (Macek, 1935a, 150) and likewise his concept of monopoly, especially that of land, and the concept of land reform (Macek, 1918, 5–6).

Nevertheless, from 1912 by the latest, Macek began to read in English and studied in detail all the sources of inspiration of Oppenheimer himself, especially the English land reformers Henry George (1839–1897), Thomas Spence (1810–1877) and William Ogilvie (1846–1912); and as he himself writes, he became a socialist under their influence. Most importantly, one cannot overlook Macek's admiration for George – whether in the concept of monopoly, natural rights and land reforms as the basis for solving social issues or the ethical establishment of economy and the emphasis on the progress of ideas (Macek, 1935a). The Russian liberal nationalists and liberal Marxists, especially Pjotr Berngardovich Struve (1870–1944) and Michail Ivanovich Tugan-Baranovsky (1865–1919) also had an influence on the formation of Macek's opinions: The former with his notion that Russia would avoid the capitalist phase of its development and jump to Socialism through *agricultural communes* as forms of common land usage, the latter by rejecting revolutionary activities.

And finally, the utilitarian tradition also had its influence, especially Jeremy Bentham (1748–1832) and J.S. Mill as did the founder of American institutionalism, Thorstein Veblen (1857–1929) and the new Liberalism of the British Liberal Party expressed by David Georg Ritchie (1853–1903), John A. Hobson (1858–1940) and Richard Henry Tawney (1880–1962); Macek assumed from Ritchie his notion of natural rights, and Tawney's consideration on the problems of British Socialism actually inspired him to consider the problems of Socialism in Czechoslovakia (Macek, 1933). In 1928, in the foreword to the first Czech edition of Smith's *Inquiry into the Nature and Causes of the Wealth of the Nations*, Macek finally also shows his inspiration from the father of modern economics. He emphasizes Smith's concept of monopoly and rejection of land monopoly and land rent, his evolutionary approach and democratic thinking, but also common good as the vanishing point of all economic relationships and the moral level of every economic action (Macek 1928).

On the shoulders of these giants, Macek built his liberal socialist concept of economics standing on four pillars: Justice and free competition as one of the instruments thereof; the notion of Socialism as developed or complete Liberalism; freedom and equal opportunities, including the concept of social rights; and the communitarian approach to the solution of social problems as a middle way between individualism and collectivism that takes into account individuals but emphasizes their embedment in society. Macek was clearly the first who placed on the table the imperialistic demand of economics when he termed economic issues as the most important social issues of all. According to him, every social institution and every human act has its economic aspect. Nevertheless, the study of social phenomena cannot be reduced to economics: Social reality is an internally connected whole. Rather than a form of causality, these connections have the form of correlations or interdependences. He thereby continued Bráf's holistic approach to social reality and Kaizl's notion of the organic composition thereof.

According to Macek, every economic order stands on the concept of justice as 'the proportion of equivalence between merit and retribution' (Macek, 1919, 417) which is common to Socialism and Liberalism. But while Liberalism assumes that justice will be ensured by free competition, the socialists demand the kind of conditions (the kind of economic order) in which all people would have equal opportunities to produce, or more precisely, to earn money (Ibid., 420). Hence Macek's positive delimitation of freedom as freedom 'for a purpose' (Macek, 1946, 83). The same path is followed in 1924 by Macek's argument in favour of economic democracy. But consequently, Macek's explanation of the need for fundamental land reform, the broadening of employee rights, the support of cooperative enterprises, expansion of the possibility for education and perhaps the equality of women was guided by the classic liberal demand for equal opportunities, albeit with the awareness of the natural limits of such an endeavour.

A special aspect of this problem, then, is the issue of income inequality – Macek understood it as justified if it is the consequence of varying qualification, whilst one of the aims of the economic democracy project was for everyone to have the possibility to acquire and perform this qualified labour (Macek, 1924). This is why fulfilment of economic freedom and the actual completion of Liberalism are for him the concepts of planning as asserted by the British Labourists, as he writes in the review of the Czech translation of the book *Planning and Freedom* by Barbara Wooton (1947). For Macek, natural rights are measured by the interest of society and should at the same time be recognized generally, regardless of whether they have been enacted as particular acts in this or any other state. Among them are the right to life, to satisfaction of needs in the sense of the right to a certain minimum living wage of a person on the current degree of culture, the right to work and preparation for it, that is, to education, and finally, the right to the fruits of one's labours in the sense of the right to a just price for cooperation (Macek, 1925b).

From the epistemological perspective, Macek was an empiricist (Polášek, 2011). In this sense he is the successor of the demand which Čuhel placed over science when he began the pertinent paragraphs of his theory of needs with the sentence 'Experience teaches us' (Čuhel, 1907, § 52). Macek's empiricism is proved both by the fact that the sign of scientific quality was, for him, provability, and scientific proof was only the proof stemming from experience, the sensory grasp of reality and the processing, with critical reason, of data thus acquired. Or his statement that the permanent happiness of the largest number is the measure of action in utilitarian philosophy is, according to him, a question of experience, not an *a priori* principle. He understood economics as a social science, and defined it according to L. Robbins as a science of human behaviour, the content of which is the relationship between purposes and limited means (Macek, 1946, 18). Economics should discover regular connections between economic phenomena and at the same time help to reform society. In this point, an important role is played in economics by ethics, which – referring to Smith – he considered to be an integral part of economics. According to Macek, economic action should be not only frugal, but also moral. But frugality is a subjective category and is the satisfaction of needs from the perspective of adequacy of purposes and means. Need is the feeling of a certain lack, conditioned by the natural and social conditions in which a person lives and connected with the desire for the removal thereof. Besides material needs, he here includes also social needs such as justice, freedom, sympathy and love, honour or fame, solitude and affiliation to the collective. In Bráf's intentions, he divides economics into theoretical and practical – the latter uses the insights of theory for the choice of means towards the accomplishment of social goals. Theoretical science is free of value judgements – it helps to uncover the truth, not to decide what is good and what is bad. But at the same time, Macek admits that empirical testing, which is the fundamental instrument of science, is always sort of limited testing; a scientist must therefore select and choose, i.e. in a certain sense evaluate between facts and the methods of the discovery thereof (Polášek, 2011).

A key category of his ethically-based economics, for which he uses the term *social economy*, is that of welfare or Comenius's happiness of humankind, as he said, in the definition of which he anticipates the fulfilment of certain material conditions, although he see its substance in interaction with other individuals, and he considers the condition of the fulfilment of welfare to be a change in the thought on social phenomena: According to him, the world needs a new economic philosophy (Macek, 1933). Because he was of the impression that a purely liberal approach to delimiting social welfare as the result of spontaneous market forces lacks the altruistic perspective, he sought a solution in balanced social policy.

He focuses first on the problem of land ownership (Macek, 1918). He considers the just division of land to be the condition for further social reforms in society. Yet Macek did not see the roots of all social evil in private ownership itself or in the redistribution thereof, but in the institution of large estates. The key to changes in social conditions therefore lies in the removal of land monopoly both through 'economic coercion' through progressive taxation and strict limitation of inheritance rights and through the voluntary change of people by education and ethical influence; he estimated that this period would span more than 200 years. His interest spread then from the monopoly to the broad spectrum of social issues: Poverty, its sources and the ways to solve it, the reform of employment rights, revenues and their distribution, the cyclic fluctuations of economy, social insurance, the policy of full employment and the constant purchasing power of money. In all these issues, Macek places emphasis on private solutions, based on morality and the sense of belonging. Like Bráf, he was of the impression that the strengthening role of the state was a common factor of importance to them all. And he emphasizes the fact that the state first has to acquire adequate financial funds and then distribute them in the sense of economic rationality.

In the area of public finances, he thus returned to Kaizl's notion that all funds which the state redistributes are private. The state economy is only one of the methods for organizing human activity, whilst the household is the original organization. He divides the expanding tasks of the state into three large groups which cover the area of security (police, military, judicature, the prison service, but also health and social institutions), economy (when the state enters into various market relationships as a buyer and seller) and culture (not only education and science, but also care for the conditions of market competition and control of private monopolies, for all of these aspects attest to the cultural level of the state). In contrast to his contemporaries, he did not particularly focus on tax principles and considered taxes to be the instruments of economic and social policy, not just a means to fill the state treasury.

As regards state budgets, he considers it important to monitor not only individual numerical data, but where state expenditures go and whether the state does not disturb freedom of private business. Every expenditure should have a previously intended meaning and thereby also material, moral, health, aesthetic, technical and political consequences. The budget should be gross and contain all revenues and expenditures of particular administrative departments, institutions and enterprises as the net earnings of their activity, i.e. deficits or surpluses. He did not consider an accidental or small deficit in the state budget to be a serious problem; he recommends solving a permanent deficit either by increasing revenues or lowering expenditures, whereas he allows for solving a temporary deficit with a short-term loan which would be repaid from revenues from the next period. He maintains a distinction between public and state debts and was markedly more careful in the defence thereof than was the standard of the period. Even with debts, he always wanted to know whether they arose due to productive or unproductive purposes.

Macek offered the entire breadth of his scope in his *Sociální ekonomika* [*Social Economy*], his unplanned Czech swansong, a five-volume opus which he published in 1946–1948. Because it was intended as a university textbook, it includes all the themes on which he had hitherto focused – from the definition of economics, its subject, the character of economic laws, the delimitation of the basic needs of life (originally dependent on a reference group) through the category of capital and the critique of measurement of national income through to the significance of foreign trade in the context of the freedom of economic competition and considerations on the share of employees' profit in the context of considerations on the transformation of capitalism into a system in which capital does not hire labour, but labour hires capital; Macek speaks of the *autonomy of labour*. According to him, it is from this that the maxim to accept decisions of state economic and social policy in favour of the mainstream voter stems.

In all issues on which he focused, Macek manifested a realism that prevented him from becoming attached to great visions that could not be realized and relying on a change in the social establishment. He was a tireless and feared debater, especially for the ministers of finance. Engliš knew his fair share about this. Macek deepened all the questions that had been opened with urgent necessity in the Czech environment by Bráf, whose grateful student he remained; he had the bravery in February 1940 to go on air on Protectorate broadcasting to commemorate Bráf's merits in the fight to elevate the Czech nation. A few years later, in 1947, Macek's students organized a grand celebration of Macek's 60th birthday, to great public attention. But as little as two years later, Macek became the subject of sharp criticism of young Marxist economists who branded him a reformist and opportunist, the advocate of capitalism, the traitor of socialist ideals, a bourgeois servant, the enemy of the USSR and a propagator of fascism. The article *Reformismus v politické ekonomii* [*Reformism in Political Economy*] was written by Ota Šik, the later author of perhaps the most famous reform of socialist economy and one of the main representatives of the *Prague Spring* of 1968. Macek did not wait any longer and at Christmas in 1949, with a prepared pretext of tourism, he crossed the snowy western border of Czechoslovakia on cross-country skis with only one bag, in which he had the manuscript of the book he had begun writing, *On Effective Proof*. . . . Twenty years later, Šik himself would be branded as a reformist and rightist opportunist – and he emigrated too.

Between capitalism and Socialism

The beginnings of Czech Marxism

The work of Karl Marx was not unknown in the Czech intellectual environment. T.G. Masaryk devoted his university courses to it as well as the two-volume work *Sociální otázka* [*The Social Question*] (1898, 1946). In it, he writes that the social question is today specifically and practically a question of Socialism; and 'in our conditions socialism is mainly Marxism' (Masarayk, 1946, 3). Marx was also well known to Czech economists, who in principle distinguished themselves according to whether they understood his teaching as an interpretation of mode of production and distribution or the tactic of the *2nd Red International*. Kaizl and Bráf were also familiar with him. Kaizl had read *Capital* during his studies in Strasbourg, and in one of his letters to his uncle and supporter he writes that it is very heavy reading, but an exceedingly enlightening and instructive book. Although he rejected Marx's practical conclusions, he considered extreme liberal thinking to be equally harmful (Kaizl, 1909, 335). This was also the case with Bráf, who in his *Listy o studiu národohospodářském* [*Papers on the Study of National Economy*] (Bráf, 1923a), published a year prior to Masaryk's *The Social Question*, referred to Marx as the most perspicacious spirit of his time. While Kaizl read Marx in order to familiarize himself with the intentions of the *Red International* and Masaryk with the aim of carrying out a revision of Marx and Friedrich Engels (1820–1895), Bráf thought through Marx to the end with regard to the correctness of his theory and its implementation. If Marx's uncovered 'collectivist future' was the correct theory, writes Bráf, a law of development would ensue with unavoidable necessity from the present state, 'independent to wills and resolutions, even if the very proletariat had no sense for it' (Ibid., 34).

The first part of Marx's *Capital* was originally published in a Czech translation just prior to the Great War. During the interwar period, Marx's ideas were propagated either by publishing Marx's and Engels' main works or by applying Marx's theory when evaluating the economic situation in Czechoslovakia, the development of capitalist countries and the position of the working class in them. Because Marx's teachings were being popularized mainly on the pages of the communist press, most of the readers were mainly confronted by Marx's theses on the class struggle rather than by his theoretical concepts. They were introduced only in 1924 under the title *Základy Marxovy nauky hospodářské* [*Introduction to Marx's School of Economy*] in *Komunistická revue* [*Communist Revue*], which was an official platform for spreading the ideas of Marxism-Leninism, established by the Czechoslovak Communist Party. During the previous year, works of Marx, Engels and Vladimir Ilyich Lenin (1870–1824) started to be published in a newly established edition of *Leninova knihovna* [*Lenin's Library*]. The first Marx text that was translated was *Hodnota, cena a zisk* [*Value, Price and Profit*] (1923). It was a manuscript of a Marx lecture that he gave for the General Council of the International Trade Unions in 1865. His theory of value and prices, surplus value, profit and wage is outlined here in its basic characteristics. Also the second Marx text, again revised by Engels, which was first published in 1891, *Námezdní práce a kapitál* [*Wage Labour and Capital*] (1929), was mainly used to propagate Marx's criticism of the existing political economy amongst the working class. Karl Kautsky's (1854–1938) *Karla Marxe ekonomické nauky* [*Karl Marx's Economic Doctrines*] was reprinted (first published in Czech in 1889) with certain reservations. In the piece, Kautsky offers his interpretation of the first volume of Marx's *Capital*, but does not devote any attention to topics such as primitive accumulation of capital or the proletarian revolution. The translation was hence accompanied by Lenin's 're-narrating' of Marx's teaching on the question of the economic essence of imperialism and proletarian revolution.

During the 1930s, Engels's works began to be published as well and in 1933 Karel Borecký's publishing house began publishing Lenin's collected writings in 20 volumes. The same publishing house published the first textbook on Marxism, *Základy marxismu-leninismu* [*Introduction to Marxism-Leninism*] a year previously (Reimann, 1932). Any interpretation of Marx's teachings therein is completely subordinate to popularizing the Russian Revolution. This more than anything shows the defining characteristic of this part of Marxist literature, and that was a popularization of the successes of socialist development in the USSR More than a theoretical discussion, it was rather a narration of the Russian Revolution and refutation of opinions about the existence of state capitalism in Russia, usually as a polemic with another – mainly the social-democratic – interpretation of the Russian Revolution and the development of Soviet Union.

The second direction of the development of Marxist political economy in Czechoslovakia was the application of the Marxist-Leninist thesis on economic and social development in Czech Lands and Czechoslovakia. During the 1920s, communists were mostly occupied by interpreting the development of a bourgeois Czechoslovakia from their 'Marxist' position: Czechoslovakia was defined as a part of the European imperialist system and as an imperialist state with exploitative economic elites who were following only their own goals and who were harmful to the working class. In this regard, however, not all communists were unified and they interpreted the same facts – unreflectively – in a completely different manner. This applies, for example, to the appraisal of the role of monopolies, mainly that of banking, in the economic development of newly established Czechoslovakia and its position in the European economy. Not even President Masaryk evaded criticism, since he was labelled as a bourgeois reformist.

The key text of this direction was Antonín Kamenický's (1899–1942) (under the pseudonym Jan Ulrych) popular and once again textbook-like explanation of Marxist political economy, applied to the specific situation of Czech Lands and Czechoslovakia – for instance, in the question of primitive accumulation, Czechoslovak imperialism, in the criticism of Engliš's teological approach and Bráf's concept of the social question (Ulrych, 1937). More than a discussion, this direction of developing Marxist political economy was, however, a series of attacks against supporters of other opinions that were described as bourgeois, opportunistic or reformist. Communists who declared themselves to be the only protectors of the only correct interpretation of Marx's teachings resolutely refused any reformist concepts of an 'organized' capitalism, economic democracy or a theory of cooperative Socialism (Nikl, 1961, 747).

For the future development of Marxist thought in Czechoslovakia it is significant that various interpretations of Marxism were not unified by theoretic discussions on Marx's teachings, but rather by the resolution on the imperialist character of Czechoslovakia that was passed by the 5th Party Congress in February 1929. That is how it was to continue – and future Communist Congresses put forward further and further economic resolutions: On the

Great Depression consequences, on devaluation, on state budgetary policy, on the situation in agriculture. The latter area of interest is closely connected to an essential Marxist-Leninist thesis on the class union of workers and peasants. The discussion on this topic had already begun in 1926 on the pages of the *Communist Revue* and was further elaborated at the 6th Party Congress in 1931, that expressed in its resolution demands on how to 'liberate' small peasants from exploitation by financial capital: To annul direct taxes for cottagers and smallholders, to abolish all their debts and seizures, to register all the diminutive land allotments free of charge, to distribute the land owned by the state, the church and the large farmers into hands of small tenants and to gain insurance of all types free of charge (Doležalová, 2008). It is therefore nothing but a formulation of the principles of the primitive socialistic accumulation and the abolishment of the obligation to pay land taxes for one group of population. Nevertheless, the Agricultural Plan passed by the Party in 1935 interpreted these points as the economic justification of the common interests of peasants and those of the proletariat. The relationship between workers and so-called working intelligentsia, as the middle class was referred to by Marxist-Leninist terminology, underwent a similarly utilitarian process of justification. In the communists' interpretation, they were a group of day labourers (state, public and private officers) that live only from their income, but were not a bourgeoisie. All attempts at analyzing the problem would typically cling to the sophistry of trying to differentiate bourgeois thinking from that of the petty-bourgeois.

Klement Gottwald (1896–1953), the chairman of the Party, was placed into the position of the most important theoretician of Marxism-Leninism, analogically to Joseph Stalin (1878–1953) in the Soviet Union. Marx's authentic opinions were gradually degraded to be just a storehouse of arguments for such an interpretation of Czechoslovak economic development when all the economic-political decisions of coalition governments without any role for the communists lead to the further impoverishment of the working class. Even during the first half of the 1930s, communists were not attempting to explain Marx's concepts of various economic terms and the Marxist interpretation of current economic events, but rather to compile Marx's opinions, frequently put out of context, which were meant to support communist criticism of all reformist efforts of governments, including, for example, economic planning: According to the communists, the goal of all the proposed concepts of planning was nothing more than a way to consolidate the dominion of bourgeois cartels and to facilitate further exploitation of the proletariat.

To change the system: the cooperative Socialism

Ideas about self-help cooperativism can be traced in Czech economic thought back to the middle of the 19th century. Czech cooperative thought drew inspiration from almost every idea about cooperatives that was emerging at that time in Germany, France and England; despite the similarities between

Czech considerations and their foreign models, it cannot be overlooked how often the ideas of F.L. Chleborád surfaced in the writings of Czech cooperative theorists. From the outset there the principle of self-help is stressed, while also respecting the profit motive in conformity with the ethical principles of economic behaviour. The Czech cooperative concepts were not just a specific type of economic thought, but rather an attempt to find a practical solution to the economic difficulties faced by a certain part of the population and to improve their material well-being and intellectual level.

Czech cooperative concepts can be divided along three lines. The first line distinguishes between a respect for or opposition to the principle of private property; the second reflects the relationship to the state and its role in implementing cooperative ideas; and the third line leads between the introduction of cooperative ideas into the sphere of production or consumption. These dividing lines give each cooperative theory its shape and determine its instruments. Based on these lines Czech cooperative concepts can be divided into three streams.

The first stream viewed cooperatives as part of the larger associational movement, rejected interference from the state, and was not opposed to the institution of private property. The second stream saw the place for cooperatives in the production sphere and savings and credit activities. Figures in this stream who advocated active state intervention also called for changes to or restrictions on private property, were more critical of capitalism than of Socialism, and looked at production as their main sphere of interest. Conversely, those who rejected state interventions proposed the creation of cooperatives based on real self-help and they also respected private property, were as uncompromisingly critical of Socialism as of capitalism, and were primarily interested in consumer sphere and credit activities. Representatives of both streams nevertheless stressed the need to establish harmony between labour and capital, mutual help, sense of belonging and competitiveness.

In the 1880s it became fully apparent that the worker movement was in the sway of the Czechoslavonic Social Democratic Party, whose support for both producer's and consumer's cooperatives was primarily influenced by Ferdinand Lassalle's (1825–1864) notion of a worker's right to the full value of his labour. For their criticism towards socialism traditional cooperative theories began to serve as an example of the direction in which workers should not proceed; by the 1890s the first ideas about expropriation in the state interest began to appear. And significantly, a new branch of cooperative movement formed that sought to change the very nature of capitalist society – *cooperative Socialism*. This third stream of cooperative thought, while it, too, rested still on the principle of self-help, put forward a strategy that envisioned the transformation of society into a more socially fair society based on collective ownership, wherein each co-owner occupies an equal position. Two social democrats, František Modráček and Josef Macek, introduced theoretical elaborated concepts on this. They were inspired by each other's work and both were influenced not only by Lassalle, but also by Charles Gide (1847–1932), Pierre Joseph Proudhon

(1809–1865) and Eduard Bernstein (1850–1932), and especially by the views of the *Fabians*, who were extremely popular in the Czech intellectual milieu until the middle of the 20th century; in 1947 a Czech translation of George Cole's *Fabian Socialism* (1947) was published, with a recommendation in the Introduction that Fabian ideas suited the Czechoslovak path to Socialism. New and original Czech elements can be found in the view on agriculture and in the emphasis on ethical and social issues, and most notably in the search for harmony between labour and capital; all this is clear evidence of the influence of Chleborád.

František Modráček (1871–1960) trained as a wood carver and furthered his education through autodidactism. He became acquainted with cooperative ideas in the late 1890s while in Germany and France, and when he returned to Prague he became the publisher and editor of a socialist revue *Akademie* [*Academy*]. His own work comprises approximately 600 texts. It was around the year 1914 that he developed his concept of cooperative Socialism, and in it he drew inspiration mainly from the teachings of E. Bernstein and his followers, with whom he shared not just a similar notion of cooperativism but also opposition to any form of state Socialism and especially Marxism. Modráček also found an important source of inspiration in *Czech socialism*, which was introduced in the 1890s by politician and journalist Antonín Pravoslav Veselý (1873–1904). For Veselý, *Czech socialism* was the version of Socialism best suited to the specific nature of the Czech worker movement that was closely tied up with cooperativism. Veselý delimited himself against revolutionary Marxist Socialism, the class struggle and revolution (Veselý, 1895). In the first two decades of the 20th century the term *Czech socialism* became publicly widely known, but it gradually came to be based less on the ideas of its original author and more on Modraček's principles, which were not, however, aimed at implementing a *Czech version* of Socialism – according to him, Socialism was a general phenomenon. Nevertheless, the vision of a specific *Czech path to socialism* survived right up until the 1960s.

The key to understanding Modráček's concept of cooperative Socialism, the so-called *self-government of work*, is his book of the same title (Modráček, 1918), where he called for the reconstruction of society into a socialist-cooperative system, that he saw as the best and actually the only possible path towards resolving the basic opposition inherent within society – the opposition between labour and capital – without undoing the achievements that had been made by civilization and culture. According to Modráček there were two stages in this path: first, wage labourers were to become co-owners by forming cooperative enterprises or by *cooperativization* of existing private firms. As the workers gradually obtained a share in production capital, labour would assume primacy over capital until it eventually controlled the entire system of production. After that, Parliament would pass legislation establishing the new socialist-cooperative order and would entirely suspend the wage-based system that had previously existed. On this point he was respectful of the irreplaceable role of the state on the legislative level, but on other matters he was strictly against the state's intervention. According to him, it is not for the state to fix capitalism's maladies or offer solutions to them; the state could be an important ally and a useful tool for the working class's political organizations, it could have a beneficial legislative, legal and political role to play, but it is not realistic or desirable for the state to assume control over the vast and diverse national economy.

Modráček moreover rejected *state socialism* established by nationalizing the means of production; in his view, concentration of economic power in the hands of the state was an unsuitable and dangerous idea that constrains individual freedom and increases bureaucracy. Workers would only go from being wage-earners in a private factory to becoming wage-earners in a state factory, while their status would otherwise remain entirely the same. Socialist-cooperative reform was not meant to undermine existing private property but rather to transform people themselves through education in socialist ideals and thereby gradually alter their way of thinking.

The cooperative itself, which was to be a key unit in the future socialist society, was not clearly or consistently conceptualized in Modráček's writings. His first real attempt to define a cooperative came in the late 1920s, when he described it as a collective enterprise, the purpose of which was to provide economic services to its members and with their cooperation (Modráček, 1931, 25). Modráček originally did not envision the diffusion of his concept outside industry; he believed that peasants had not reached a level of thinking and awareness where the people could understand and accept the purpose of this kind of reform. Nevertheless, under the influence of Josef Macek and the rhetoric about the *hunger for land* that had seized the public space in connection with land reform after Czechoslovakia was established (Doležalová, 2018a) he incorporated agricultural cooperatives into his concept.

The ideas of Josef Macek on cooperative Socialism, which he called *self-help Socialism*, are similar to Modráček's at the very least in that Macek based his concept on an evolutionary process of implementing social reforms with the goal of creating a socially just society through the introduction of 'co-partnership', the distribution of shareholding rights to workers and their profit-sharing. With this, however, Macek's self-help Socialism ran up against the opinions of the leaders of the trade union movement and the supporters of class struggle; the former were opposed to the risks of entrepreneurial activity and the responsibility it involved, while for the latter the idea of workers participating in capitalist enterprise was treasonous. But the point of departure in Macek's idea was consistent with that of the Marxists: A declaration of the dying of capitalism (Macek, 1925a, 182). Macek, however, argued that as long as the development of parliamentary democracy and universal suffrage were accompanied by economic democracy (which included the introduction of just price as fair equivalence in the exchange process) on the cooperative basis, the transition to a socialist society would occur gradually; he clearly rejected the dictatorship of the proletariat and a revolutionary path to Socialism.

Although Macek regarded transition of society to be a moral issue, he refused abolition of wage-based relationship to work through legislation that would turn employees into co-partners. The reason was that he regarded this as ineffective. In his analysis of inequality and exploitation he showed that real change required abolishing the land monopoly, because private ownership of land on even a small scale could become a wealth-generating resource based on the labour of others. The way to address the problems of achieving a just price and eliminating land monopoly was in Macek's view – like Modráček's – to expand the scope of self-help-cooperative enterprise and to increase the share of employees in the workplace conditions. In this Macek turned his attention not just to one type of cooperative. Besides agricultural, consumer, production, sales and credit cooperatives, he saw manifestations of self-help efforts in mutual insurance companies, trade unions, self-help and self-education associations, as well as in cartels and employers' organizations. For him, self-help was an ideal approach to organizing people in such a way that individuals in pursuit of their own interests do not harm the interests of others, rather that everyone be of help to one other (Macek, 1923, 31).

To rationalize humankind: Laboretism

In his *Úvahy a projevy* [*Considerations and Speeches*] (1990) the founder of Bata Company, Tomas Bata (1876–1932), recalls that he mistrusted cooperatives, for as a child he joined one such 'cooperative' event – a Rattle Parade on Good Friday – and the proceeds were divided unfairly. By the time he completed his primary school and began his apprenticeship in his father's business, he had already become well aware of the unequal distribution of wealth within society. 'I was a collectivist and a communist of sorts but never a socialist. I considered the existing capitalist society to suit only bad people, such as the greedy and the people with aversion to work. I dreamt of Tolstoy's modest life' (Bata 1990, 25). This is an interesting piece of business inspiration since Tolstoy did not only write *War and Peace* and *Anna Karenina*. He was an unconventional intellectual with ambitions to reform not just his serfs but also himself, his own family and the whole world. As Paul Johnson states (2007), this is a strange, fallacious idea, advocated by intellectuals. Regardless, it may well have been this intellectual approach by Tolstoy which Bata had copied in his paternalistic relationship towards his workers. And it is also the explanation as to why we find Bata among the founders and supporters of the original stream of Czech economic thought, *Laboretism*.

When the Laboretist Club was established in 1927, its first members included not only Bata, but also Miloš Havel (1899–1968), founder of the Barrandov film company and the uncle of the future Czech president Václav

Havel (1936–2011), the President of the Supreme Administrative Court at the time, and other entrepreneurs, scientists and artists. They followed similar intellectual directions to Europe, especially *fatism*, a Danish movement of economic thought established in 1925 that implemented the transformation of joint-stock companies in such a way that employees owning non-transferrable shares became majority shareholders (Máče, 2001,585). They were loosely inspired also by American technocratism, and a Technocratic Society was even established in Czechoslovakia in 1934, but they criticized it for inhumanity, although they later granted that the Russian Revolution gave it a more democratic direction (Šmejkal, *et al*, 1962, 126).

Since respected intellectuals and entrepreneurs from a broad political spectrum were among *Laboretism* supporters, it was in a position to attract interest from a wide range of people. *Laboretism* concerned itself with the position of the working man within society and aimed to transform the capitalist' society into a less 'problematic' form (Máče, 2001, 584). It strove to solve social problems by seeking social reconciliation between employees and employers and later also reconciliation between the organization of society and new forms of business, for the pace of technical progress exceeded the pace of organization changes – with all the economic, social, political and moral consequences. The laboretists always emphasized education and morals – the term *Laboretism* itself was created by combining the words labour and ethos (Verunáč, 1923).

The starting point in the laboretists' thinking was the ideal of a healthy, happy and moral human being. This ideal was to be accomplished by organizing and planning the economy and the whole of the society, as societies based on Liberalism were falling short of achieving this goal. One of the prominent proponents of *Laboretism*, Václav Verunáč (1893–1960), characterized it as 'a movement of thought, borne by the principles of technical thinking, by an ethical concept of work and by the principles of scientific organization' (Verunáč, 1928, 3). In contrast to Taylorism, for instance, the implementation of principles of *Laboretism* would not be limited to industrial enterprises only. It would significantly affect all areas of human activity and thus also the agricultural, financial and public spheres. Scientific organization was meant to encompass society as a whole. A society-wide plan, complemented by a system of checks, was to be the instrument of such wide-ranging organization.

Most laboretists continued to adhere to the principle of private ownership, although their trust in the functioning of the invisible hand of the market was minimal. Their hopes for making economic activities more efficient were projected into planning by placing the central role in all stages of planning in the hands of the state and its institutions. Although they agreed with other theorists of planning in the use of the methods of credit and monetary expansion and forced syndication, they always emphasized the role of the *board of experts* that should not only issue regulations on planning and direction, but also carry them out. The economy should not be a sphere of power struggle, but a science controlled by the instrument of the scientific direction of society. It should not be in the hands of political authorities, but 'experts of social laboratory' (Verunáč, 1933, 67). At lower levels, this form of planned economy was to be managed by industrial intelligentsia, the so-called social engineers – technical cadres familiar with technologies of production as well as social issues; so future states would look back in amazement at the previous dilettante epochs, where the philosophizing of everyone on everything or the fight of everyone against everything was considered to be 'the summit of development' (Václav, 1934, 115).

The laboretists reached the conclusion that planning is only an organizational system which can function under capitalism and Socialism; in the 1930s many laboretists were clearly inspired by the Soviet model of planning but also by Italian corporatism and the German concept of central management and planning.

The state as an entrepreneur

It was Josef Kaizl who established the majority of the attributes of public finance in the Czech environment. There are several general features to theories of public finance in the period that followed. First, there were two standard rationales for the existence of a state financial economy. One was the fact that the state endures longer than any private economic subject. As Kaizl put it, municipalities do not die. The other was that there are some needs that people are unable to meet and fulfil by themselves. Although economists had different views on how great a range of duties they considered it necessary for the state to perform, the duties they did outline almost always included basic education and an education in trades, housing, and the enacting of health and social legislation. They also had different answers to the question of what really distinguishes the state economy from the private economy or what principles the public economy should adhere to.

Second, according to Kaizl, financial science should be engaged in the study of 'what should be' and act as a kind of instruction for practical financial policy. Later, a consensus formed on what should be the objective of financial policy, which was to cover the expenditures of the state and thus fulfil the state's intended purpose. It was – even after the Second World War – general welfare, sometimes referred to as the common good. Defining the meaning of this term, however, again lay outside the interest of economists, one exception being Karel Engliš, who defined the purpose of the state as achieving the ideal with respect to both the individual and the nation.

Third, because taxes were the only subject of financial science, only some economists devoted any space to the question of the nature and role of state budgets.(Doležalová, 2007). It was not until the interwar period that economists began to more broadly discuss the question of whether financial science should study also state expenditures – that is, the state budget as a whole. The impulse to include the state budget within the concept of financial science came from Josef Drachovský (1876–1961), Josef Macek and Vilém Funk (1875–1955), who were influenced by the English tradition. The first two translated and wrote the introduction to the Czech editions of the best known interpretations of public finance at that time by Charles F. Bastable (1855–1945) and Hugh Dalton (1887–1962).

But Czech economists did not look for limits to the expansiveness of the state sector. That is why crucial to understanding the concept of public finances in Czechoslovakia is the entity defined as *state enterprises*, state-owned and state-run subjects (SOEs). Alois Rašín (1867–1923), the most famous Minister of Finance in Czech history for he introduced monetary separation from Austria in 1919, was the only one to express unambiguous opposition to the existence of SOEs, citing their monopolistic character, inefficiency, surplus employees and political influence. Macek, Funk and Drachovský also criticized SOEs, but they conceded that society as a whole benefited to a certain degree from their functioning. For this reason they wanted to impose a legal responsibility on their management to ensure that they benefited society as a whole. According to Funk, however, these disadvantages are in no way offset by some of the advantages offered by SOEs (Funk, 1923).

His appraisal of state enterprises and his approach to them in general was one point in which Karel Engliš differed from the rest of the economic community. On one hand, he referred to state enterprises as thoroughly capitalist institutions in a state that is based on solidarity, but on the other hand he understood state enterprises as an element of a cooperative system that seeks to maintain a balance between production and consumption (Engliš, 1932a). Reasons for expanding their scope should not be to help to cover the expenditures of public administration, but rather for an objective that is related to the general purpose of public demonstration, which Engliš referred to as a public social objective. SOEs are also an instrument in his concept of social orders; he acknowledged their strong political influence, which in his opinion 'sufficiently' explains their poor profitability; therefore, he recommended in at least some sectors favouring instead regulation and the political oversight of private enterprises, and only if this does not work proceed to state entrepreneurship (Engliš, 1938). To sum up the reasons for state enterprises to exist, the four most frequently mentioned reasons were: 'Becherian' reason that SOEs are exemplary enterprises, generating state revenues and lessening the dependence of the state on the private sector; that they reduce prices in sectors that are not of interest to the private sector; that they offer *non-private* jobs and jobs secured by the state; and that politically distinguish state sectors according the spheres of interests of particular political parties.

Three more points should be noted about the concept of SOEs in Czech economic literature at that time: First, all of the economists basically set out in their reflections on SOEs from the belief that the public economy differs from the private economy primarily by the temporal limitedness of the existence of the private economy, while the state endures, and therefore the tasks and duties it engages in can produce benefit in a longer-term measure. Second, only some economists regarded the public economy as 'an element alien to the individualistic economy' drawing its resources from the latter but using them for a different purpose than what the private economy would do. And third, all of these economists engaged in *contradictio in adjecto* when they deemed SOEs to be elements of the private economy acting in the state economy.

Facing the crisis

The first Great Depression and poor relief

Czech economists first grappled with an economic crisis as early as 1873, when a crash on the Vienna stock market brought the liberal period to a grinding halt. The ensuing depression prompted tradesmen and small entrepreneurs to return to more careful strategies and the state to a certain degree of state interventionism. It was into this situation that the then 22-year old Bráf entered. He thus experienced a time when economic science, itself quite young, was faced with distrust over its ability to solve economic problems successfully, and over the dispute on methods between Menger and Schmoller that also elicited doubts regarding the goals of economics.

At the same time, the crisis opened an entirely new phenomenon for economics, the social question. And as in other themes, in this one too Bráf defined the field for the next decades (Doležalová, 2014). A fundamental role was played by the fact that Czech economists were subject to a certain tension between Catholic tradition in Bohemia and Protestant-borne modernizing social policy, for it was in German states that social measures were implemented, giving an impulse to the reflections of Czech economists. Poor relief was the most discussed question. We can divide the discussion into three directions which overlap to a marked degree: Searching for the content of the term poverty, explaining the cause thereof and proposing possibilities to solve it, and more precisely, discussions on the possible instruments that could solve poverty (Doležalová, 2017).

The meaning of the term poverty was unclear. It can generally be said that it was related to the subject of minimum wage, influenced by Malthus's population theory and was submitted to the first attempts at statistical quantification. The issue remained primarily an ethical question; it was connected to reflections on the moral improvement of society. At this moment, at the turn of the 19th and 20th centuries, the notion of poverty as insufficient income was asserted; poverty thus expressed inequality in the distribution of incomes (Engliš, 1909, 209). But because insufficient income had not been quantified and a unified poverty line did not exist, it was a locally expressed indicator which was given both by the relative concept of a tax-exempt status and basic income in various segments of the economy and by a socially respected exclusion of certain population groups from poverty relief (gypsies and tramps). It was also limited by the period development of statistical methods. The concept of poverty thus included both purely normative aspects (poverty as an evil) and positive ones (the quantification of poverty as derived in part from the distribution of income in the economy).

Because they were unable to give a satisfying definition of the term poverty, economists concentrated more on the identification of factors which led to the rise of population groups who met the conditions for poor relief; these factors were considered to be the causes of poverty. According to Bráf, the causes of poverty were subjective and objective. Among the objective factors he included such factors as the legal code, geographic and climate conditions, progress in science and technology and the ensuing changes in the division of labour, the economic cycle and economic policy. These were factors that could not be influenced by the position of an individual. Among subjective conditions he included people's physical and psychological dispositions and their moral and volitional attributes. But he took into account that these are not always in the individual's own hands (Bráf, 1923a, 140). At the beginning of the 20th century, Engliš argued that the causes of poverty are the same factors that affect the distribution of income, and he distinguished between individual and social causes of poverty. By means of this characteristic, Engliš tried to distinguish the causes of poverty on the one hand, and the conditions for granting poor relief on the other. He then determined that the ruling economic-legal order was the main social cause of poverty (Engliš, 1909). Poverty was thus no longer explained merely as a consequence of alcoholism, laziness, inability or moral decline, but also as the result of a certain social reality, or more precisely, of an institutional and economic framework that also fundamentally influenced the individual causes of poverty.

At the end of the 19th century, unemployment moved to the centre of attention among the social (objective) causes of poverty. At the time, economics distinguished between three categories of the unemployed – persons unable to work, people with aversion to work and a third new category brought about by industrialization. That is, people who are able to work and would like to work, but cannot find work; the term *social pathology* was coined. It was indeed the surfacing of this third category that was usually the argument for deeper state engagement. We thereby arrive at what is, from the perspective of economists, paradoxically the most frequent cause of poverty, that is specific acts that emerged to solve the problem of poverty. Economists criticized the unclear law delimitation of poor relief and the ways in which it was to be fulfilled in practice. This paradox – referring to legislative steps to solve poverty as the cause thereof – brings us to a discussion on the specific ways of solving it.

Solving the problem of poverty was to be secured either through statehelp or by self-help. There was therefore discussion on the extent of state intervention and the ability of the state to solve the problems of the poor. Behind all the proposals there is a clear humanistic endeavour to change care for the poor from charitable to socio-economic. They shifted from the proposal to change the world into a more just version through proposals for better poverty statistics to proposals for specific instruments to eliminate poverty. In the case of the former, these were closer to ideologically-coloured proclamations which usually lacked an objective perspective. Proposals to improve poverty statistics were by their character more technical than economic or social-economic. Finally, the proposals of specific instruments went from insurance, through poor relief legislation and public work, to a systemic solution of issues of municipal finance and securing a harmony between state aid and private charity.

The view that private solidarity and self-help precedes state care and that the state should intervene only when self-help and charitable activities fail began, at the end of the 19th century, to be considered by economists to be an 'outdated' view, although they respected its place and significance; only a minimal warning was voiced against the liquidation of private and community instruments and the replacement thereof by those of the state. The most broadly discussed manner of solving the problem of poverty was social insurance; it was once again Albín Bráf who formed in his work a basic guidepost for the comprehension of the effects and instruments of insurance (Bráf, 1883) and other economists continued it or merely reproduced it, but only occasionally brought forward new proposals.

The Great Depression of 1930s and the beginning of planning

The main motivation for considerations on planning, which in its early days corresponded in content to controlled economy, was to give the current capitalistic system the necessary energy and an alternative way of face-to-face control with the situation when the market mechanism fails. Concrete proposals or planned projects were usually focused on limited territory, but also on economic branches. At the same time, the requirement for creating an entirely new human generation was put in the form of planning related to economic processes, with a higher degree of responsibility than that to which the previous generations had been exposed – the idea of pan-human usefulness was to be at the core of planning. The first planning proposal was put forward in 1924; it was an economic plan that set out to be the foundation for a new social order of state regulation of the economy without offending the principle of private ownership. In 1925, the proposal to create a plan appeared even at the level of government negotiations. These proposals had their roots in the conflicts between industrial and agricultural capital and the plan was to secure the coordination of the requirements of both groups. (Šmejkal *et al.*, 1962, 88) But soon opinions began to prevail that planning could also be the means of stabilization of the economic cycle, and that planning had become an instrument aiming to remove crises and unemployment. The state was to become its bearer.

The Great Depression dynamized these thoughts. Czech economists understood it as a paralysis of the existing mechanism of how 'normal' economic life had functioned until that point and as a disruption of its balance. Observing the Czech interpretations of the causes of the Depression, we can define the Depression as a disproportion between production and consumption; besides that, the emphasizing of the lack of trust in the capitalist system itself is striking. That is where the two streams of thought on solving the Depression originate: That of price (deflation) and that of rationalization. The first stream saw the cause of the crisis in price decrease and the second in production and its organization. The scale of corrective measures was diverse and varied from application of interventionist measures on both the domestic and international level, through acceleration of deflation and decrease of the interest rate to corporatism and planning. Virtually all of them anticipated greater state engagement. A strong, intervening state became the synonym for progress.

When the translation of Barbara Wootton's books *S plánem či bez plánu* [*Plan or no Plan*] was published in Czechoslovakia in 1936, Josef Macek greeted it by emphasizing that Czech readers needed this encouragement to contemplate the prerequisites of a planned economy in Czechoslovakia. After all, he was neither the first nor the only one among Czechoslovak economists who offered planning not only as a means of post-Depression therapy, but as a form of further state economic activity (Loewenstein, 1931). For instance, Jaroslav Nebesář (1882–1952) suggested an active economic policy of the state and the Central Bank to support economic growth and to overcome the social consequences of the Great Depression; from here it really is but a small step to the idea of direct state control of which Nebesář would become both the creator and the apologist after the next war. Karel Maiwald (1902–1979), who in the second half of the 1930s was an admirer of J.M. Keynes, as was Nebesář, thought that alongside the deepening knowledge of the liberal economic order, the injustice and in some respects even pointlessness thereof was becoming manifest. In his work, he repeatedly stressed his demand that economic life be intentionally controlled by society and, for the interests of a collective, be effectively protected from the selfishness of individuals. After the war, he also entered into the services of directive control of the economy; in 1949, he emigrated.

In the mid-1930s, Karel Engliš expressed, on the basis of his concept of three economic orders, his opinions on the nature of planned economy (Engliš, 1935). He differentiated between *organized* and *planned* economy. While the first term refers to all the modes of productions and its main characteristic being that it grows only from below and is a solution to individual interests, the second term refers to orders from above, from the superior central will – the state. Through every single intervention, the state gives rise to a different order than one which would be created 'from below', says Engliš, and he also deduces that planned economy refers to a set of measures that the state chooses in order to maintain or improve the economy. Such an effort can be activated not only by a critical situation in the economy, but also by state endeavour to completely liquidate the *individualistic orders* and replace it with *collectivism*: 'There is a critical point that can be reached without the disintegration of the entrepreneurial system and exceeding it entails its disintegration' (Ibid., 40).

In 1930s, calls for planning ceased to be a voice calling into the desert and became a war cry. Whilst Czech politicians spoke of capitalism that was sick unto death, of the chaos and the desperate madness, Czech economists wrote about the collapse of the *laissez-faire* system, and on planning as a way of resisting it; some of them warned against the danger of revolution (Hejda, 1932). In principle, the authors did not distinguish between the modes of planning in the USSR, the USA, Italy or Germany – these were all countries on the road to planned management, and they asserted that planning was possible in various political regimes.

The effort to restore the economy quickly put another programme's demands on the table: The demand for large state investment when economists evolved their concepts of planning into a form of *forced syndication* and *public investments*. This exact syndicalism was referred to by Karel Engliš (1935) as an impulse to controlled economy, for it placed ahead of the state 'unforeseeable' new tasks: The first syndicate would outline as a goal efficiency in this or another specific branch. But when the state undertakes forced syndication the control of economic processes from above begins. The breaking point is the moment when the state assumes responsibility for an imbalance in the branch. The state covers its liabilities through state budget expenditures and the spiral in their growth necessarily starts to turn. Syndication does not mean the possibility of achieving efficient production, argues Engliš; nor does it mean maximum employment or maximum consumption; but sooner or later it can lead to changes in the economic system itself.

Theoretically and practically, the more influential considerations were those on lending, the leading representative of which was Josef Macek. In his study *Cesta z krize* [*The Way out of the Crisis*] (1935b), he writes on the necessity to find the bravery to uncover fundamental errors in human thought and action which caused *poverty in abundance*; one such mistake, according to Macek, was the concept of money. The issue of money appeared to him, most importantly, as an issue of credit money – banknotes and the administration thereof (Ibid., 174). He proposed that money should stop being considered as a good and that the crisis should start to be treated by state monetary and credit policy. Others joined in this view: According to Nebesář, 'planning by credit is the foundation of all planning' (Nebesář, 1939, 136); according to Maiwald, 'credit is the key to putting latent economic forces into motion'. (Maiwald, 1937, 19).

For them, the connection of currency with gold became a barbarian anachronism. The bank of issue, not bound by gold, was to influence the economic cycle in a decisive way with its monetary and credit policy. This was closely connected also to the interpretation of the role of 'cheap money', i.e. operation on the free market; 'buying and selling partial bonds', as Macek defined it (Macek, 1935b, 61–62). According to him, operations on the free market support private and public enterprises by supplying the money market, which is then able to provide credits at reduced interest levels. He and Nebesář agreed that money should appear in the expansion of state investments, for a bank of issue can, until a time of full employment, issue long-term money for its investment purposes, i.e. implement 'a planning credit expansion with the aid of credit' (Nebesář, 1935, 79). According to Macek, the saturation of the money market and public investments were two paddles which one had to operate simultaneously; 'if only one is operated, the boat spins in circles' (Macek, 1935b, 80). Thoughts on the active role of the state budget in the process of the economic cycle, influenced by J.M. Keynes, and the requirement of deficit financing (which had been an economic reality as early as from the beginning of the 1920s (Doležalová, 2007)) in the interest of *planned* development, together with the first thoughts that planning should span 'at least' 5 years thus found their way to the Czech environment.

Under pressure of Nazi occupation

The Munich Conference in September 1938, the formation of an independent Slovak State and the occupation of the remainder of the Czech Lands in March 1939 entailed a shift of political and economic conditions, which economists had to respect. From the foundation of the Second Republic in September 1938, we can observe a shift in Czech economic thought. The main theme of economists became the consolidation of the economy in connection with territorial changes. Economists focused on themes such as the state budget, taxes, prices, tariffs and foreign trade, and they upheld expressly opportunistic views, speaking in a predominating measure only on the advantages of connection with the Great German Reich. But some of the economists still took a critical stance to state interventions, whether a critique of domestic reality or of economic policies in other countries was at issue. Engliš's pupil, Alois Král, expressed his doubts that bureaucratic governance could effectively supplement private business initiatives and unrestricted decision-making and he stressed unity and economic cooperation with Slovakia that tried to enforce decentralization 'in an idealistic belief in full national independence and self-sufficiency' (Král, 1938).

The turning point in economic thought was in the next year, when the shift towards central-directive economic ideas became the distinct characteristic in economic thought. Land reform, the nationalization of key industries and an active role of state in economic processes appeared therein. Under pressure of repressions, or more precisely, under its threat, some economists gradually became silent. Some of them were executed or died in concentration camps. Publication of the most significant field journal, *Economic Horizon,* was halted in 1941.

Even so, the Protectorate economics included a broad spectrum of economists that can be divided into three streams: The first acted for the regime with a non-critical view of the new measures; the second consisted of current topics without the authors' own opinions; the last stream consisted of economic contemplations without a connection to practical affairs. But the plurality of opinions was strongly suppressed and theoretical contemplations about interventionist models became predominant.

The fundamental theoretical theme was the German theory of living space. But its economic connections were discussed without regard to its political aspects. Engliš's student, Miloš Horna, identified the problem of living space as one of raw materials, and saw three ways to the solution thereof (renewal of international exchange, scientifically controlled production of the substitute raw material industry, and the new division of natural resources). He considered new territorial redistribution through expansion to be the only one possible, for it was the most suitable for a strong and militarily equipped super power (Horna, 1939, 440). At that time, he saw the elimination of customs and foreign exchange boundaries as unsuitable for the Czech Lands and Moravia; a few month later he labelled the incorporation of the Czech Lands and Moravia into the customs territory of the Great German Reich as 'a significant milestone of our currency history' and as the beginning of an entirely new currency system in Central Europe which would be further based on the leading currency (Reich mark) and controlled currencies (e.g. Czech koruna (crown)) (Horna, 1940, 489). He assessed positively the way in which the Reich government postponed the complete connection of currencies until the time when both economic areas had converged closer to one another. He even expressed belief in the protection of divergent economic signs of an ethnically Czech space – if it was in the interest of the entire Reich. The connection of the Czech crown to the mark, or more precisely the overvaluation thereof (by 14.8%), and the change in currency exchange relations towards other currencies was, however, only occasionally the subject of criticism (Klimecký, 1940, 455).

Another typical example was the formation of the *Customs Union*. Only its benefits (a larger selling market, opportunities for greater specialization, connection to a dynamically developing German Reich) were emphasized. The decree on the ban on exporting certain types of goods from the Protectorate was characterized as a tool of protection of the internal domestic market. For example Zdenko Fafl (1881–1961) and Leopold Chmela (1894–1962) thought of the customs incorporation as an essential part of a future plan of a 'large program of new economic order' of Europe (Fafl, 1940, Chmela 1940), for it removed obstructions of free market. Fafl, moreover, declared that the *Union* works as an important means of achieving economic autarchy in the framework of the unified Reich emerging in Central Europe. He expected a future Europe formed by great modern geopolitical wholes: 'Small states will form a customs union with the great leading states which need for their development a sufficiently large living space for the possibility of the development of their own political, cultural and economic needs.' The *Customs Union* can thus serve as a way towards 'a reasonable and correct arrangement of world economy' (Fafl, 1940, 463).

Leopold Chmela, the Governor of the Czechoslovak National Bank after 1945, also viewed the *Customs Union* as a well-considered step beneficial to both sides. He considered as its positive aspect, progress in the rationalization and growth of the technical level of production, but also the reopened possibility of Czech expansion to new markets. Abolishment of customs barriers also brought new trade agreements with states with which the Reich had a contractual relationship - Haiti, Manchuria, Costa Rica, Nicaragua, Panama and Paraguay (Chmela, 1940). He failed to notice that, at the same time, the Protectorate lost contracts with states which were excluded from the *Most-Favoured-Nation Clause*: Great Britain and its colonies, France and its colonies, the USA and Iraq. The only critic of the *Customs Union* was therefore Vladimír Klimecký (1901–1968), who explored the process of economic interconnection and equalization of both countries and defined its barriers: tax structures, transport rates, social transfers, a similar structure of economy and natural conditions; but especially the extent of competitiveness (Klimecký, 1940). Other authors relativized this aspect (Chmela, 1940).

Likewise, the order of the day was organization of economic self-administration in the Protectorate, when German and Italian experiences with corporatism were being discussed. Hopes were even put into corporatism as an ideology corresponding to specifically Czech conditions and national character (Kliment, 1938). Liberalism was a subject of interest only as a failing ideology that leads to social inequality. Socialism was thought to be too simple since it shows preference for just one particular group of society (Potužil, 1939).

The understanding of state interventions as a necessity became the common denominator of all the streams of economic thought. For instance, in the scope of price formation, an intervention by the *Nejvyšší cenový úřad [Highest Price Office]* is the last but one best option with regards as how to react to the war needs of an economy that had become a part of the Reich's controlled economy (Černý, 1940). Besides price-forming influences, the regulatory function of prices and similar terms, expressions such as *administratively set prices, administrative cost control* and *costs recognized as useful* slowly found their way into the Czech economic dictionary: Expressions typical of a centrally-controlled economy which was often characterized as a replacement of the liberalistic structure by structure based on national solidarity, where the state asks its members to prefer the interests of the whole. When authors 'discovered' some negative aspects of controlled economy, they themselves then counter-argue the 'advantages' of it (Chmela, 1940, 467).

Short way from capitalism to Socialism

The three years between the end of the Second World War and the taking over of power by the Communist Party became the touchstone of all the more or less theoretical streams from 1918–1945. For most of the Czechoslovak economists this period was connected with searching for a way to a quick post-war reconstruction. The economic texts attest that they tried to follow the pre-war tradition. The 'new economists from exile' came in from London with practical instructions on how to deal with the problems of post-war reconstruction, including the involvement of Czechoslovakia in the international division of labour. And others came back from Moscow – they were more Party functionaries rather than theorists; however, to put policy into practice, the Party recruited two excellent young economists that came back from London, Ludvík Frejka (1904–1952) and Josef Goldmann.

The core of the contemplations of communist economists was mainly the question of the relationship of the proletariat with the non-proletariat classes of society and their revolutionizing. It therefore was rather a political than an economic question. The thought of mainstream economists could be characterized by somewhat of a naive belief in a self-acting mechanism of economy that is capable of absorbing market shocks and institutional changes. The prevailing feature of published texts was not an economic analysis of these changes, but rather a description of the present situation.

Leopold Šauer (1901–1983), the chief editor of the once again published *Economic Horizon*, pointed that out in his first editorial. He observes changes in economic life, most of which 'were not sufficiently theoretically studied before, neither was it possible to gain reliable information from abroad' (Šauer, 1947, 2): *Horizon* was supposed to be focused on the history of economic theories and the history of institutions. The journal did indeed become a space for open discussion quite quickly, but only for the next couple of years. It stopped being published in 1951.

The *Horizon*, first, brought information about the development in economics through reviews of the newest economic literature. The reviews weren't focused solely on Czechoslovak books, but also on the books by West European and Soviet authors and on various fields of economics. Second, the journal published texts written by foreign authors (Hicks, 1947) and in the texts of the Czech authors, we can find a number of quotations from current issues of foreign economic journals and the newest books. It can be argued without any exaggeration that during this period, Czech economics was still an open science with overlaps to not only economic practice but also to philosophy and sociology. It therefore still appeared in 1947 that the development of economic thought in Czechoslovakia followed its inter-war trajectory. But it is *Horizon* that represents distinct evidence of changes that started in economic thought at the end of 1947 and in the first half of 1948: In the book reviews Czech and Soviet books began to dominate at the expense of the Western ones; practical economic questions at the expense of the theoretical; and practical question began to focus almost exclusively on practical economic issues in Czechoslovakia and the Soviet Union.

The approach to planning illustrates the changing paradigm and 'tightening the screws' of an open discussion. A large number of titles addressing planning began to be published straight after the end of the Second World War. Disregarding the titles that had the character of a summary and used a more clichéd language with regard to the building of Socialism rather than the specialized language of economics, Czech economists pursued planning in accordance with the pre-war discussions: The term planning was an ambiguous one. It was always supposed to help the optimal use of the labour force and other sources and it had the character of a field tool being created from below. Hence, it was a non-directive planning and it presupposed the preservation of the highest possible level of freedom: 'Strictly speaking, we don't wish to renounce either the right to free consumption or the right to freely choose one's occupation' (Doležel, 1947, 66).

Economists were still wary of attempts at direct planning and creating a planning centre, even though they generally acknowledged that such planning could be successful. For instance, the reviewer of Lipson's book *A Planned Economy or Free Enterprise* (1946) on the relationship between the planned and market economy characterized the author's approach as having too much confidence in controlled economy and warned that the state can be a bigger danger to freedom than the feudal state once was. He therefore considered finding harmony between social security and economic progress while keeping political freedom as the key question linked with planning (Blažej, 1947). Economists stressed that the prerequisite of successful utilization of the plan in both the controlled and liberal economy is longevity and asked whether it was even possible to presume that long-term anticipation (as a base for long-term planning) could have better results in the planned rather than in the liberalistic order. They argued that even in planned economies breakdowns of balance must occur so 'a plan without political directives is but an empty diagram'. Although they didn't deny that large investments taking place without considering rentability couldn't overcome any crises, they came to the conclusion that:

> This world full of chaos is not very compatible with stability and a high level of prosperity. Let's not delude ourselves! Not a long-term plan, neither a policy of full employment represents a way out of the chaos of today straight to the garden of economic stability and prosperity.
>
> (Doležel, 1947, 67)

In this study, the author followed up on his prior book on planning (Doležel, 1946) in which he focused on the question of price creation in a planned economy when the free market is paralyzed or even eliminated. This question was the second continuous area of interest to Czechoslovak economists. Planned economy was considered – in accordance with Western trends (Robinson, 1934) – to be a sort of perfect competition. Together with perfectly balanced prices perfect competition is regarded as a mere theoretical prerequisite that can never be accomplished in the real world. Economists conceded that the economy is transferring from the theory of automatic creation of prices in the free market to *price manipulation*. But that assumes that the price policy is carried out on a rightly understood scientific basis, or in other words, that it must be fully aware of the effects of individual prices on the expansion or restriction of money circulation (Svoboda, 1947, 159).

If by the first half of 1947 emptiness and platitudes can be seen in some articles, articles published during the end of that year and in the first half of 1948 often had the character of being merely a transcript of the Party theses. The reason for this discursive change lies in the fact that in 1947 planning became a subject of discussion in the *Ústřední výbor* [*Central Committee*] of the Party. Until then, an unquestionable priority in the practical policy of the Party was nationalization and the Party discussions were subordinated to that. Economic questions were not even on the programme of the Party Congress in 1946, but Ludvík Frejka, who took over the function of chairman of the Economic Council of the Party, endeavoured to include them in the talks. In 1947 he managed to push through a discussion on long-term planning. The *Central Committee* then entrusted Frejka to prepare a proposal for a 5-year plan that would follow a number of viewpoints: The dependency of the Czechoslovak economy on the West, the state of both the private and the nationalized industrial sector, the state of consumption and the strengthening of the role of industry workmen.

February 1948 opened new areas of interest not limited to communist economists and shifted economics to a subservient role. Publications of questionable quality began to be published in droves, only ever descriptive and critical of previous economic conditions and announcing the future successes of the socialist economy, controlled by just one Party (Frejka 1948). But the emptiness of Marxist-Leninist political economy began to be on show for all to see. It began to be almost exclusively identified with the theory of a socialist revolution and used as an ideological support in the struggle for political power. Just as so far respected economic theories began to be questioned, so did the figures and institutions that cultivated them during the previous periods. The interwar economists still commented on new economic issues, but their voice continued to lose its relevance. Economics was losing its prestige and this process was finalized by the loss of social position and professional autonomy of the economists themselves.

Teaching economics across the centuries, states and political regimes

The year 1882 marked a year of major institutional change in the history of Czech economic thought: A full programme of lectures and seminars in Czech was introduced at the Czech part of Charles-Ferdinand University, and only Czechs could hold professor positions. Nevertheless, no dramatic changes occurred in the content of the curriculum. The economic courses had been already established at the Faculty of Law, at the Czech and German polytechnics in Prague, and at the polytechnic in Brno, which became a university in 1873. There a department of law in trades, commerce and exchange and national economy was set up, followed later by the Institute of the National Economy, Financial Science and Statistics. The polytechnics offered lectures in national economy, political science, business and industrial statistics, and commercial and exchange law. At the university there were lectures in political science, political economy, industrial policy, financial policy, state administration, financial science, the history of economic literature and the philosophy of law.

When the deaths of professor Richter (1878) and professor Jonák (1879) occurred in quick succession, those professors were replaced by Emil Sax and Karl Theodor Inama-Sternegg (1843–1908), who after a short time was replaced by Fridriech von Wieser, a student of Carl Menger. The teaching of economics thus fell into the hands of professors who in the next few years would play a fundamental role in the development of the economics itself. At that same time there were already two young Czech private senior lecturers, Josef Kaizl and Albín Bráf; both of them lectured in Czech and German.

Bráf lectured in Czech on financial science, national economy and the history of economic literature, and in German on the theory of money. Kaizl lectured in German on national economy, the history of economic literature with a special focus on Socialism, the history of the commercial policy of Austria, the system of commerce and a subject called *The Study of Wages and the Question of the Working Class.*

In 1875 teaching at the university began also to be provided in the form of seminars; later they were also introduced at the polytechnics and at the commercial academies. The purpose of seminars was to deepen the knowledge students acquired at the lectures, to better prepare them for practical work, and also to support students in pursuing independent research work (Krameš, 2013). The Faculty of Law offered sixteen seminars, three of which had an economic focus, and these were led by Bráf, Kaizl and Wieser. Under their influence the last remnants of the cameral sciences and classic economics faded from the economics curriculum and the study of economics began to be strongly influenced by both the younger German and the Austrian schools; after the university split into separate Czech and German parts, the latter remained the domain of the Austrian school, especially after Menger published his paper on method in the early 1880s, and the Czech university maintained the spirit of the historical school.

While Kaizl limited his teaching at seminars in order to pursue his political activities, the energy that came out of the seminars taught by Bráf generated a large circle of Czech students around him, many of whom later chose to make their own careers as economists. Through his personal recommendations Bráf helped many of them obtain jobs teaching at academies, universities or polytechnics or in well-paid positions in the state or private sector. And it was students of Bráf who after the founding of the independent Czechoslovakia in 1918 came to occupy literally all the key posts.

It was to Bráf's credit that students of law discovered economics even within the limited number of hours that economic subjects made up within the law curriculum. Although the seminars were not always harmonious, those who took part in them remembered them in a very positive light later on. With Bráf, economics shifted into the private sphere again, but for altogether different reasons than a century earlier, as the seminars were held either in Bráf's flat in the centre of Prague or in his summer house in Roztoky near Prague. Participants used to receive Bráf's personal invitation. Dinner was part of the seminar programme, after which the gentlemen relocated to Bráf's private library. There, surrounded by his books and pipe in hand, he guided the students in discussions of theoretical and practical economic issues. The students, with a pipe and coffee to fortify them too, had the feeling that Bráf was speaking with them as peers, an experience incomparable to any of their other courses: 'Argument was the only truth. Those were beautiful, unforgettable evenings' (Mildschuh, 1927, 19).

As an inspector in the Austrian commercial academies Bráf also helped to shape their system; in 1903 Bráf drew up the teaching curriculum for them that remained in place until 1948. The commercial academies enjoyed considerable prestige in Czech society and many Czech economists, including Bráf himself, started their careers as teachers at one of them. This did not, however, prevent him from voicing criticism. Bráf criticized the commercial academies for not educating future businessmen but officials, who were not even drawn from the cleverest batch of students – in his days the children that arrived at the academies were usually those who had failed to gain admission into one of the *gymnasium*. Bráf was not so much concerned with adding theoretical subjects to the curriculum of the schools as he was with introducing practical ones – such as accounting, correspondence, merchant counting; he asserted this idea in 1898. He believed that the lack of practical economic skills was the reason why Czechs were lagging behind Germans. He proposed to introduce economic lectures at the theology faculties, because for him priests remained a major channel of communication in the monarchy and a main element in the economic education of the population (Bráf, 1923a, 61–67).

Nevertheless, when the *Export Academy* was founded in Vienna in 1898, Czech economists began calling for the creation of a Czech commercial college and Bráf supported this idea. He was opposed to setting it up as a separate faculty at the polytechnic, because he feared that that would undermine the ties of economics to the social sciences and economics would become a technical discipline (Ibid., 10). Realistically, however, he understood that this was the only way that a university education in economics would ever see the light of day. He was well aware that there would not be a sufficient number of students interested in studying economics or qualified teachers. From the 1907–1908 academic year a course on commerce – albeit just a 2-year course – for future teachers at commercial academies began to be taught at the Czech Polytechnic in Prague. They were provided by one professor and a few external teachers; some lectures – in national economy and the law of commerce and exchange – were held at the Faculty of Law. Evidence of the strong interest in this form of study in economics is that 830 students enrolled in these courses there. However, it was no secret that the graduates sought employment as anything other than teachers of economics – as state officials or bank clerks.

On the eve of the Great War there were three possible variants on the table for the direction education in economics could take in Bohemia: As a separate field and with a move from the Law Faculty to the Faculty of Arts; the Law Faculty could split into two fields of study – law and economics; a department of commerce and insurance could be set up at the polytechnic. In the spring of 1919, after an independent Czechoslovakia was established, the Revolutionary National Assembly made a decision about the founding of *Vysoká škola obchodní* [*Commercial College*] and it chose between two proposals – one suggested locating it in Prague, the other in the city of Olomouc. The supporters of each of these locations used the same justification in support of their proposal, grounding their arguments in the national-economic needs of the new state in view of the changing economic and political world order: They argued that even nations that have a long commercial tradition, whose national character is thoroughly practical, mercantilist and calculating, whose physical location almost forces them to be oriented towards business by nature, that is, the English, not to mention the Germans, devote the greatest attention to education in commerce, even 'our' age-old rivals in Hungary already had two commercial colleges, and in Vienna the *Export Academy*'s transformation into a commercial college was reaching completion. Czechoslovakia, it was claimed, had no other choice but to also join in the international competition in 'education' because it was supposed to be the leader of all the Slavonic nations in the area of economics (Doležalová, 2011, 10). Ultimately the proposers agreed that given the substantial amount of interest from students that was predicted, it would be a good idea to set up both colleges. But because the final debate on this bill was on the agenda on the same day as legislation relating to land reform, PMs did not devote any attention to the bill and in the vote the 'Prague' proposal won.

In the autumn of 1919 the first year of teaching in economics began at the *Commercial College* in Prague, which was set up as a faculty of the Czech Polytechnic; as such the graduates of the college received – and still do – the title of 'engineer'. The school offered a 3-year study programme in which the first 2 years comprised compulsory foundations (languages, accounting, commercial law, technology, the study of goods, economic theory and the principles of private enterprise), upon completion of which students could take their first final exam and proceed to the third year of the programme to study one of four specialized areas, banking, industry, commerce or political and diplomatic studies. Two definitions of economic education alternated at this time: While the dominant effort in the early years was to create a school to educate skilled merchants and businessmen, and potentially also state officials, over time voices called more strongly for a deeper theoretical approach to economics. According to critics at the *College*, and elsewhere, learning chiefly centred on rote memorization instead of seeking to provide students with a practical grasp of the basic principles of economics and management. In the 1930s they added the criticism that because of the eclectic nature of Czech economic education the Czechoslovak government was unable to effectively deal with the independent state's economic problems and later with the effects of the economic crisis (Albrecht, 2011, 42).

Among those who had the biggest influence on how tuition of economics developed before 1948 was Bráf's student, Josef Macek. He exercised this influence not just as a professor at the *Commercial College* (1919–1939, 1945–1949) but also as PM. Macek called for changes that would adapt economic education to meet the needs of the time – that is, the needs of the private as well as the expanding state sector. He believed that teachers at lower levels in the education system could naturally serve as advisors not just for their students but also for their parents. According to Macek, adults, too, even after they had completed their formal schooling should be given a proper education in practical knowledge of economics and social affairs. Macek also saw economics as the best way of introducing self-education in various areas, as the topic has a close connection to the everyday experiences of every reader (Polášek, 2011).

All thoughts of reform and practical efforts were brought to a halt when the universities in the Protectorate of Bohemia and Moravia were closed down on 17 November 1939. With the exception of the polytechnic in Brno, which was shut down by Presidential Decree, all the other universities were reopened in May 1945. Economics, however, experienced the awkward pressure of having its very science status and its key figures and teaching methods questioned and revised. The loss of professional prestige was reflected in the salaries and living standards of university professors, changes in the organization of the university undermined its traditional autonomy, especially in the area of granting professorships, and economists lost the influence they had had on the public discussion of economic issues. Relations between economists themselves became more complicated as they each in their own way tried to navigate the straits between academic values and the pressure coming from the emerging regime, which in the first years after the war was represented by new communist experts who did not belong to the same social or oftentimes even intellectual milieu. The *Commercial College* in particular was hit with institutional and personnel changes, as well as changes in the content of the tuition. The changes were not systematic but rather erratic; the impact on individual teachers and on economics itself was all the more painful (Albrecht, 2011).

At the same time both nationalized and private enterprises were in urgent need of economists and the number of students applying to the schools grew considerably because in addition to recent graduates of secondary schools that would normally apply there were also students who had been unable to study or to complete their studies when the universities were shut down during the Protectorate. In the 1945/46 academic year, more than 5,500 students enrolled in the *College*, compared to 1,200 students in 1939. Classes were held in cinemas, and they were organized into two shifts, like in a factory (Závodský, 1999, 47).

The reopened schools faced a shortage of teachers. Some teachers had emigrated, some had died in the concentration camps, and a few had discredited themselves by collaborating with the Nazis. After the war all teachers had to prove their 'unimpeachable' commitment to the nation – that is, that they had never collaborated with the Germans or supported Nazi opinions. Evidence of collaboration was considered as even involvement in organizing a holiday job for students in Leipzig in 1939 (Albrecht, 2011, 44). After the war, there were three groups of teachers teaching at the *Commercial College*: The older generation was connected with the interwar period; this group includes Josef Macek, who during the 3 years after the war went from cooperating with the government headed by communists through participating in excluding politically 'unsuitable' students all the way to emigrating himself. Also in this group was Jan Maria Novotný (b.1898), who had established himself as an expert in public finance. He obtained his doctorate in financial science from the Faculty of Law in Prague and in 1923–1925 studied at the Wharton School in Philadelphia. In 1934 he was made a senior lecturer in finance and in 1946 he became a professor. In 1948 he emigrated to Canada. The second group was made up of teachers who had studied during the interwar period, many of them abroad, but had not worked full time in academia before the war. To the extent that they were 'politically' compliant, they ascended all the more quickly up the academic ladder. They supported the idea of state interventions and expropriation. This group included, for instance, Karel Žlábek (1902–1983), a graduate of the doctoral programme in management at the University of Zurich. In 1946 he was quickly promoted to the position of professor. Josef Blecha (1908–1964) was appointed as a senior lecturer in finance and Leopold Šauer a senior lecturer in statistics. The third group was formed by new, Marxist-oriented economists, who became senior lecturers without completing the standard academic process of writing and defending their habilitation thesis. This group includes Jaroslav Fukátko (1898–1956) and Jan Janáček (1904–72) (Ibid., 46–49).

To adapt its curricula to the changing economic system, in 1945 and 1946 the *Commercial College* introduced a new selection of subjects, which included enterprise planning, the history of the USSR, the trade union movement and the cooperative system and thereby accommodated the needs of the nationalized and, up to that point, private economy. Novotný was the most resolute advocate of reforms aimed at strengthening the democratic and capitalist orientation of economic education. In 1945 he proposed changing the *Commercial College*'s name to the *Vysoká škola věd hospodářských* (*College of Economic Sciences*). One of the reasons why Novotný suggested abandoning the name *Commercial College* was that it was a literal translation of the German *Handelsschule*.

The cool reaction from colleagues to his suggestions is proof that Novotný remained relatively isolated in his opinions, and he had to collaborate with Žlábek on reform in a committee that was set up for this purpose. Novotný and Žlábek represented two altogether different standpoints; Žlábek stressed the importance of the area that was his own academic province, business administration, arguing that the modern era needs 'engineer-economists' and cannot manage with the philosophizing kind. Most notably, however, he often quoted Soviet economists' statements that in the planned economy enterprise must remain the basic unit of the economy. This naturally fit well with the interests of the Party, and with those of communist economists Frejka and Fukátko, who developed a theory of *socialist business administration*.

Although the school worked on reforming studies, the changes originally proposed by Novotný did not occur until the end of February 1948 and under very different circumstances. By then, however, there was no longer a place for Novotný at the school, or even in the new society. Žlábek's ideas only survived for a few years before they were replaced by a more directive approach to planning that was introduced by the *Central Committee* of the Party.

Economic sentiment in the time of national emancipation (and de-emancipation)

Describing Czech university graduates' preference for seeking comfy positions in state administration and the financial sector, Albín Bráf referred to it as the *Czech disease*:

> If someone manages to get into the Land accounting office or banking institution, with fixed working hours and hope of a pension, this is the height of all ambition. They want to join banks and offices, just never to get behind the counter or desk of a shop.
>
> (Bráf, 1907, 2)

Compared to Germans, the Czechs struck him as having little entrepreneurial initiative and little willingness to take on the risk of business. This prompted him, but also others before him, such as Chleborád and Havlíček Borovský, and others after, such as Macek, to feel the need to try to boost Czech economic revival through education. A shared feature of almost all the economists who were working in the Czech Lands from the late nineteenth century up until the communists seized power is their deep interest in public affairs. They were not just scholars and teachers, but also politicians, journalists and organizers of public life. They sought to popularize economics in the wider strata of society and to link economics to the practical needs of the emerging Czech entrepreneurial class. In short, they were men who had their finger on the pulse of the time. They understood social activism as a moral imperative.

These heroic efforts assumed concrete form and can only fully be appreciated when we realize that these figures were acting in a time when it was claimed in the Czech environment that formal education was of no benefit to trade and enterprise. The best businessman or entrepreneur could only be someone who had started out from nothing, a self-made man, educated in the school of life.

The first level of public activism economists pursued – alongside helping to create and develop education in economics – was to advance awareness and understanding of economic issues among the general public. Bráf and Macek, in particular, underlined the importance of an education in economics for anyone embarking on any kind of economic activity or working in any area of the economy or social policy. Bráf even gave lectures on political economy at Prague Castle to Archduke Karl Ludwig of Austria (1833–1896), the younger brother of Emperor Franz Joseph (1830–1916), while Macek regularly took part in the meetings of the famous *Pátečníci* [*Friday Men*] that writer Karel Čapek (1890–1938) organized in his house and that President T.G. Masaryk also attended. However, their work to promote knowledge of economics was also more far-ranging in scope. Their endeavour is best characterized by Macek's observation that the authority of rulers derives primarily from the ignorance or errors of the people ruled. A broad spectrum of institutions formed the platform for this work of spreading knowledge of economics and they sought not just to promote economic awareness but also to support entrepreneurial activities in Czech society. These economists penned the entries for encyclopaedias and dictionaries, organized informative lectures all over the Czech Lands, and most notably wrote extensively for journals and magazines and commented in the press (both the central and local) on current economic (and political) issues.

The most prominent economic journal in the late 19th century was *Economic Horizon*, which originated as a vehicle of the *Industry Union* and the *Exportní spolek* [*Export Association*]. The journal's subtitle was 'a journal devoted to national-economic and socio-political issues' and it continued to be published for 50 years. The first issue was published in 1896 by the publishing house of Jan Otto. A year later, and for almost the next 30 years, its editorship was taken up by Bráf's student Josef Gruber, who was followed by another of Bráf's students, František Hodáč (1883–1943). The journal soon became a professional platform, which attracted contributions from everyone who wanted their opinions to be heard. In addition to theoretical writings it also published papers on current issues and statistical data and reviews of domestic and foreign economic literature. During the Great War the journal had to contend with interference from the imperial censors – sometimes the problem was just a few sentences, but other times it was an entire article. It was forbidden to write about the financial and economic situation of the monarchy and especially about the Central Bank's tariff policy, the prospects for post-war economic cooperation, concepts for a Central European economic space, the shortage of coal in the monarchy, or the increase in the number of Russian inhabitants, and it was prohibited to even make mention of the Bank of England, Masaryk or Serbia (Gruber, 1925). During the Second World War publication of the journal was halted (1941–1946) and in 1951 the communists banned the journal altogether.

Among the institutions that contributed most to elevating prestige of economists in public, reference must be made to the *Česká společnost národohospodářská [Czech National-Economic Society]* and the *Národohospodářský ústav* [*National Economic Institute*]. The *National-Economic Society* was founded in 1896 as an association aimed at the systematic education of the nation into entrepreneurs and consumers. The impulse behind its creation came from the *Jubilejní zemská výstava* [*Land Jubilee Exhibition*] in Prague in 1891, which marked the start of a new wave of collective activities aimed at promoting Czech enterprise and disseminating economic ideas in general, but also, to some degree, of national solidarity; in the same year the *Export Association* was established to promote the export of Czech goods. The creation of the *National-Economic Society* grew out of the first congress of theoretical and practical economists in Bohemia in 1895, the organization of which was directly inspired by what was by then the third congress of Polish economists in Lvov in 1894. Czech newspapers and magazines reported on this event and campaigned for a similar event to be held in the Bohemian Crownlands. Three hundred people from Bohemia, Moravia and Silesia attended the congress in Prague. Albín Bráf was not in attendance, but – and perhaps for that very reason – Josef Kaizl spoke and pressed upon the audience that it would be impossible to acquire political weight by any other means than 'relying on our own economic strength'. Other speakers roared from the stage that Czechs were the most wasteful nation in the world, Czech women the most preening, that swindling behaviour was epidemic in society, but that no-one was actually interested in pursuing business (Gruber, 1921).

The congress provided the *National-Economic Society* with stores of enthusiasm and heaps of far-reaching advice, but produced very few individuals willing to support the *Society* financially or through actual work; as it was establishing itself the *Society* did not have a membership base of even 150 people. The reason was no doubt the fact that the *Society* was boycotted by the Social Democrats, who wielded influence over leaders in the trade union movement, and by the Old Czech Party, which held sway over some large entrepreneurs. And because the *Society* was established as an association and therefore on membership fees, its activities never developed into what was originally planned. Such plans had included lectures, courses and talks on economic issues, the publication of journals and books, the setting up of libraries and reading rooms specializing in economics, the organization of walks in which participants could learn about important economic objects in the landscape, statistical survey, the awarding of scholarships to study economics abroad, the formulation of proposals to improve legislation, and the provision of professional consultations on economic issues and conceptual and material support for setting up enterprises. The majority of activities, however, had a limited lifespan, as no-one signed up for them. It is moreover very hard to put together a board out of just 21 candidates, many of whom did not like each other on the grounds of the fact that they belonged to either the Young Czech Party or the Old Czech Party, so in the end the board was made up entirely of theorists. It was not until the start of the 20th century and the arrival of Josef Gruber in the position of chair (1900–1920) that the situation began to change, even though education and publishing remained the *Society*'s primary activities.

The foundation of the *National Economic Institute* was another example that reflected the complicated situation that existed in Czech society at the time. In this case, however, the animosity was not political but had to do with nationality – or more precisely, with the absence of the expected nationality-based animosity that is obviously associated with Czech economic emancipation. In 1895 Karel Rieger, an entrepreneur, died and in his will from 1888 left the substantial sum of 100,000 gulden to the 'Czech nation' to be used as determined by the current chair of the Old Czech Party. This was a remarkable legacy, because Rieger's parents were Bohemian Germans and Rieger himself had been brought up in German schools, his mother tongue was German, and his wife was German. Nevertheless, Karel Rieger became friends with František Ladislav Rieger (the shared surname is a coincidence and they were in no way related to each other), who, together with his son-in-law Albín Bráf, came up with the idea to establish an institution to support young entrepreneurs travelling to acquire experience abroad. They contacted the President of the *Česká akademie císaře Františka Josefa pro vědy, slovesnost a umění* [*Czech Academy of Sciences, Letters and Arts of the Emperor Franz Josef*], Josef Hlávka (1831–1908), a prominent Czech entrepreneur and philanthropist, who donated double that sum, and along with 14 other figures (and with Hlávka, Bráf and Gruber as members of the board) they founded the *Institute* as a part of the *Czech Academy of Sciences, Letters and Arts*. The Emperor approved the foundation charter that had been secretly under negotiation for months (in order to prevent the plans from being thwarted by the Young Czechs in Vienna) in October 1906 (Doležalová, 2013).

The *Institute* had a very different profile from other bodies. It was wealthy compared with other voluntary associations. With a founding capital of over 330,000 krone (invested at 4% with the Land Bank, behind the foundation of which was also Bráf), the *Institute* had an annual income of over 21,000 krone. Its members were established businessmen and academicians. Although the statutes called for 50 members, originally only 40 were selected, because 50 successful Czech business and economic leaders could not be found in 1907, when the *Institute* began its work. The *Institute* was primarily engaged in the work of granting stipends for study abroad. From 1907 to 1914 the *Institute* awarded 231 stipends, of which 120 were for students to study mining and industry, 61 for studying modern agricultural techniques, and 50 for studying banking and commerce. In most cases the stipend recipients were headed to Germany, England, France and the USA. Efforts to expand the role of the *Institute* during the First Czechoslovak Republic were successful to only some extent. The *Institute* was dormant during the Second World War and was shut down by the communists after 1948 (Albrecht, 2013). It was revived in 1992 to support research in economics in two different ways: As *Centre for Economic Research and Graduate Education (CERGE-EI)* and *Národohospodářský ústav Josefa Hlávky* [*National Economic Institute of Josef Hlávka*].

The second level on which economists were involved in public life was politics, and their political activities usually reflected the areas they specialized in on a theoretical level, and this was especially so when they were in the position of an elected representative. They initiated and had an active hand in formulating socio-economic legislation in the Habsburg monarchy and then in Czechoslovakia. It is impossible to overlook the role Bráf played in developing a system of public hospitals and insurance institutions and in founding the Land Bank, Kaizl's role in creating Austrian financial legislation, the part Engliš paid in getting legislation passed on the appropriation of forests and large estates as part of land reform in 1918–1919 (Doležalová, 2018a) or his contribution to systematizing taxes and state budgets (Doležalová, 2007). A relatively large number of them also occupied ministerial positions: Bráf and Kaizl were ministers (of agriculture and finance, respectively) in the monarchy's governments, Engliš was a minister of finance and a governor of the National Czechoslovak Bank, and Macek worked at the Land Office, which managed the process of land reform. A significant share of the ministers in all 17 Czechoslovak interwar governments were economists, and in the first years after the Czechoslovakia was established, in particular, some government meetings must have looked similar to Bráf's seminars from the decades before, as there were so many of Bráf's students present.

Friends and enemies

With regard to the size and population of the Bohemian Crownlands and the Czech Lands and the number of Czech law graduates, it is not surprising that all economists, at least until the 1930s, knew each other. After all, the first reformers of the 15th century were bonded by friendships, and also the scholars of the 18th century across all disciplines knew each other well. The real 'troubles' occurred when Albín Bráf married the daughter of the leader of the *Old Czechs*, the economist F.L. Rieger, whilst one of the other most important economists of the time, Josef Kaizl, was a *Young Czech*. The dispute arena was mainly in the Prague press as well as in the Imperial Diet, where Carl Menger also entered the game. While Kaizl criticized Menger, Bráf always remained fond of him, they even supported each other when voting on various laws. This infuriated Kaizl and Masaryk, who then did not hesitate to judge him in the Czech public arena. In their correspondence, they called Bráf 'The Small'. Although it is necessary to point out that they also called other Czech intellectuals uncomplimentary names, those who they did not find fired up enough for the 'Czech' matters in Vienna. Masaryk writes to Kaizl referring to some of Bráf's letters for him to read: 'You see how small he is: Using such diction to write to a man who can barely read' (Bílek, 98). On the other hand, Kaizl was criticized by Bráf's brother-in- law, Bohuš Rieger, for being ambitious and not a gentleman. He labelled his pieces of work as compilations. And Bráf criticized Masaryk for putting his oar into every discipline, even though he has not a clue about any of them; and he was said to tell this anecdote: 'What is the difference between the Lord God, the German Emperor and Professor Masaryk? The Lord God knows everything, the German Emperor knows everything better, Masaryk knows everything best' (Bráf, 1922, 27). The grudge continued in the period of the First Republic, and it impacted primarily relations among the changing economists in the post of the Minister of Finance. The 13 replacements in this post were definitely not harmonious whilst passing on the baton, although outwardly they showed mutual respect. Those who tended towards the most vehement assaults were Karel Engliš along with Cyril Horáček, Alois Rašín and Josef Macek.

The permanent involvement of economists in affairs in the public space has to do with the politicization of the economy itself. A theme that was at the back of every idea about the economic betterment of the Czech nation within the monarchy *sui generis* became a political question in the 1880s, and that was the idea of 'Czech national economic needs'. In the public space this led to claims about the need to support Czech products and the coining of the slogan '*svůj k svému*' (*everyone to his own*), which Bohemian Germans countered with the slogan '*Deutsche, kauft bei Deutschen*' (*Germans, let us buy only German goods*), and discussion about the need for Czech economic emancipation. Among economists this opened the question of the distinction between the individual, the national and the state economy and discussion about the legitimacy of the existence of a state economy in a situation where a particular nation does not have its own state. The first contribution to this discussion were texts Chleborád had written two decades earlier focusing on the search for the best Czech translation for the German term *National* or *Volkswirtschaft*.

In 1896 Čuhel chose this subject for the introductory article he wrote for the first issue of *Economic Horizon*, where he formulated a kind of theoretical manifesto of economic independence. Written in a form intelligible to the wider reading public, he made a distinction between the state economy and the national economy and was the first to set out what the needs of a national economy are (Čuhel [Šimek] 1896). It is more than likely, moreover, that it was events in the current life of Czech society at that time that led Čuhel to formulate his theory of needs. He could have been presented with no better example than that of Czechs enthusiastically contributing to the costs of building the National Theatre, but refusing to buy more expensive lower-quality goods just because they were Czech, for him to realize that economics cannot study how and why people choose their goals, but only what paths they choose by which to fulfil them. Instead of an ambitious and unrealizable basis of production, the slogan in the public space became *Everyone to His Own*, a kind of bonus attached to products that had their own quality and use-value, and economic emancipation transformed into a kind of Czech-Austrian compromise, this time in an economic form. And Bráf proclaimed the economic emancipation of Czechs within the Austro-Hungarian Empire as the third phase of the Czech National Revival after linguistic and political emancipation (Bráf, 1909, 27).

Even though Czech economists were preoccupied less with considerations about the *national* character of the economy and Czech economic emancipation and more with consideration on social justice, social conciliation and fair wages, the connection to the struggle for national emancipation meant that not only did the social prestige of economists rise but hand-in-hand the interest in economic issues generally did as well. The culmination point was the establishment of an independent Czechoslovakia. A good example is the process of preparing monetary reform at the start of 1919, which was to separate the currency of the new state from the Austrian krone. Dozens of economists, whether teachers or state or private clerks, along with interested persons from the wider public, applied to take part in a survey announced by the *Chamber of Commerce and Trade* in Prague, in which people could express their opinions. What is significant is that they commented most on whether the new currency should be named the *lion* or the *dollar* ('koruna [crown] never again!'), and everyone rejected the idea that Czechoslovakia should contribute to paying for war debts incurred by Austria-Hungary. They enumerated the negative consequences that being connected to the Austro-Hungarian currency would have for the economy of the new state, which they based on arguments regarding the natural wealth and the advanced level of industrial and agricultural development in Czechoslovakia, thanks to which 'we will recover more quickly on our own' (Engliš, 1919).

The public enthusiasm for the economy as a route to national emancipation reversed by 180 degrees within just a few years – as a result of the Great Depression. The Depression had a decimating effect on the economy of the young state and its consequences cast economics in a bad light. Although economists, and foremost among them Macek, criticized manifestations of distrust in economics and its simplification as a medium for the accumulation of property, and Macek emphasized repeatedly that it was not the economy that had failed but the politicians who had refused to listen economists' advice that is necessary to change the approach to economic processes, trust in the economy and economists turned down a route back to the time when economists were nothing but *exponents* of the bourgeoisie. Voices began to be heard as well that Socialism was not the music of the future but was becoming the reality of the present day, and the newspapers devoted extensive space to considerations on planning and even an appreciation for Germany's planned economy. Even the newspaper of the right-wing agrarian party, *Venkov* [*Countryside*], reported abundantly on the advantages of state debt as a way of overcoming the crisis and combating unemployment.

At the end of the 1930s it was clear that the Great Depression had altered the way the public viewed economic issues. Entrepreneurs were regarded as exploiters, and there was even talk suggesting the state set a maximum permissible profit that could be made. There were calls for state control of the economy and state interventions. In 1938 economists still largely failed to see the real change in public discourse and tried to offer psychological and historical explanations for the public's outlook and also to draw attention to the negative aspects of Russian economic development: 'There is no state or public apparatus– has Russia taught us nothing? – that has the ability to replace the creative inventiveness and the work of thousands and thousands of entrepreneurs who – running their plants while under the risk of loss – work for the common good' (Jak, 1938, 282–283).

The war only seemingly put a halt to this trend; it was during the war that the belief that development towards central control and a planning economy is inevitable won out in the minds of a decisive majority of the political spectrum. Eduard Beneš (1884–1948), President in exile in London, commented himself in 1942 that liberal society is theoretically and practically a thing of the past and that 'we are in the transition from one phase of society to another' (Doležalová, 2010). In this he was probably not referring to the end of democracy as a system for the exercise of power, but to Liberalism in the economic sphere. He felt himself to be a true democrat when he was announcing the onset of 'an uncompromisingly classless and full socialist society' and the end of a society based on a market economy and private ownership. Beneš – and along with him a whole range of other Czechoslovak politicians who were not communists and described themselves as democrats – was convinced that the development of a classless society was the only path forward into the future. An idea began to take shape that envisioned for Czechoslovakia a unique path to Socialism through a *people's democracy*. This concept, with a pleonastic name, embodied within itself the idea that the defeat of fascism meant both the defeat of private property as the dominant system and a strengthening of the Soviet Union not just as a country but also as the model for the state system. The newly formed *people's democracy* was supposed to serve as a confirmation of the Marxist idea that the Russian-style proletarian dictatorship is not the only path to Socialism.

Soon after the war the shift in discourse manifested itself in every area of society. The Party's propagation and agitation on the pages of the economic section of the Party newspaper *Rudé právo* [*Red Right*] and also on the pages of other periodicals had been newly adjusted to this task; articles revealing the 'positions' of the private business sector, its manoeuvres, fishy practices and unfair profits started to regularly appear as well as criticism of the 'old bureaucracy' and its incompetence and corrupt nature. At the same time, the agitation was supposed to point out only the positive aspects of nationalization and to popularize agreements with Slavonic countries as a protection from crisis and a guarantor of a standard of life. The film director Jiří Weiss (1913–2004) was even picked to shoot a film in 1947 about the great life of 1953 – when the first 5-year plan would be completed. Economist Josef Goldmann was responsible for the popularization of the economy according to communist ideas and at the same time for the preparation of news about the approaching crisis in the West in the *Central Committee*.

Economics became a public affair in a way that the first generation of Czech economists had certainly never dreamed of. Economics became a tool of the political fight.

4 Between theory and ideology

Economics as a political tool (1948–1989)

'We who were enraptured by the wave of passion, who awakened the enthusiasm of the people on the general political field and then on that of the military, we anticipated that we would carry out directly on the basis of this ardour equally great. . .economic goals. Life showed us our error'.

V.I Lenin (1955, 49)

25 February 1948 changed Czechoslovakia. It departed from the path of its version of Socialism and began to build Communism. In its political and economic relationships it gradually reoriented itself to the countries of the emerging Soviet bloc. The Communist Party became the only leader of the nation. Total nationalization of all industrial sectors and services, violent collectivization of agriculture and a devastating monetary reform took place. A planning system of an administrative-directive type that included all economic sectors was implemented. The Soviet system was not systematically described anywhere at that time; the Soviet experts and advisors only knew the system from within their narrow field of specialization and were able to introduce technical procedures. Therefore, the Czechoslovak plan even included items such as *Care for Camels* as a Means of Transport, or *Elimination of Illiteracy*, although there never was a desert in Czechoslovakia and there was no illiteracy at that time. However, they had both in the Soviet Union. Of course, the Soviet experts also brought the ideological apparatus to explain each of their steps taken on the basis of power. But already in 1953 and 1954, serious faults in the operation of the national economy appeared; shortages grew and national revenue totally decreased. The regime reacted with an attempt to create pressure for effective usage of allotted funds by means of the so-called *normative of material interests*. Nevertheless, the reform did not lead to a change in efficiency.

Communists labelled the international situation as the reason for the failure, which led to the rise of the joke (popular to the present) about the existence of the five enemies of Socialism: spring, summer, autumn, winter, and – capitalism. The decrease in economic efficiency continued; in 1962–1963 there was a total drop in real salaries. Yet there was a strange equalization of salary, where 80% of fully employed workers were concentrated in the earnings range of 1,000–2,500 crowns (Návrh, 1965, 52), whilst salaries of nomenclature cadres, from the district Party secretaries through to the President were, respectively, six and 60 times higher. Work productivity did not increase, dependence on imported raw materials did not decrease and there were no technological innovations. The onset of the scientific-technical revolution had been missed.

The changes which later entered history as Šik's reform stemmed from the acute need to prevent the loss of the economic efficiency of the economy and its decline to the level of developing countries. This was meant to prove an extent of market relationships which would not threaten the leading role of the Party (Kosta, 1996, 22). Two documents were enacted that were to implement a new system of control and lead the Czechoslovak economy out of a long-term unsatisfactory state (Návrh, 1965; Principy, 1966). The reform finished with the violent ending of the *Prague Spring*, when Warsaw Pact troops entered Czechoslovakia in August 1968 and commenced a period of new purges in the Party. The normalized and re-Sovietized Czechoslovakia awaited the beginning of Soviet *perestroika*.

After 1948, so-called Marxism-Leninism began to be almost exclusively identified with the theory of both the socialist revolution and the socialist economy. Significantly, economists (and scientists generally) were, analogically the *National Front* of political parties, labelled the *Theoretical Front*. Economics became, rather than a science based on objective arguments, a religion in which the terms faith and betrayal would be used in its deliberations. Economic pseudo-innovations were partly based on ignorance of world economic development and on the deliberate overlooking thereof and partly on the emptiness of the substance of the political economy of Socialism. This shift of economy was accompanied by a loss of prestige, professional autonomy and social position of economists.

If we determine outside of this group those economists who were connected with the interwar era, who did not buckle in their views and were rapidly removed from scientific and public life, three groups of economists remain. The first group was comprised of those who had received their education during the time of the First Republic – some had studied at Western European universities and after the Second World War joined the services of the Party. The second group was comprised of economists who had studied in the first years after the war and had been active Party supporters from the beginning. Finally, the third group was comprised of economists who had received education at schools based on the theory of Marxism–Leninism from the 1950s onwards. Some of them acquired the experience of studies at Western universities from 1967–1969.

These three groups delimit the main heroes of this chapter. Although burdened with incomprehensible terminology and endless spiral-like sentences, in their hands, Marxism-Leninism was not just dogmatic; the search for Socialism with a human face was not just a dream; the grey years was not just a period without any intellectual joy. And this took place in existential situations which troubled souls and ruined human lives.

The Stalinist fifties

February 1948 shifted the production of economic literature to a lesser role. Publications of questionable quality began to be published in droves, always just descriptive and critical of previous economic conditions, proclaiming the future successes of a socialist economy controlled only by the Party (Frejka, 1948). The new economy was to be built on the foundations of so-called Marxism-Leninism and was to be the confirmation of it in practice. The majority of publications were addressed more to the masses rather than to intellectual opponents and had a strong ideological content and used strong ideological language. According to these publications, Marxism-Leninism was the application of Marx's theory to specific conditions in Russia. Lenin was called the successor of Marx, and one who had in some aspects surpassed his teachings. Lenin's most important contribution in developing Marxist political economy was considered to be his critical analysis of the new phase of capitalism, i.e. imperialism. Nevertheless, in the terminology of the first post-war Marxists, it was Stalin who 'generalised Soviet experience and discovered in it the economic laws of socialism' (Frejka, 1951, 65). The plan, as the primary regulator of the socialist economy, was considered the primary economic law of Socialism. The second law was the necessarily proportional development of a socialist economy (in contrast to the necessarily disproportional development of a capitalist economy, which may only occasionally be proportional – in an unorganized and partial manner). All post-war Marxist-Leninist theses define the principal difference between capitalist and socialist ways of production as follows: In capitalism, all economic laws function spontaneously, thus creating regular crises. The socialist way of production is also subject to economic laws, but their nature is known and people have the opportunity to use them to transform reality consciously: 'When man recognised them [economic laws - AD], he created the means to master them' (Frejka 1951, 55).

The implementation of planned and proportional development was based on the single-minded activities of the Party and state institutions. The progress of Socialism was directly proportional to the level of collective ownership of production means eliminating the antagonistic disharmony typical of capitalistic production. Expropriation, therefore, was regarded as a theoretical necessity. Apart from the aforementioned two principal laws, Socialism was to be subject to many additional laws, such as the law of socialist industrialization and the law of agricultural collectivization, the law of primitive socialist accumulation, the law of the allocation of means of production and the law of increase of living standard. All of them were supported by a truly unique scientific axiom – the practice in the Soviet Union.

Study of these laws was the content of a stand-alone research field called Political economy of Socialism that was included in all state examinations at all universities in Czechoslovakia in the form of given truths that were not subject to discussion. Capitalism itself mutated to the form of one of the *pre-socialist economic formations* and if it was the subject of deliberation, then only as the last phase (of imperialism) in the development from *primitive communal society* to *Communism*. Books were filled with examples of its unavoidable defeat, offering an inexorable logic: The capitalist entrepreneur does not implement a machine in order to facilitate labour for the workers in order for them to fare better, but rather to augment his profit; in Socialism, the fact that a machine saves human labour suffices to have it implemented. This is why it is possible to implement more machines in Socialism than it is in capitalism, and the superiority of Socialism over capitalism is given by as little as this (Hrubý 1951, 92–93).

Almost all these theses were based on a textbook published in the Soviet Union and approved by Stalin. Every new text by Stalin became the subject of celebratory discussions (Šik, Kazda 1953). Only exceptionally do we find quotes from Marx's *Capital* (usually from Parts I and III) or from Lenin's *Imperialism* (1948); of the 'bourgeois' economists, only Malthus managed to penetrate. According to the Soviet pattern, research had to be isolated from the universities. In particular, 'fundamental' research in economic theory was concentrated in the *Československá akademie věd* [*Czechoslovak Academy of Sciences*]. In that scope, the *Výzkumný ústav ekonomického plánování* [*Research Institute for Economic Planning*] and the *Ekonomický ústav* [*Economic Institute*] were founded in the early 1950s.

The golden sixties

Reform discussion during the late 1950s did not exceed the framework of Soviet textbooks (Boreš *et al.* 1957). The influence of Evsei Liberman's (1897–1981) study, published in 1956 was obvious even if this source was not explicitly quoted (Havel *et al.* 2002, 220). Advancing even entirely formal adjustments could not succeed, for the political economy of Socialism was built on a structure of laws which were not discussed. In the 1960s, however, voices began to sound saying that these laws could be contravened: 'The people have a certain power; they can, at least for a time, work against social laws' (Brus, 1964, 135). The platform for discussions was formed especially by the*Economic Institute* environment, led from 1961 by Ota Šik, who concentrated around himself young, talented economists. Discussions related mostly to the government-issued official materials and oscillated around the key theme they contained: The relationship between the market and the plan and the two factors that influenced it – price formation and so-called material interest.

In relation to the plan, economists were from the beginning divided into two groups. The first saw the decisive area of developing the state establishment in perfecting the objective content of planning; the second group, which gradually dominated, emphasized issues of a systemic character, including reorganization of the system of control. Within this group there was a dominating consensus that the main problem of planning was, first, overestimation of the role of the *planning headquarter*. Indeed, in a situation where prices do not fulfil their informative or allocative function, it was that decided which productions would take priority – and hence about allotted raw materials, employees and capital (Turek 1967, 31). And second, overestimation of planning. The economists argued that a detailed schedule of plan tasks had both clear technical limitations and also led to state enterprises (SOEs) concentrating all their activity into the fight for high allotments of resources. They fulfilled the constantly new directive indicators only formally, overvalued their needs and undervalued their production capabilities; but the link to the (societal) needs which every SOE was to secure was lost.

The new concept of the plan thus had to respect the 'current level of development of production forces', respect SOEs interests and their activities. The market and the plan were to divide the field of activity in such a way that the plan would dominate on the macro-level and the market on the micro-level. The obligatory character of the plan was to limit itself only to 'necessary' tasks (R&D, limits of investments, export, production necessary for securing basic societal needs, defence and security). After almost 20 years the consumer was to receive space in the economic structure: State-determined prices were only to be of an orientation character. This would of course require changing the concept of the plan as a law.

The first considerations on this theme were very cautious. Among them the proposal to make SOEs independent in the scope of simple reproduction and to concentrate all of the profits into the hands of the centre which could influence changes in production on a societal scale (Vejvoda, 1964). The superiority of the plan to the market was meant to be understood only in the sense that the plan regulates but cannot operate against the market (Kožušník, 1964). In 1965, the market was already being labelled as the only way that labour could be expended in accordance with needs (Mošna, Horálek, 1965, 11), and the plan was meant to be able to anticipate the tendency of the market and fix it by a structure of goals and at the same time operate actively on the future market (Kouba, 1965, 295); a mere addition of the market mechanism into the control instruments hitherto was labelled as an attempt to mix fire and water (Ibid.).

Over the next years, the dictum of official proposals determined the playing field. The plan was still the fundamental instrument for managing the socialist economy, although in its new conception and connected with a consistent utilization of the law of value (under Socialism) and in 'a certain framework of market relationships' (Návrh, 1965, 17). A year later, the plan was still the fundamental instrument of control, but it was now a plan which stemmed from knowledge of the market and provided sufficient space for the development thereof. The market and plan were now two 'indivisible' reciprocally conditioning and influencing sides of economic control (Zásady, 1966, 16).

Immediately afterwards, economists carried out the fateful *salto mortale*: Planning something to which the market leads is pointless. The plan to them began to become utilitarian, a necessary instrument for perfecting the market (Kouba, 1967, 779). The market was the foundation of the economic mechanism, the plan its superstructure (Kouba *et al.* 1968, 131). The market was the place for the free decision of the consumer and the economic calculation of the SOEs. It was to work in all branches, albeit not the same in all; the predominant part of the economy was to be faced with the 'threat' of the world market and employees with the threat of job position loss; the SOEs themselves were to be faced with the threat of dissolution (Turek, 1967). Economists even recommended making the market superior to the plan, albeit for a limited time only (Ibid., 295). The market was to become the instrument for transferring the economy from extensive growth to a state of market balance (Ibid., 288). Otakar Turek (b.1927) proposed forming an economic model based on the market mechanism, with so-called *parametric prices*, that could be considered the predecessor of the *hard budget limitations* of János Kornai (b.1928). The central plan was to have the form of a prognosis and its goals were to be asserted only by market-confirmed instruments of economic policy.

Economists were thereby saying nothing less than that Socialism was still a market economic system, albeit with a plan as a regulator. Although the authors always repeated that it would be merely a 'transitional' state, several fundamental laws of Socialism were being shaken to their foundations. The plan began to be labelled as an instrument which was 'ahead' of its time: People's needs do not change once in every 5 years and within the intentions of the plan, and the attempt to dispense with need as a market category belongs more to the communist manner of distribution (Turek, 1967, 30).

The issue of prices was closely connected with the change of the plan and market. Prices were – theoretically and practically – considered to be a *recording category*, the task of which was to measure and express the production volume. These were always firmly fixed for several years ahead regardless of changes in production conditions and consumption. Moreover, there was a price dualism in the form of variously constructed retail and wholesale prices (the latter did not include so-called turnover tax, a period term for value added tax); with time, there was a growth in the number of products for which the wholesale price was higher than that of retail and the state had to subsidize the given production. The actual costs of the producer thus did not have a reliably comparable national-economic dimension. Now, the prices were to become a criterion of success.

The first proposal for changes considered price as an economic instrument and anticipated the formation of a 'space' for setting prices on the basis of agreement between the supplier and buyer (Návrh, 1965, 43). But there was still to be a plan for price formation and, for the SOEs, the price was to be the preliminary information by which they were to adjust their costs. Fixed prices, prices circulating within state-given limits and free prices stemming from supply and demand were to co-exist side-by-side. The *Zásady urychlené realizace nové soustavy řízení* [*The Principles of Accelerated Realisation of the New System of Management*] (1966) placed price liberalization on the agenda sheet. This disturbed a further axiom of Marxism-Leninism, in which the economic content of price is the value of abstract labour, thus labour 'socially necessary' for the production of a given product. Economists thus had to confront the effect of the law of value under Socialism. Its conceptwas not to change, but was to be subjected to the criteria of efficiency (Komenda, 1965). Although they considered the market mechanism to be the most effective 'utilization' of the law of value, prices were to arise 'spontaneously' in any case. Economists thus did not condemn the headquarters to passivity in price issues. It was to utilize *manoeuvring* by prices so as to lead SOEs into fulfilling the plan (Burešová, 1966, 288). This is why it had to be equipped with knowledge of past and future economic processes, including the situation on the foreign market. This was to be simulated in the event of need (Turek, 1967), which was nothing less than an administratively-set price on the basis of world prices.

Price *manoeuvring*, however, was threatened by the rise of inflation pressures. These would be implemented not by the world market, but by the domestic enemy, SOEs, whose products would not be the subject of interest as a result of price fluctuations (Klaus, 1967, 131). Fears of sharp price fluctuations were shared by all economists. They distinguished between two types of instruments for maintenance thereof: Economic (free entrance into the branch) and administrative (*fixing a price ceiling*) (Kožušník, 1967, 308), although in principle a consensus dominated that if the headquarters was to enter into price formation, then it was only to be in the event of protection against speculative price growth (under Socialism this was misuse of the monopoly position of SOEs by their directors). Only as late as in 1968, was a revolutionary thesis published that prices should be influenced only by the relationship of supply and demand; the thesis was substantiated by the fact that optimal planning was impossible without a rational price structure and it exposed socialist society to the risk of irrational economic activities (Kouba *et al.* 1968, 210).

The second condition for a normally functioning market was, according to the diction of the official proposals, so-called material interest, expressing the relationship of people in the socialist society to material impulses of labour; it was also in this area that economists broke many taboos. Initiative in this sense was a sentence by Ota Šik that 'material interests are always a reflection of an existing production method' (Šik, 1964, 104). Economists emphasized ever more urgently that the socialist economy too was still and totally production of goods; in many texts we find a Smithian-sounding sentence that those following their immediate interests do not necessarily act anti-socially. For the Marxist-Leninist economists the way to an interconnection of individual and social interests came through the connection of the incomes of workers with those of the corporations in which they worked – with the reasoning that the labour of the individual gains meaning precisely as a part of the labour of the collective (Komenda, Kožušník, 1964). Although critical views also appeared that rejected the system of material interests, with the argument that it could work only when expanding market relationships to the entire economy (Ježek, 1967; Mlčoch, 1976b), the concept was in principle accepted as a way for people to become aware of existing economic relations.

In this issue, The *Návrh nové soustavy plánovitého řízení národního hospodářství* [*The Proposal of the New System of Planned Management of National Economy*] (1965) offered just phrases on 'constant perfecting', 'flexible adjustment', 'maximum workforce productivity' and the 'principle of distribution according to labour'; the main direct instrument remained central regulation of tariff salaries and standardization of labour consumption. The *Principles* (1966) placed the *enterprise* at the position of the fundamental economic cell of society, delimited the salary issue by implementing enterprise taxes from salaries, which were to increase the price of *live* work and thereby motivate implementation of new technologies, and connected material interest with the work of the collective.

After years of ideological condemnation, even the experience of the Yugoslavian worker autonomy could thereby become a topic of discussion (Kocanda, Pelikán, 1967); others argued more in the favour of worker participation in management (Levčík, Kosta, 1968). The principle of the interest of management in profit was both rejected as the ground of managerial Socialism (Turek, 1967, 287) and also supported (Mlčoch 1967a). A decisive role in the system of material interest, however, was to be played by a system of transfers to the state budget – in terms of a unified aim for all SOEs. This elicited discussion on the possible consequences of unified transfers – the liquidation of incapable SOEs, although it granted in principle that this was a necessary part of the real market environment. The year 1967 saw the emergence of official material on the standing of SOEs (Demokratizace, 1968) that counted with their de-etatization, their management through works councils and the formation of a pluralist ownership structure (state, enterprise, cooperative form). But discussions never reached a consensus on the necessary existence of private ownership of an entirely radical form, leading to the isolation and separation of individual parts of the economy.

In all the discussions described, the phenomenon of material interest was considered to be a collective phenomenon; but it was to manifest itself very individually. At the level of the individual, the concept of salary in Marxism-Leninism was understood as the workers' plan-determined share in the created national income, whilst the specific amount thereof depended on the amount and quality of the labour; it was thus declared as a means towards the realization of distribution according to labour as a legal attribute of the socialist economy. Two concepts of personal material interest emerged in the course of 1967–1968.

The first upheld a gradational profit-share according to length of employment, with the substantiation that a fixed share would lead to rivalry among employees (Kocanda, Pelikán, 1967). The second concept distinguished between the consumer and entrepreneurial interests of the workers that were to lead to the removal of fears of modernization (Rusek, 1968). Even truly heretical views on *feudal socialism* were voiced, saying that Socialism had not eradicated estranged labour but had only produced it in another form which had, moreover, been deformed by phrases that everyone had to work to their best ability, by impressions that mere planned distribution of the workforce was sufficient and by notions that the workforce no longer had value, for the opposite would entail granting that even under Socialism the workforce had become a good (Fišera, 1967, 339–340). Besides this, as some had noticed, the used differentiation of salaries according to the societal significance of occupation was no more than a deformed relationship between supply and demand for labour (Jüngling, Nachtigal, 1967). It should be added that although Socialism considered participation of the people in control economy as one of its greatest merits (through societal ownership), this remained practically on the sidelines of the discussion. This was clearly connected with the fact that it was a public secret that the 'low professional and cultural level of the leading cadres is one of the main barriers to the economic development of our country' (Rychetník, 1968, 353).

But the 1960s were not only a period of searching for new (possible) ways of developing Marxism-Leninism. Notions inspired by the current development of political economy in the world were also born. There were three sources. The first were international contacts, based on research teams of scientists from socialist countries. It was thence that the opinions of Polish and Hungarian economists-Michal Kalecki (1899–1970), Oskar Lange (1904–1965), Wlodzimierz Brus (1921–2007), András Bródy (1924–2010), and J. Kornai-permeated into Czechoslovakia. Thanks to these teams, economists could also begin to travel abroad (first to socialist countries) for conferences and seminars. Several of them also travelled abroad for foreign scholarship, especially to Cornell University, where Jaroslav Vanek (1930–2017), Czech by origin, worked in a leading position. The second source was foreign economic literature, when libraries (especially the *Economic Institute* Library) began to purchase not only the latest foreign economic literature, but also texts which had already become classics and books forming the core of contemporary 'non-Marxist' economics began to be translated into Czech.

The lost library

Until the second half of the 20th century, the Czechs were missing a specialized economic library. However, in fact, the foundation had already been laid at the end of the 14th century, when one of the first Czech commentators on Aristotle, Iohannes Wenceslai de Praga (d. 1400), left his house and his library to the 'Student College of the Czech Nation'. Four centuries later, Josef Sonnenfels received state support for the purchase of economic literature. Nevertheless, when his students wanted to transfer these books to the university library in Prague after his death, they found out that there were a lot of books (719), but very few books specializing in economics. Contrariwise, Joseph Kopetz's library did not only contain the manuscripts of his lectures, full of notes on contemporary events, but also dozens of other authors' books that illustrate the breadth of his work, as well as the knowledge of the then students of economics; there were Stuart and Smith books, Smith's German perception and German interpretations of physiocrats. Still, even in the middle of the 19th century, Chleborád complained about the insufficiency of the University Library in Prague, claiming that it neither had H.Ch. Carey in the original nor a translated copy of Bastiat. A unique economic library was not compiled until J.M. Novotný attempted in the interwar period. Its extent is evidenced by the fact that he brought around 6,000 volumes with him to Canada. Approximately 10% of this collection is now in the Syracuse University Library. He left another 10,000 volumes in Czechoslovakia, where the books probably became a part of the collection of the National Library (Markovski, 1987).

And finally, the third source was the *Graduate School* of the *Economic Institute* (GS) from the second half of the 1960s, at which non-Marxist political economy began to be taught in the framework of the Ph.D. programme. Almost all theoretical economists went through its gates; after 1989, many of them would become leaders of the Czech transformation, politicians and ambassadors.

At the *GS*, P.A. Samuelson's textbook, *Economics*, then in its 6th edition, was also translated. The translation was published in internal *Economic Institute* publications, although its book edition was thwarted by the forthcoming normalization of 1970. In the same year, the activity of the *GS* was also ended and its director, Luděk Urban (1927–2013) had to leave the *Economic Institute*. A similar fate was shared also by numerous economists connected with the discussions on economic reform, especially those who had gone so far in their considerations that it had threatened the Party's power entitlement and had cast into doubt Socialism in its fundaments. Economic reform remained an open, unfinished process of searching for the optimal form of the mechanism of the functioning of economics in the principle of trial and error (Šulc, 1998, 77), which would not be discussed for another 20 years.

The grey seventies and eighties

Purges in the Party and society began after the Soviet occupation. Half a million members who were in any way connected with the events of the *Prague Spring* or, as the case may be, rejected the interpretation of Soviet occupation as liberation, were excluded from the Party. For the theoretical economists, especially those from the *Economic Institute*, this entailed transfer from theory to the working class sphere, to substandard positions of warehouseman, maintenance man or official; several of them chose instead to emigrate. Economics as the core of 'counter-revolution' was put under strict ideological supervision. Scientific contact with foreign countries was discontinued entirely. Ideologically incorrect books, including translations of foreign titles, were withdrawn from the press; over the next years, only a few Western authors, such as Joan Robinson (1903–1983) (Robinsonová, 1975), infiltrated among the production of Soviet books. Open discussion was unthinkable, censorship supervised the content of professional articles and books, and editors were supervised directly by the Party. Even the themes of masters' and doctoral thesis were the subject of Party supervision. All texts, including student theses had, in the first paragraphs, to be shielded with the 'classics' of Marxism-Leninism.

The *Economic Institute*, which was able to restart tuition at the *GS*, remained the most significant place from the perspective of cultivation of economics. The lecturers based their lectures and seminars on publications by the leading economists from the West (Havel *et al.* 2002, 239). Research tasks assigned by the government began to be carried out in the 1980s; their results were often labelled 'secret' or 'for internal use only'. Under the evident influence of Kornai, the Václav Klusoň's (b.1926) team solved the issue of the shortcomings of the system of planning (Ibid., 245). In the second half of the 1980s, space slowly began to open for public discussion on economic issues. Informal seminars began to emerge, in the scope of which discussions that surpassed the limits of the current official doctrine took place (Tříska, 2011). Not only the two future Czech presidents, Václav Klaus (b.1941) and Miloš Zeman (b.1944), but also future representatives of all political parties – both left and right-wing – that would emerge after the *Velvet Revolution* in 1989 met there.

In 1984, the *Prognostický ústav* [*Prognostic Institute*] within the *Academy of Science* headed by Valter Komárek (1930–2013) began to form. A group of economists, especially from the *Economic Institute*, gathered around him, as did several economists who were engaged in the reforms of the 1960s, including some chief figures; some of them would go on a few years hence to occupy key positions in Czech industry and in state leadership. Their major research output was a long-term forecast up until 2010. Originally, the whole text was declared secret. However, after it had been leaked to Radio Free Europe (Kosta, 1995), the journal *Politická ekonomie* [*Political Economy*] devoted a monothematic issue to a discourse on the main points of the prognosis.

Whilst Komárek outlined therein the difficulties of the Czechoslovak economy, he also saw a comprehensive plan as the path to correction, and stated in the list of literature texts by Michail Gorbachev (b.1931) and by the highest Party representatives at the time, some of the members of his team offered a critical analysis not only of the state of the economy, but of the results of the prognosis itself. Even the first principle of the intended changes – a change in the relationship between planning and the market – was the subject of criticism. Václav Klaus criticized the fact that there would not be a relationship between two autonomous subjects in view of the role of the planning headquarters. He proposed its separation from fiscal and currency operations and a departure from the idea of a 'comprehensive plan' (Klaus, 1989).

The feeling of *deja-vu* is necessarily elicited in this context by the translation of the last official Soviet textbook of the political economy of Socialism published in the same year (Medvedev, 1989). Sentences similar to those from the 1950s version with an interpretation that seems as though copied from Czech texts from the second half of the 1960s: The economic mechanism is based on planned control, thanks to which society achieves proportional development; plan is the main tool for 'implementing the Party's economic policy into life' (Ibid., 175); the Leninist principle of democratic centralism is the basis of the construction of economic control in all socialist countries; *democratism* is a powerful instigator of the initiative and creativity of the masses; *enterprises* are the basic economic cells of society; and *perestroika* is to be realized by a radical reform of the economic mechanism, including expansion of the independence of enterprises, of the organizational structure, of self- government '(The more self-government, the more socialism' (Ibid., 218)), and of the activation of the human factor. The new quality of centralism is to overcome the one-sidedness of planning, and changes cannot succeed – as experiences in socialist countries demonstrate – without a 'multilaterally' developed market (Ibid., 181). A strange mixture of phrases and theses of the *Prague Spring* is proof of the closeness of Gorbachev to the Czechoslovak reformers of the 1960s

(Brown, 2009). And it is also proof that open public discussion over economic issues had for the time being – despite *perestroika* – not taken place and the horizons of economic thought remained beyond the horizon of the possible – with only a few exceptions (Klaus and Tříska 1988).

Four faces of the Czech version of Marxism-Leninism

Josef Goldmann: the macro-economic analysis of real Socialism

Goldmann stands out among the economists who had fallen into Marxist clichés without being able or willing to give content to the terms they used in their texts. Experience of life in the Czechoslovak borderlands, the Great Depression, the occupation of Czechoslovakia (his mother died in a concentration camp); all this led him to the conviction that there could be a better world, and this could only be under Socialism. Not even the experience of a communist prison had shaken him.

Josef Goldmann (1912–1984) was born into a German Jewish family in Carlsbad. His mother tongue was German, and it was always easier for him to write in German or English – Czech was his third language. Even in general language he found English terms more easily and always got angry in German. He studied economics at the LSE in London and at Charles University in Prague. He worked for the Economic Committee of the Party in its exiled headquarters in London during the war; at the same time, he was employed at the Statistics Office at Oxford University and the British Institute for Public Opinion Research. In 1945 he became a member of the Party. From 1945–1949 he was a planning official for its *Central Committee*, and over the next three years he was the Deputy Minister, Chairman of the State Planning Office and the representative for Czechoslovakia in COMECON. A steep fall came at the beginning of the 1950s – in one of the last political trials – against 'national' economists – he escaped death by just a hair's breadth. Yet his conviction was given as late as 1954, i.e. after the deaths of Stalin and Gottwald. He was dismissed in 1960 and rehabilitated in 1963, but he would never again allow himself to be tempted to hold a political post. When he left for Great Britain on invitation from the University of Cambridge in 1968, he even considered going into exile. But 2 years later, a psychological illness, bipolar affective disorder, began to appear, which is why he returned to Czechoslovakia on the exhortation of his family. Surprisingly, the Party purges did not affect him and he could continue to work.

Acquaintance with Keynes's students in London, Richard Kahn (1905–1989), J. Robinson, and especially with M. Kalecki during the war had a fundamental influence on the formation of Goldmann's economic views. Apparently, the beginning of his own scientific career was a column proofreading Kalecki's book *Studies in Economic Dynamics* (1944); his (Goldmann's) first scientific article (1943) was later republished in Kalecki's collection of papers, *Studies in War Economics* (1947). In the same year, Goldmann's first book in Czechoslovakia was published; it was published in English and concerned Czechoslovak experiences with planning. It was successful especially abroad, for Western Europe tensely waited to see how successful this experiment could be. In view of its industrial structure, Czechoslovakia could have been a significant precedent also for their economic policy. Through planning, however, Goldmann aimed for a solution of the more general problems of the socialist economy; the plan was for him a directive instruction, and he rejected the French way of indicative planning. But he had already realized by the turn of the 1940s and 1950s that a planned socialist economy would tend to create shortages (*narrow profiles*) which to a capitalist economy are unfamiliar (Goldmann, 1949, 53).

After his rehabilitation, he returned to economic research in the framework of the *Economic Institute* and it was as though he had never ceased working, and as though he had never experienced the political trials and communist imprisonment, he immediately assailed a 'heretical' theme: The price level and fluctuation of the pace of growth in the socialist economy; once again, he published the results in English (Goldmann, 1965). Goldmann's analysis was based on the existence of unproductive supplies; he labelled them as the 'escape channel of the reproduction process'. The expansion thereof entailed that SOEs formally fulfilled the plan, but there was no market for their products. He therefore saw the main problem in the existing system of planning and control, especially in large investment projects; his assertion that in their consequences, the economic cycle existed even under Socialism (Goldmann's estimate was 8–10 years), was truly revolutionary.

Goldmann further deepened his analysis when he concentrated on an elaboration of the factors of economic growth and their reciprocal relationships. He once again entered into lively discussions with Kalecki, but also with Brus and other – even Western – economists, and newly also brought into the discussion Russian economist and planning theorist Grigory Alexandrovich Feldman (1884–1958). He thereby also broached – for the first time in the Czech environment – the issue of the legacy of the economic thought of the Russian Revolution, the New Economic Policy. From Feldman, Goldmann adopted the notion that economic growth is subordinate primarily to two limitations: The capacity of capital goods and systems of payment with foreign countries (Čihák, 1997, 10). The determining inspiration was once again Kalecki. Although Kalecki's model is non-mathematical, Goldmann's intention was to apply it to Czechoslovak statistical data (Goldmann, Kouba, 1967).

On this basis, he then identified the difference between growth models of socialist and capitalist economies: While under capitalism, the pace of growth is influenced by demand, under Socialism it is by supply. This is why the cyclic movement of a socialist economy is given by the side of supply. The substantiation may at first glance be identical with Frejka's theses at the turn of the 1940s and 1950s on the (currently) insufficient knowledge of socialist laws, but the sense is of one other than ideological agitation. Goldmann did not, for one, hesitate to assert that cyclic fluctuations are greater in Czechoslovakia than in Great Britain or France, where they were moderated by Keynesian stabilization policy, but most importantly, his thesis aimed towards an analysis of the limits of the efficiency of a planned economic system and the manners in which it functions; as a Marxist he considered it to be a real and functional variant of a capitalist economy. This is why, perhaps surprisingly in the context of the proceeding 'reconstruction of economic mechanism', he warned against attempts to improve the current system instead of a replacement with a more effective mechanism. This was to him the model, based on the law of value and the market mechanism. He completed his analysis with an expression of a six-equation model of the fluctuation of the pace of growth of the socialist economy: Fluctuation develops from investments to the physical capital, which are an exogenous factor and are not correctly allocated. The measure of fluctuation is given by the relationship between the pace of production supply growth, the expectation of this growth and by the amplitude of fluctuations. Foreign trade enters into the equations as a further factor – for Czechoslovakia as an example of a small open economy (Goldmann, 1973).

According to Goldmann (Goldmann, Kouba, 1967) the absence of effective economic criteria and/or limits on efficient allocation of investment gave rise to close ties between investment and inflation. At the beginning of every 5-year planning cycle, there was a considerable tendency to increase the investment ratio and to start new investment projects financed through the central budget. In the third year of the planning period, this investment faced serious constraints in the capacity of the investment-producing sector and started to delay. These delays had an inflationary impact that was documented in the 1950s and 1960s (Drábek *et al.* 1993, 6).

Together with his students in the course of the 1970s, Goldmann published a book on the state of the socialist economy in 1990 (Goldmann *et al.* 1974), an initiative work of Czech prognostication, with several remarkable notions. First, the standard of living is ceasing to be a goal and is becoming a factor of economic growth; second, the natural environment is becoming a factor of economic growth; third, the role of services will grow in the context of consumption; and fourth, the problems of the Czechoslovak economy require, over the next 20 years, a harmonization of scientific central planning and commodity monetary relationships (Čihák, 1997, 16–17).

Over the next few years he published a trilogy focused on the theoretical concept of the socialist economy as a complex, dynamic system placed into the international division of labour (Goldmann, 1975, 1978, 1985). The expression of the goals of the socialist economy became a key issue for him (Goldmann, 1985): Goals should not be an exogenous factor in the socialist economy, determined by a superior body, but a project which is discussed. He referred to this emphasis on aiming as his innovation, although it corresponded with Engliš's considerations which were 50 years old; as a graduate of the interwar Prague Faculty of Law Goldmann certainly knew Engliš, but never referred to him in any way. The book was withdrawn from sale after several weeks, for the regime became aware of its implications; but it reached readers once again as late as the summer of 1989. Even so, his conclusions on the economic crisis threatening Socialism could not be published in Czechoslovakia; the study was published in Hungary (Goldmann, Kouba, 1984).

From the 1970s, Goldmann surrounded himself with such a group of students and colleagues that he gradually established a school (Čihák, 1997, 3) focused on a macro-economic analysis of real Socialism from a Marxist position. Goldmann brought his students to a precise knowledge of Marx's work and to an emphasis on the role of empirical research. Since his students will partake in the transformation of real Socialism into capitalism after 1989 as ministers or directors of major banks and privatized SOEs, Goldmann's legacy would perhaps be the reason why the Czech transformation would emphasize the macro-economic dimension and why it would be successful in this regard.

Ota Šik: from Stalinism to the third way

In 1947, when Šik took a hard stance against economists connected with the Czechoslovak interwar environment and the 'bourgeois political economy' (Šik, 1949) he certainly could not have known that in 20 years he would be branded with the mark of Cain of a revisionist and a counter-revolutionary, and, moreover, would also have to emigrate. In the interim, however, he managed to become a respected expert on Marx's teaching, a successful economist whose books were translated into numerous languages, even a politically exposed person – but most importantly, a leading personality preparing the best-known reform of socialist economy that would bear his name.

Ota Šik, original named Otto Schück (1919–2004), was born in Pilsen to a German-Jewish family. Experience of life in Sudetenland in the time of the Great Depression would bring him – similarly to Goldmann – to the communist movement and the study of Marxism; Ulrych's marxist textbook (1937) became his 'Bible'. From 1941, he was imprisoned in the Mauthausen concentration camp, where he made acquaintance with the future second president of communist Czechoslovakia, Antonín Novotný (1904–1975). It was indeed this moment that influenced his political engagement and the face of the entire reform effort of the 1960s. After the war, he studied at the *Vysoká škola politických a sociálních věd* [*School of Political and Social Sciences*] established as a Party project to train *new cadres* for the nationalized economy. After February 1948, he worked at the Party's Department of Culture and Propaganda. After he was accused in 1951 of anti-socialist opinions, he was spared from punishment (at that time, the death sentence) by Novotný's intervention. Šik nevertheless had to leave the Party secretariat. After a several-year intermezzo in academia (he became a professor of political economy) Novotný pushed him through to the position of Director of the *Economic Institute* in 1961, where from 1963 he managed a team for work on economic reform. During the *Prague Spring*, he became the Vice-chairman of the Government and the Minister of Economy. After the August occupation in 1968, he emigrated to Switzerland, where he worked from 1970–1989 as a professor of comparative economic systems at the universities in St Gallen and Zürich.

At the turn of the 1940s and 1950s, Šik studied Lenin's and Stalin's works intensely (although he does not state the latter in his memoirs); the latter was the object of several of his first texts. On behalf of the entire *Theoretical Front* he squared up with the revisionism and reformism of the Czechoslovak political economy (Šik, 1949). A day after Stalin's death, he explained Stalin's economic contribution to his students (Šik, 1953). Not even in the years that followed did his notion of Socialism and planning diverge from the acceptable Party limits. Nevertheless, experience from working in the Party apparatus and from a stay in the USSR, slowly awakened him from his illusions about the Socialism in which he lived. He began to identify in it a totalitarian, despotic and bureaucratic system. 'I gradually departed from the propagandistic rumination of Stalinist dogmas,' he wrote on this topic in his memoirs (Šik, 1990, 56).

He immersed himself in a thorough study of Marx (he took part in the translation of the first three parts of *Capital* into Czech), but also non-Marxist economists such as J.M. Keynes, J. Robinson, E. von Böhm-Bawerk, J. Schumpeter and K. Engliš. It is indeed in the context of his background of newly formed insight that one has to interpret his dogmatic-sounding theses from that time. When Šik writes of the 'constant fight of Party bodies to arrange fulfilment of the plan', the inspiration of Engliš and his thoughts on the 'fight of political parties when setting societal goals' manifests itself clearly. When he writes that the laws of the socialist economy would not in themselves ensure prosperity, that the masses of the working class had to be involved, it is a careful expression of notions on the role of the 'spontaneous' market under Socialism. And he could find among many Western European economists the notion that it is not possible to plan everything from the centre to the last detail.

There is also no doubt that his analysis of Marx's theory of ownership relationships, on which he built a fundamental critique of the concept of societal ownership, also belongs to the same notional current. He arrived at the opinion that Lenin's and Stalin's concept of ownership has no support in Marx, for in Marx's concept, the character of ownership corresponds to the degree of the development of production forces, and Marx never writes that the form of socialist socialization of work should be state, bureaucratically controlled enterprise. To put it differently, Šik asserts that the given state of economic development does not enable central planning and control of the economy. In view of the character of work during Socialism, it is still not possible to satisfy all needs, and it is therefore necessary to solve through a real market the disparity between the producer and the consumer on the side of demand. These considerations clearly aimed to cast into doubt the Stalinist dogma of state ownership and thence led to the expression of the role of interests and motivations in socialist society.

This was not a new theme. Šik certainly knew the goal of Kurt Rozsypal's (1916–2013) economic reform project of the 1950s: Achieving 'a full harmony between the interests of the individuals and those of the whole society' (Boreš *et al.*, 1957, 21); perhaps it was indeed this that inspired him to consider this issue more deeply. According to Šik, interests and motivations arise from needs. Needs are the immediate impulses of human action which always aim towards a certain goal; in this sense, they are intentional and are the result of the decision-making process; need (material and non-material) is a shortage felt by people that is reflected in their consciousness and that elicits a certain endeavour to remove it (Šik, 1962, 291). If certain, objectively evoked need require a relatively more permanent, concentrated attention, desire for the satisfaction thereof constantly employs the mind of the person, for satisfaction thereof evokes (by strength of emotion and feelings) exceptional attention and a repeated, possibly deepening personal desire for it, it then is an interest (Ibid., 304). And this interest could be both individual and social in the sense of the interest of a broader group. The interests of the individuals could come into conflict with social interests and lead to 'social contradictions'. Two years later, he added that the notion that socialist interests that can have only people that have known and become aware of the existence of long-term social interests is a typical sectarianism (Šik, 1964, 106).

Although Šik in his analysis took into account such authors as Leon Trotsky (1879–1940), Nikolai Bukharin (1888–1938), Evgeni Preobrazhensky (1886–1937) and Max Weber, he continued innovatively in searching for generally valid rules of human action, the fruit of the Austrian subjective school and Czech economist Čuhel at the beginning of the 20th century. A few years later, Šik's theory led historian Miroslav Hroch (b.1932) to express – the internationally respected – theory of national movement (Hroch, 1968). For Šik himself the theory of interest was a bridge in the search for ways to transform Socialism of the Soviet type, for Socialism remained for him the best of possible worlds. This was why he accepted membership in the *Central Committee* of the Party in 1962. In his memoirs, Šik writes that he opted for this 'agreement with the devil' in order to open a space for a change in the system from within the Party so that reform-oriented economists and politicians could receive a share in power (Šik, 1990, 77–79).

And this truly happened. While in Rozsypal's team at the end of the 1950s, of which he was also a member, his views on the necessity of a comprehensive concept of the change of the economic system was given no space whatsoever, as a member of the *Central Committee* he gradually brought to his team at the *Economic Institute* young, talented economists alongside Jiří Kosta (1921–2015), and with them he embarked on work on his own notion of economic reform. One more test, a very personal one, awaited him: To defy Novotný, his friend from the concentration camp. During the XIII Congress of the Party (1966) Novotný, at that time representing the orthodox wing in the leadership, tried to prevent Šik from taking the floor. Novotný's manipulation had a boomerang effect: A large majority of participants responded with standing ovations to Šik's radical criticism of the halting reform strategy pursued by the authorities and to his plea for an accelerating reform drive (Havel *et al.* 2002, 229).

Šik published his notion of economic reform at the end of the same year and worked very hard on its realization over the next 2 years. He based his theory on the concept of *market Socialism* as a synthesis of *macro-economic planning* and the *market mechanism* (Šik, 1968). During 1968, he supplemented his thoughts with a third fundamental element: *Workers' board*. However he may have considered the market to be an element of the capitalist system, he considered its presence in Socialism to be necessary due to the existence of production of goods. But it was to be a market regulated by a plan, as a macro-economic instrument which was indeed constructed in the centre, but democratically. He did not hesitate to defend his notions with the assertion that a return to capitalism was no longer possible in Czechoslovakia, for society no longer desired it. This is very reminiscent of the 200-year old argument of Maria Therese's, that craftsmen from Protestant countries could no longer overturn re-Catholicization in Bohemia and Moravia. Orthodox Marxists soon lost pace with Šik (and his team). But Moscow, too, soon noticed that Czechoslovakia had returned, after 20 years, with Šik to a search for a Czechoslovak version of Socialism. The events of the *Prague Spring*, the occupation and Šik's departure into exile followed.

In Šik's exile considerations, the concept of market Socialism grew into an alternative form of socio-economic development of contemporary developed society, which he called a *third way* (Šik, 1972). Its foundation was the market, participation of workers in management and in profit, a macro-economic planning of income distribution and market regulation. At the end of the 1970s, under the influence of the ideas of the entrepreneur Ernest Bader (1890–1982), his notions shifted to economics based on self-administrated enterprises (Šik, 1979). In his concept, a human economic democracy was to be founded on three pillars: The market, self-administration and distributive macro-economic planning.

In the 1980s, Šik developed his notions on precisely these three pillars and argued in favour of a socialist market economy. Yet he understood the market mechanism as a precondition of growth of economic prosperity and macro-economic planning as an instrument to remove unemployment (Šik, 1989). In his opinion, it is necessary to overcome the estrangement of workers from capital and capitalist economic institutions through co-ownership of capital and co-determination in enterprises; conditions for real democracy would thereby be formed. He still considered ignorance of the economic motivations of economic subjects to be a fundamental error of Marxist political economy, which was encoded already in Marx's rejection of the positive role of the entrepreneur. According to Šik, overlooking motivation is the reason why socialist countries economically lag behind capitalist ones.

Whilst Joan Robinson raised her eyebrows in surprise at his lecture at the University of Cambridge in 1970, the communists secured for the purposes of their studies in the regime a 'highly confidential' translation of his works. After 1989, however, Šik did not find an audience for his ideas in the Czech Lands. Socialism with a human face was no longer the order of the day.

Karel Kosík: philosophizing economics!

Understanding the changes in Czech economic thought that occurred in the 1960s is not possible without framing them in the development of Czech philosophy. Indeed, starting in 1956, after the XX Congress of the Soviet Communists, discussions in the field of philosophy began to open onto the theory of socialist society. A programmatic idea of Karel Kosík (1926–2003) lies in its foundation: To stop contemplating the ideas of Socialism and to start analyzing Socialism as a reality. His ground-breaking *Dialektika konkrétního* [*Dialectics of the Concrete*], first published in 1963, is an original philosophy of human action. For Kosík, economic action is the model of it; it was as though he said, with Marx, that the task of philosophers is to explain the world, and the task of economists is to change it. But as a philosopher, he questions not only the socialistic reality that had been experienced, but also the *objective* truth by which the reality is ideologically framed.

Kosík's departure point is the term *pseudoconcrete*; that is, the collection of phenomena of the everyday human life which includes: The world of external phenomena on the surface of the fundamental processes; the world of procuring and manipulation, i.e. of the *fetishized* man's praxis; the world of common ideas as a product of fetishized praxis; and the world of fixed objects which are not immediately recognizable as the results of human social activity. By employing the dialectical-critical method of thought, the task of philosophy and social sciences is to discover the nature of things hidden behind the *pseudoconcrete* by *deconstructing* it. This *deconstruction* can be realized through first, the revolutionary praxis of humankind, second, dialectical thought penetrating to the *thing itself*, and third, realization of the truth through an individual's life as appropriate to his own culture. The real world, concealed by the *pseudoconcrete*, is the world of realization of the truth. The truth is not given in advance but truth which happens. With Husian ethos, Kosík speaks of truth, as truth pertaining to the substance of things, the truth of being, of the world and of reality. According to Kosík, societal-historical reality is a complexly structured *concrete totality*. Yet his concern was not the completeness of facts, but rather the fundamental question: What is reality? And is it possible to change it revolutionarily?

From the outset, Kosík involves economics in his grand philosophical narrative, he dynamizes and contextualizes the subject of economics and its greatest abstraction, *homo economics*; before man masters economic manuals, he already lives in economic reality and understands it somehow, he writes. The first example Kosík introduces to explain the difference between *real existence* and *phenomenal forms of reality* that are reproduced as categories of *routine thinking* is money: People use it and carry out the most complicated transactions with it without ever knowing what money is. The elementary mode in which economy exists for man is *care*. *Care* is the involvement of the individual in a network of relationships which place themselves before him as a practically utilitarian world, it is the activity of the individual in the form of caring and procuring; caring and procuring is the phenomenal side of abstract labour. The transition from labour to care and procuring reflects a process of the deepening fetishization of human relationships.

Homo economicus is an expression of the mental process of the science that transforms a human being into an object; it is an abstract unit integrated in a scientifically analyzable and mathematically describable system. At the same time, it is based on the idea of the existence of such a system. This is why economics as a science can emerge only in capitalism, which is a system in itself. This is why *homo economicus* is equipped with characteristics which are unavoidable for the functioning of such a system: rationality and egoism. But the actual reduction of man to the *homo economicus* abstraction is not affected by theory, but by reality itself. According to Kosík, 'economics is a system and a set of laws governing the relations by which man is constantly being transformed into the *economic man*' (Kosík, 1963, 52).

The question as to the qualities of *homo economicus* in the scope of capitalistic systems opens the field for argument in favour of a necessary and logical development of economic formations in the direction of Communism. It is obvious that the word *capitalistic* can be replaced by the adjective *socialist* or *communist*: What the qualities of *homo economicus* in socialism or communism are? Yet Kosík rejects the penetration of psychology into economics, as he does the concept of economics in a quantitative sense – as wealth, property or 'making' money, and investigation of different aspects of social whole as separate categories he refers to as 'immature thought'.

In the third part of the book, *Philosophy and Economics*, Kosík's question turns to reading Marx's *Capital*. Yet the relationship of economics and philosophy is not only one of the aspects of reading Marx, but enables access to the very essence of *Capital*, and thereby capitalism – first and foremost through the composition of the work as a whole. For the logic of *Capital* – in the same way as the logic of every other scientific work – has to correspond to the logical structure of the researched reality; this is indeed why the category from where Marx begins in his analysis is the category of a *good*, says Kosík. And *Capital* pursues this category as an odyssey. Just as *Phenomenology of the Spirit* (1977) of Georg Wilhelm F. Hegel (1170–1831) is 'the path of the natural consciousness to true knowledge [. . .] so that through the complete experience of its own self it may arrive at the cognition of what it is in itself', so *Capital* appears to Kosík to be an 'odyssey of concrete historical *praxis* [of good – AD] which proceeds from the elementary labor product [. . .] to conclude its journey not in the cognition of what it is in itself, but rather in a *revolutionary* practical action based on this cognition'. (Kosík, 1963, 111). According to Kosík, *Capital* is not a theory but a theoretical *critique* or a *critical* theory of capital (Ibid., 112).

From there, following Marx's example, Kosík embarks on a journey to discover the nature of economics itself. If economic categories are *forms of being*, their analysis uncovers *social being*: Economy is the totality of the process of producing and reproducing man as a social-historical being; economy is not only the production of material goods but also of social relations, i.e. of the context of this production. Finally, in this concept labour is not the work activity of man which in turn influences his or her psyché, habit and thinking; to comprehend labour as labour assumes its distinction from work activity, work routines and the historical form of labour. Labour is a *happening* permeating his or her *entire* being and constitutes his or her specificity. According to Kosík, the question of what work is, like the question of what man is, is an ontological question. And further, in harmony with Hegel, ontology and the dialectic method are inseparably connected.

The intention of Kosík's *Dialectics of the Concrete* is not a revision of Marxism, but a return to the 'original' Marx, searching for what had become lost over the decade that had passed or, as the case may be, what had not been said at all; plentiful citations from Marx's *Grundrisse* (1961) confirm this thesis. And at the same time, Kosík's concept is built on a critical reflection on the 200-year tradition of the development of European philosophy from Hegel through Marx to Husserl and Martin Heidegger (1889–1976), and likewise on their main thought currents in the 20th century, including existentialism or structuralism. He cites Hungarian Marxist György Lukács (1885–1971), the representative of the Frankfurt School Herbert Marcuse (1898–1979), philosophers Ortega y Gasset (1883–1955) and Ernst Cassirer (1874–1945) and sociologist M. Weber, but also economists F.A.von Hayek and John von Neumanna (1903–1957) and opens Czech economics to new thought horizons. And ultimately, Kosík's work is an endeavour to return economics to the scope of social science as the science of human action.

Miroslav Toms: scientific star

Miroslav Toms was a 'scientific star' even as a student at the *Vysoká škola ekonomická* [*University of Economics*]. That was in 1961–1966, when the problems of the socialist economy could not be overlooked. He published his first professional study in his third year (Toms, Hájek 1965), and it caused a commotion. He was soon able to gather around himself students and followers; paradoxically, these were often his peers or even older colleagues; he astounded them with his ability for theoretical abstraction and knowledge of Marx's teaching and contemporary Western economic theories.

Miroslav Toms (1944–1988) settled permanently at the *Economic Institute* after his studies. In 1967, he left for a scholarship in the USA (University of Michigan), where he lectured a course on the theory of growth of the socialist economy based on Marx's reproduction schemes and Feldman's and Kalecki's model of growth. It was indeed these economists who were the source of his fascination with economics. Its result was 135 professional texts, of which 52 were published in what was then the most prestigious economic journal, *Political Economy*. In the 1980s, two volumes of this journal were devoted to a dispute over his books. In his texts, Toms focuses on the efficiency of the socialist economy and concepts of economic growth, factors influencing its transfer from an extensive to an intensive model, the theory of prices and utility value, but also the comparison of economic systems. His goal was a new interpretation of the central themes of Marx's theory with the language and media of neoclassical analysis (Mlčoch, 1989, 421), whilst respecting the function of scientific-technical progress.

Toms's methodology was based on the connection of Marx's qualitative analysis with a quantitative analysis; to put it otherwise, a dialectic-materialistic approach with an econometric approach. Toms's endeavour aimed to build an internally consistent system of economic disciplines, starting from the most general questions of political economy and ending with broadly evolved practical applications. Referring to Marx, he asserted that theory and practice mutually condition one another dialectically, which is why scientific knowledge has to be implemented into economic practice. His usual reaction when solving a problem was apparently 'let us first ask what theory has to say about it' (Klacek, 1989, 402).

Toms was able to free himself from the need to see the laws of political economy of Socialism everywhere. With one exception – *the economy of time*, i.e. the *theory of efficiency* – in Marxist terminology, the maximum rationality of expending societal labour in conditions of common ownership. Marx spoke of the economy of time as the first law of socialist society, and although this thesis had entirely disappeared from the work of Marxism-Leninism, it became Toms's life theme. The reason no doubt lay in the fact that the Czechoslovak reality of the 1960s showed the definitive limits of extensive economic development, and not even two reforms were able to find a remedy for this situation. According to Toms, efficiency in its substance had to be researched as a socio-economic relationship between the participants of the production process based on the contrast expressed by Marx between concrete and abstract labour, i.e. as the relationship of effect (satisfaction of societal needs) and labour costs. Two questions hence stemmed for him: What is efficiency in a socialist society (thus in specific historical conditions) and what should the economic mechanism be in order that the value criteria therein would fully express the criteria of efficiency?

Although he evolved a principally balanced theory of long-term economic growth, he did not overlook out-of-balance phenomena in the socialist economy and the overcoming thereof. Toms rejected the thesis on the so-called supply determination of the socialist and demand determination of the capitalist economy. According to him, guiding the economy to a balanced state assumes simultaneous respect of both sides of the reproductive process (Mejstřík, 1989, 429). This is why he tended towards Kalecki's view that it was necessary to distinguish between branches determined by supply and those determined by demand. According to Toms, the dynamic of economic development depends on two factors: First, on the volume of production resources and the workforce numbers; and second on the efficiency of the use thereof. Intensive growth can be based only on the second factor. Contrariwise, extensive growth leads to a *vicious circle* where an inefficient cost structure of the economy is formed. This is the point of exhaustion of the possibilities of extensive growth and becomes an impediment to further development. As a source of the *vicious circle* Toms identified the interest of the socialist SOEs in *quantitative plan indicators* (Toms, Hájek, 1965).

Developing the theme of the criteria of efficiency brought him to the issue of *utility effect*. He considered its foundation to be the (Marxist) category of utility value – a dynamic category based not only on the needs and goals of society, but also on the predominant relations of production. Toms distinguished (Toms, 1981) between *individual* and *societal* utility value, whilst the first is conditioned by the objective attributes of a product and the second, moreover, also on the range of its societal needs. On the basis of Marx's analysis of the relationship between societal utility value, price and socially necessary costs, he arrived at the conclusion that the relationship between the volume of production and societal needs has to be implemented into prices and the plan. Planning, according to him, should be able to set expectations for proportional development – without inflation and deflation pressures. The way to achieve this was the improvement of the planning mechanism, which led him to search for instruments which would change producers to profit-oriented ones; Toms used the term *special real profit*. Changing the orientation of producers also had, besides social and ecological *normatives*, hard indicators of the technical-economic level of production, for the criteria of efficiency do not work because they are required by the plan but because they are connected with the system of motivations of the activity of economic subjects.

Toms's interest in the theory of comparative economic systems (Klacek *et al.* 1968) perhaps best reflects his theoretical spirit searching for a synthesis of various theoretical systems in which particular schools were special cases. The subject of Toms's comparison was the concept of capital and the measurement thereof, the classical and neoclassical theory of value, but he devoted most attention to Marx's theory of accumulation and employment, whence later stemmed his attempt to formalize and dynamize Marx's theory of cycle and the theory of economic growth (Toms, 1976). Toms proposed Marx's original theory, which is based on the unchanging productivity of work and constant capital-labour ratio, as subjecting to changes caused by the growth of productivity of work as a consequence of scientific progress.

Toms focused on the question of scientific progress from as early as the mid-1960s in discussions with Radovan Richta (1924–1983) and other members of Richta's team for researching the scientific-technical revolution (Richta *et al.* 1967). With his concept, Toms overcame the traditional Marxist-Leninist approach to scientific-technical progress as an exogenous factor, where technical progress was to 'adjust' to the needs of the socialist economy. Toms asserted the opposite: Removal of the differences between the productive and non-productive sphere, growth of education, the development of informatization and cybernitization make science an internal factor of growth, and he attempted to develop a method to measure their effects on economic development. He thereby anticipated that the macro-economic contribution of R&D lies in the development of (societal) needs and changes in the quality of the satisfaction thereof. As a Marxist, he led this question to considerations on the intergrowing of Socialism into Communism, on the spontaneity of this process and the factors that influence it.

Thence he arrived at his last scientific topic, the issue of needs. His considerations were founded on a fundamental questioning of one of the essential laws of Socialism – the law of satisfying needs and the growing standard of living: How can one fulfil the communist motto of *to each according to his or her needs*, asks Toms, when Socialism is neither able to secure remuneration according to labour nor a state where everyone holds a post that corresponds to their knowledge and skills? In the 1980s he brought these considerations to an analysis of needs as a dynamic factor in the socialist economy and attempted to capture the needs in terms of their structure, mutual interdependence and the dynamic of their development (Toms, 1981). From the perspective of the real Socialism in which he lived, he expressed the heretical question as to whether the current imperfections of Socialism are given by an imperfect knowledge of social reality or whether the existing state is an *Orwellian* society of equal and more equal, where the others illegitimately benefit from the advantages and privileges the state provides them and therefore knowingly support steps leading to stagnation. He called for an analysis of dark sides of Socialism such as clientelism, corruption, incompetence – and the victory of mediocrity.

Teaching economics in the time of Marxism-Leninism

February 1948 established a period of rapid changes in economic education. Not only did busts of the first Czechoslovak President T.G. Masaryk disappear from the hallways of schools, the professorial body and students were 'cleared' of 'reactionary' elements in two waves of purges. The syllabuses and the aims of education were gradually totally subordinated to the ideological needs of a centrally directed economy and adjusted to the Soviet model of organization of science and education. The content of tuition uncritically reproduced Marxist-Leninist clichés and was substantiated by the works of Marx, Engels, Lenin and, until a certain time, Stalin.

As early as the evening of 25 February, the building of the *Commercial College* (*ComC*) was occupied by members of the so-called People's Militia and, apparently on request of the student's action committee that the school should lose its connection to its original German inspiration, it was renamed the *Vysoká škola hospodářských věd* [*College of Economic Sciences*] (CES). The first wave of political purges in the professorial body followed. Teachers troublesome to the regime had their pay reduced, often by more than 50%, or they were transferred, pensioned or dismissed. Influential positions were allocated to politically reliable Party supporters.

At the same time, a discrediting campaign on the theme 'who teaches economics today' was running in the daily press. The Dean of *ComC* and *CES*, Gustav Švamberg (1880–1958), was sent on holiday and resigned a month later. Václav Šada (1904–1980) became the new Dean, J. Macek was appointed

Vice-Dean, L. Šauer became president of the action committee, and associate professors Fukátko and Janáček were appointed regular professors. On the other hand, J.M. Novotný was dismissed from teaching and emigrated to Canada with his family in 1948. He there worked at McGill University and later transferred to Utica College in New York (Albrecht, 2011). The positons of Žlábek and Blecha weakened. Although Blecha was appointed as a regular Professor of finance in 1949, he had to undergo political training.

Students were subject to 'study checks', which took place from autumn 1948 to spring 1949. And as one of the students of the time remembers, students who could be branded as 'class enemies' disappeared. Only communists were left unscathed by the checks; although everything took place under the pretext of expelling weak students, even top students were expelled (Němec, 2011). More than a third of the students screened (898 students, i.e. 37%) had to leave *CES*, which significantly increased the entire Prague average, which was 22% (Devátá, 2011). As the Czech novelist Milan Kundera (b.1929) in his novel *Žert [Joke]* (1967) shows, the students were hit by a wave of denunciations which were often of an entirely personal nature – for instance, an inappropriate joke aimed at the president of the Faculty Committee of the Socialist Youth Union. Nevertheless, the subject Fundamentals of Diplomatic Service was allowed at that time even though it was coloured with jokes on how to incorporate the General Secretary of the Party into diplomatic protocol. And in the context of business correspondence tuition, students would still receive advice that if 'Your most humbled servant' ought to be written in the letter then you ought to write 'Your most humbled servant' and not 'Good Luck to the Five-year Plan!' (Němec, 2011).

New subjects had already begun to appear in the syllabuses: Marxism-Leninism began to be lectured under the name *Social Science* and was lectured more or less by external lecturers; a course on economic planning was announced as early as March 1948. Subjects such as *State Defence Doctrine*, lectured by a real Czechoslovak Army general, found their way into the obligatory curriculum. By contrast, mathematics became voluntary, and the previously obligatory three foreign languages were reduced to two, with the first being Russian. The autonomous *Institut pro ekonomické plánování* [*Institute for Economic Planning*], led by Janáček with the support of Goldmann, was established in autumn 1949. Summer courses in economic planning were quickly organized for students in their last year. Soviet textbooks were the only literature. Deeper connection of theory and practice was to be achieved by the participation of workers at lectures, connected with discussions on their work experiences or the assignment of practical topics for seminar thesis.

In May 1949, the Party formed a programme to 'train the new socialist intelligentsia' (Devátá, Olšáková, 2010), the fundamental principle of which was the positive discrimination of students from worker and peasant families; in its consequence the class-political composition of students was to be changed. A new round of purges in the professorial body followed at the end of 1949, which affected Macek, who had several months previously participated in the expulsion of ideologically 'inflexible' students. Nevertheless, his courses on social policy were criticized by communist students for being too oriented on British models. All teaching staff now had to be screened by the Party. Most of them had completed their economic education before 1938, many had foreign experience and were broadly respected, such as Goldmann and Frejka, Klimecký, Vladimír Kadlec (1912–1998) and Rudolf Margolius (1913–1952). They were joined by Soviet professors to teach Soviet-type planning (Albrecht, 2011).

Despite all efforts of the teachers to pass through – even at the cost of moral and professional compromises – the traps of Party intentions, the school was closed by law as early as the summer of 1949, regardless of the fact that 1,561 students were studying there at the time. The remaining employees were dismissed. Švamberg had to go into retirement; work in a dairy was recommended to Žlábek. Only the Dean, Janáček, could stay on to supervise the remaining few theses and examinations. The last state final examinations and graduations took place in July 1953 (Šauer, Šauerová 1984, 37).

Tuition of economics was, by the same law, transferred to the newly established *Vysoké školy politických a hospodářkých věd* [*School of Political and Economic Sciences*]. If the school just closed had been the bearer of the establishers' ethos of Czech economic thought, with roots at the end of the 19th century, this school was the project of the Party. It became the legal successor of the *Svobodné školy nauk politických* [*Free School of Political Doctrines*], which had been founded in 1928 and was transformed into the *Vysoká škola politické a sociální* [*Political and Social School*] (PSS) immediately after the war. Its goal was meant to be education of qualified state officials. It had three faculties – political, journalist and social. As a guarantee of 'political correctness' the pedagogic body was compiled according to the Party's key; it included candidates of political parties assembled in the *National Front* in 1945.

Lectures, especially from the history of political ideologies, economic theories and economic methodology soon became Party recruiting events. These were aimed primarily at students, who were accepted without having completed secondary school education. The *PSS* thus became a base camp for the training of loyal communist officials in the period after 1948. Quite fundamentally in the quantitative sense – in the first academic year 1945/1946, the school accepted over 7,000 students and lectures took place in cinema halls and a heated circus tent. While only three lecturers (of a total number of 18) who were members of the Party worked in *CES* in 1949/1950, the proportion of Party members at *PSS* was 86% (72 of 84 lecturers) (Devátá, 2011). It is therefore not surprising that it was precisely at this school that a sharp attack started to rise against Karel Engliš as the newly elected Rector of Charles University and generally against the level of university education in the country. 'Universities often do not provide even the education a worker receives when he reads the communist newspapers', wrote Václav Kopecký, one of the Party ideologists (Pousta 1998, 264). Despite the fact that economics itself was not a study field there, the most significant future Czechoslovak economists of the 1960s – Šik, Kouba, Kožušník and Urban graduated from the *PSS* in the three post-war years.

The role of *School of Political and Economic Sciences (SPES)* which was established as a 'pioneer Marxist school' and was managed directly by the Party, or more precisely, by its Department of Culture and Propaganda, was to educate the 'new cadres' in the theory and practice of Marxism-Leninism and to fill the programme to 'train the socialist intelligentsia'. In the inaugural Rector's speech, Ladislav Štoll (1902–1981) announced the end of antagonism between people who worked physically and intellectually and promised economists educated in the spirit of Marxism-Leninism who would pursue the heuristic work of Soviet sciences and represent in a dignified manner Lenin's great historical work and who would know how to change the world, how to make it better, more joyful and the nations happier. (Štoll, 1949) Even after many years, its graduates remember how attractive they found the idea of direct connection with current political events that clearly resonated with the marked politicization of society and with the period desire to participate actively in the building of Socialism (Devátá, 2011).

The *SPES* was organized into three faculties focused on economics, social policy, and law and diplomacy. Studying of economics was to be oriented on the training of 'theoretical' economists, with emphasis on Marxist political economy. It was a high goal. In the spirit of positive discrimination of workers and peasants this meant the education of students with an incomplete grammar education alongside sixth-formers with a good 'cadre' profile (it was necessary to open additional courses in grammar, the fundamentals of mathematics, etc.). An entirely new system of collective study was also adapted to this; it sharply differed from the hitherto free choice of study topics and, by contrast, copied the Soviet model. Students were pyramidally divided into so-called study circles, collectives and groups, which were to enable checking of the results of students' preparation for lectures and seminars which were obligatory. Every collective had its own teaching assistant from the ranks of higher-year students, whose task was to help worker and peasant students.

Teaching plans for economics, which were prepared according to the Soviet model, were submitted to the *Central Committee* of the Party secretariat for approval. Studies were for 4 years, divided into two 2-year blocks: In the first 2 years the students studied the so-called common basis – languages, the fundamentals of Marxism (historic and dialectic materialism), subjects from history (history of the worker movement and the Soviet Union), but also the economics, philosophy, history of the state and law, mathematics and statistics. In the next 2-year period, study was divided into five specializations: Political economy; planning; industry and transportation; finance; and domestic and foreign trade. The first was the most prestigious, and its focus lay in the study of Marx's *Capital*, the political economy of Socialism and a selective critical reception of the preceding economic theories.

All the faculties, but especially that of economics, suffered from insufficient personnel support, for economic specialization was, according to fixed quotas, meant to be studied by half of all of the students, i.e. about 500 students in each year. The lecturers were divided into departments, at the head of which stood a representative from the *Central Committee* of the Party's apparatus as an ideological guarantor of all its activities. The foundation of the *Department of Political Economy* was formed by young, starting-out Marxist-oriented economists Felix Oliva (1897–1977), Pavel Hrubý (1914–1994) and Vladimír Kadlec and the philosophers Karel Kosík, Jindřich Zelený (1922–1997) and Radovan Richta. Kadlec, at the time an associate professor of financial law at the Faculty of Law at Charles University and an employee of the National Economic Department of the Office of the President of the Republic, later became the Rector (1966–1968) and Minister of Education at the time of the *Prague Spring*. But the leading personality was certainly Felix Oliva, one of the founders of Czech Marxist political economy. At the beginning of the 1950s, under the influence of the political trials, he became an advocate of dogmatic Stalinism willing to write off anyone who had different views. Oliva's fears from the time of the trials, however, were based in reality. As a representative of Western communist war exiles, and of Jewish origin moreover, he found himself dangerously close to the 'fight against cosmopolitanism' (Knapp, 1998, 134).

After a mere 4 years, when it seemed that the stability of the school's operation had been accomplished, it was closed down. Seven hundred and thirty- one students of the regular 4-year study programme, of which 80 began to work as teachers or lecturers at educational institutions throughout Czechoslovakia, were their first and last graduates. The *SPES* had been criticized by the Party for not securing, despite large subsidies, even enough cadres for the internal state administration and for the new socialist enterprises. It was also criticized insofar as Czechoslovakia was still lagging behind Poland and Hungary in numbers of graduates in economics and insofar as no student had been sent to the Soviet Union for their studies. The main reason for its liquidation, however, lay elsewhere: Some of the allies of the General Secretary of the Party Rudolf Slánský (1901–1952) (with whom the Party was in the process of 'dealing') such as Goldmann, Margolius and Frejka taught there. In the first wave of the political processes in Czechoslovakia in the early 1950s, Slánský was charged with high treason and sentenced to death. The last two also followed Slánský to the Pankrác prison's gallows.

Even despite its ephemeral life, the *SPES* was able to form the foundation for the constitution of the so-called worker intelligentsia and educate professionals who in the next two decades became internationally recognized scientists and influenced not only the economic development of Czechoslovakia. It was indeed through them – and more than two hundred educational texts – that Marxism-Leninism was implemented into the entire educational environment as the new official *scientific* doctrine. The remaining economic teachings were rejected and were now to be interpreted only as a *critique of Marxist political economy*. The tradition of Czech economic thought was to be completely forgotten. The subject of interest became current Soviet works, especially Stalin's texts.

When the law on the closure of *SPES* was enacted in 1952 (it formally took place in 1955), the individual faculties, with the exception of the economic one, were affiliated to Charles University. The faculty of economic engineering was established into the framework of the Czech Polytechnic (which was how the *Commercial College* was established in 1919!), to which the majority of the professorial body from *SPES* was transferred, and Fukátko became the Dean. After his death in 1956, however, the faculty lost influence and was closed in 1960. At the same time, the same act from 1952 established the *Vysoká škola ekonomická* [*University of Economics*]. The role of preparing 'Party cadres' was assumed by the newly formed, purely ideological, if strictly selective, *Vysoká škola stranická* [*Party College*].

In the description of turbulent changes to economic education in Prague, we should not overlook the fact that after 30 years Olomouc too returned to the idea of establishing a commercial college. In 1949, the *Ústav pro plánování* [*Institute for Planning*] was established here at the Palacký University as a result of the efforts of the Rector, Czech philosopher Josef Ludvík Fischer (1894–1973), for an interdisciplinary organization of study in the form of an inter-faculties institute. It was also the result of efforts to focus university tuition on regional economy that was, in the terminology at the time, focused on regional planning and people's administration. The *Institute* organized 1-year courses to educate business and administrative planners, designated for graduates of grammar economic schools (former commercial academies). Two hundred students passed through it before it was closed in 1953 (Řezník, 2011).

In 1953, there was thus once again – as in 1948 – only one school at which it was possible to study economics. Until 1989 it remained the only one if we do not count the field of political economy – mostly in combination with the discipline called scientific Communism – at the faculties of arts at Charles University in Prague and Masaryk University in Brno designated for just a few students, and the economic faculties of technical and agricultural colleges which were focused on pertinent sectors of the economy. The *University of Economics* had four faculties, in substance copying the situation at *SPES*: General economics (with the subjects of political economy, planning, work economics, statistics and teaching), business administration, domestic and foreign trade and finance and credit. In keeping with the Soviet model, the school practically resigned from research, which was now planned and supported by the Party – it left this space to the newly established *Economic Institute of Academy of Sciences*.

The students were divided into study circles and in each of them there was a post established for a manager for professional questions and a confidant (a Party member or candidate for membership therein), whose task was to give the Party or State Security information as to what the students were discussing, but especially as to whether the communist regime was being criticized; many of the confidants were deliberately assigned to the circles. The communists gradually worked through a sophisticated system in which selected students were offered Party membership as early as in their first year in exchange either for study benefits if they accepted the proposal or for difficulties if they refused. This system endured until the end of the 1980s. Most economists who assumed control of the Czechoslovak and Czech economy after the *Velvet Revolution* of 1989 would be members or at least candidates for membership in the Party, many of them having had this 'confidant' experience.

The Marxist-Leninist content of studies, however, remained vague. On the grounds of the *University of Economics* a campaign was transferred around Stalin's articles and dogmatism in economic thought (Šik, Kazda 1953). The dogmatism was reflected even in the 1960s; Soviet economics and the Soviet economy were the only sources from which it was possible to constitute new economic disciplines and the tuition thereof. Selected students left for the Soviet Union for scholarships. Textbooks were initially only Soviet and gradually also Czech, but these were almost literally copies of the former. And although new ones were constantly published at regular intervals, the content thereof did not change. It was structured on the works of the classics of Marxism- Leninism and described the laws of Socialism and the functioning mechanisms of the socialist economy.

Tuition in economics was divided into the political economy of capitalism (based on Marx's *Capital*), the political economy of Socialism, dialectic materialism and scientific Communism. Nevertheless, a place in the structure of subjects was surprisingly also retained by the subject of history of economic theories, which had its roots in the first half of the 19th century, and paradoxically became the only possibility as to how the future Marxist-Leninist economists could become acquainted with other economic schools. And they thanked Marx himself for this, for he considered this discipline to be one of the parts of political economy.

With the exception of Richardo's interpretation of the discrepancy between salary and profit and François Quesnay's (1694–1774) doctrine, however, interpretation was in the first decade disrupted to such a degree by critical reservations that it was entirely impossible to gain a self-contained notion of the particular theories and to separate them in any way from the Marxist-Leninist critique thereof. Rosenberg's *Commentaries* to Parts I and II of Marx's *Capital* (Koderová, 2006, 64, f. 7) and later ideological textbooks by Heretík (1955) initially served as study literature. Translations of significant Western economic literature began to be published in the second half of the 1960s, when also the first interpretative textbooks began to emerge. Again surprisingly, but confirming the fully ambivalent development not only of economic thought, but also economists themselves, they were published by the Central Committee Party's Department of Culture and Propaganda, where Šik worked. But *The History of Economic Teachings* later became the standard textbook, the authors of which lectured courses at the *University of Economics* at the same time (Šmejkal *et al.* 1966).

The structure of the interpretation which the authors fixed therein remains valid to this day: The interpretation went chronologically from the economic thought of the ancient and feudal societies, through Mercantilism to the thought of the main representatives of classical economics; prior to 1989, they were consistently referred to as *classical bourgeois political economy*. The teaching of the members of the so-called Ricardo School was already considered to be the beginning of the 'vulgarization' of the classics, and Malthus, Say, Bastiat and Mill were labelled as representatives of 'vulgar' economics. 'Vulgarization' itself was associated especially with the transition from the working theory of value to its costs version, in the context of which other factors besides labour – land

and capital, and also enterprise, the remuneration for which was represented by profit – took part. But the monistic approach stemming from the determination of value, or more precisely, from price on the side of supply was retained. The interpretation continued through *petit-bourgeois* economic theory from the first half of the 19th century (Sismondi and. Proudhon), utopian Socialism, the German historical school and the Austrian school to the theorists of the Second International and Alfred Marshall and John Bates Clark (1847–1938). From contemporary theories, attention was devoted to institutionalism, to Keynes, to the theory of imperfect and monopolistic competition, to the theory of economic growth and to German Ordoliberalism.

Soviet textbooks once again predominated briefly in the period of normalization after 1968, but by the first half of the 1970s, textbooks began to be published by authors concentrated around Jaroslav Petráček (b.1929), the most significant representative of the history of economic thought in socialist Czechoslovakia who entirely changed the face of this discipline. He quickly managed two truly Hussar's escapades. With the reasoning that an opponent against whom we do not have a sufficient arsenal, and who we at the same time do not know, appears to be much stronger than he is in reality, and further, that effective critique assumes far deeper knowledge of phenomena and penetration beneath its surface (Petráček, 1974, 5), he published the first Czech book with an objective interpretation (albeit still as a 'critique') of Western theoretical theories (albeit still 'bourgeois'). But then the publication of the second volume, which focused on the macro-economic part of contemporary Western economics, was thwarted by an attentive censor.

Nevertheless, the interpretations set out by Petráček became part of tuition. This was his second Hussar's escapade. He managed to implement a modern contemporary economics and the history thereof into all economic subjects at all universities and colleges including the tuition of future teachers of so-called civil education. It was approved by the subject commission instituted by the Ministry of Education for that purpose. Petráček himself was very surprised – he proposed a broad several-semester course, for he assumed that it would be shortened to a quarter. But at the ministry they took it that a subject with such a large time allocation must be clearly significant (Koderová 2006, 69). The history of economic thought thus became the most feared part of final examinations of all future economists in Czechoslovakia. The examinations on scientific Communism or on the political economy of Socialism were a walk through a rose-garden by comparison, as they were based on the repetition of well-known phrases.

Further, in 1988, under Petráček's management, a comprehensive textbook was published which deepened and broadened the interpretations with the newest directions of contemporary Western economics, not only in the context of the mainstream, but outside of it (Petráček *et al.*, 1988). A year later saw the publishing of a volume of papers, *Současná západní ekonomie* [*Contemporary Western Economy*] (1989), which was prepared by teachers from Petráček's workplace, and in it they attempted to show how political economy was interpreted in the most frequently used university textbooks of the 'Anglo-Saxon world'. The interpretation of individual topics was divided into two fundamental approaches referred to in their general features as Keynesian and monetarist (or more precisely neoconservative or neoclassical) (Koderová, 2011). This volume became the fundamental textbook according to which economics began to be taught a few months later – after the *Velvet Revolution*.

Outside of the mainstream: economics in exile and in the underground

In the course of the 20th century, Czechoslovak economics was affected by three devastating emigration waves: Of 1938, 1948 and 1968. In the context of the first wave, which followed 1938, several economists returned to Czechoslovakia after the war; that proved to be a fateful decision for several of them. Ludvík Frejka, former name Ludwig Freund, was a typical example. He studied at the Business University in Berlin and the LSE and became a member of the Party from 1923. During the war, he worked in communist exile in London. In 1945–1948, he was the secretary of the National Economic Commission of the *Central Committee* of the Party and a member of the planning committee. In January 1952, he was arrested, accused of high treason and espionage. In November of the same year, he was sentenced in a Slánský trial and executed. In 1968 he was honoured by the Order of the Republic in memoriam.

After 1948, some economists, used the experience of their first exile and decided to emigrate again. Several professors from the *College of Economic Sciences* also joined this wave. The largest group of economists emigrated to the USA. Jan Viktor Mládek (1911–1989) was promoted to the position of Director of the International Monetary Fund, Antonín Basch (1896–1971), worked for the World Bank, many others worked at American and Canadian Universities, such as J.M. Novotný, J. Macek and J. Vanek; the latter gained particular prominence. After his studies at the Sorbonne and in Switzerland he received his Ph.D. from MIT. Since 1962, he has been teaching at Cornell University. His contribution to the debate on the Leontief paradox made him famous. Later, he developed his original theoretical concept of *labour-managed economies*. He analyzed the implications of workers' self-management for both micro- and macro-economics and critically analyzed the neoclassical school (Havel *et al.* 2002, 242).

The events in 1968 forced into exile even some of those who had previously supported the Communist regime; some of them gained prominent positions in their host institutions. From the perspective of the preservation of Czech economic thought, a decisive role was played by the *Společnost pro vědu a umění* [*Society for Science and Arts in America*] established in New York in 1957 with the intention of helping the young generation of exiles in scientific careers in the USA, especially through personal connections and regular congresses. After 1968, however, the *Society* dealt with the fundamental problem of 'two exiles'. It was the problem of the uncertain educational background of emigrants; some of them had studied only at the *Party College*.

Regular congresses (every 2 years) were first and foremost a meeting platform for practically all economists who had emigrated to the USA and, in that brief period when Czech society was drawing towards the *Prague Spring*, also with domestic colleagues who could travel abroad. The congresses were focused mostly on 'Czech' and 'Slovak' topics. In the 1960s, discussions on the possibilities of the transformation of the Czechoslovak economy resonated here repeatedly, and in 1968 and 1970, a memorial to the honour of Karel Engliš took place. The main initiators, Jaroslav Polach (b.1915) and J.V. Mládek had been Engliš's students at the Masaryk University in Brno in the 1930s.

From 1970 – when all of Engliš's books had been placed on the index of banned literature in Czechoslovakia – preparations for the publication of an annotated bibliography of Engliš's publications and translation of his main works were also underway in the USA. This work was ultimately unsuccessful, for after 1970 it was impossible to acquire materials from Czechoslovakia and there were relatively few titles by Engliš in the Library of Congress and other foreign libraries – Engliš had published most of his texts in Czech. As regards translations of Engliš's works into English, Engliš's terminology transpired to be a problem insofar as it required connecting an economist, a logician and a linguist. Even the translation of Engliš's term *logical orders* was the subject of numerous letters between *Society* members and American economists – using the terms *Logical Orders, Logical Orders of Thought, Engliš Orders of Ideas as Logical Tools of Thinking* or *Forms of Thought* were discussed in them. Nevertheless, to all those interested it seemed that Engliš's concept fell precisely into nascent comparative economics; Arthur Schweitzer (1905–2004), who was then the Head of Department of Economics at Indiana University, Bloomington, summarized the reasons why Engliš's texts should be translated into English. First, due to the fact that they surpass the limits of Walter Eucken's (1891–1950) ordoliberalistic distinction between an exchange and administratively controlled economy which does not enable distinguishing of the different subsystems of private capitalism. It was precisely this that Engliš offered with his concept of *solidarism*, when he also draws social and political elements into economic analysis and observes their interactions with economic ones. Second, because Engliš's concept is compatible with the work of Max Weber, whose social economy includes cooperatives, the nation, the state and solidarity. But in contrast to Engliš, Weber did not build an economic system (Doležalová, 2018b). Two of Engliš's books were published almost two decades later by Columbia University Press (Engliš, 1986, 1992).

Whilst the names of Engliš, Bráf and Macek returned, after 1989, to the Czech public sphere and their books to libraries, it became something of a 'post-Velvet tradition' to overlook the economists who had gone into exile. Whilst they were helpful in providing missing economic literature, namely textbooks, giving lectures and full courses of modern economics at Czech universities and offering scholarships abroad for Czech students, they were not welcome in the domestic environment and their role in the economic reform of the 1990s was not significant. Only a few of them were active in the debate on privatization of SOEs and Jan Švejnar (b.1952) established a now highly esteemed economic research centre *CERGE-EI* that replaced the former *Economic Institute* in the framework of the *Academy of Sciences*. Neither Šik's concept of the third way nor Vanek's vision of a self-managed democratic economy has been accepted in the Czech environment.

Yet another specific group, in which the traditions of the Czech economy were cultivated, formed after 1968. It was formed by economists who had been excluded from the Party and deprived of academic positions, but who did not go into exile and devoted themselves to economics outside of their main – usually worker – jobs. They met at so-called home seminars, organized by Vladimír Kadlec. From the second half of the 1980s, the group issued *samizdat* journals *Ekonomická revue* [*Economic Revue*] and *Ze zásuvky* [*From the Drawer*], and at the end of the 1980s, one of the models of the future transformation here began to emerge (Šulc, 2009). But most significantly, the most important non-Marxist political economy book that penetrated during the whole Czechoslovak socialist period was discussed here: *Stát a ekonomika* [*The State and Economy*] by Zdislav Šulc (b.1926) from 1985.

The study of Eucken's analysis of the economy of Nazi Germany, the works of J.M. Keynes, J. Kornai's book *Economics of Shortage* (1980), but especially *Budování státu* [*Building the State*] written by the famous interwar Czechoslovak journalist Ferdinad Peroutka (1895–1975) and Masaryk's *Česká otázka* [*The Czech Question*] (1895) and *Světová revoluce* [*World Revolution*] (1925) induced Šulc to consider the 'Czechoslovak way to socialism and back' (Šulc 2009, 91). Over more than three hundred pages, he drew a critical image of the socialist economic system and proposed a concept for the change thereof. Šulc's aim was the same as Kornai's: A comprehensive analysis of the functioning of a centrally-planned economy using the instruments of classical and neoclassical economics. Yet Šulc's goal was more comprehensive: To analyze specific mechanism that in a centrally-planned economy create pressures that lead to its unavoidable dissolution. This is why he defines, in the first part of the book, a concept of economic policy in the conditions of a *central-rationing system*. On the basis of Ordoliberalism, neoclassical economics and the political economy of Socialism, he analyzes the mutual interconnection of the constitutive and regulatory elements of the socialist economic mechanism. The second part of the book subjects to critical analysis the reality of the way in which a Soviet-type economy functions. From this it is clear that the state and the economy faced the same problems in 1980 as in the 1960s. He summarized the socialist system with an apt term, *inverse mini-max*. Its content was the strategy of socialist SOE which, in contrast to capitalist businesses which try to minimize inputs and maximize outputs, do the exact opposite. For the analysis of investments under Socialism, he introduced the term *investment scissors* and used a specific type of *multiplier* and the phenomenon of *extended delay*. An original contribution was his analysis of the form of the monopoly in a centrally-planned economy and the role of system-creating elements when creating the economic balance of an enterprise and macro-economic balance; he demonstrated that the forces that work towards the balance of an enterprise are at the same time forces that work towards macro-economic imbalance.

The third part of the book is entirely original and contains Šulc's formulation of conditions for the transformation of a centrally-planned economy into a monetary market economy; he speaks of a *non-capitalist monetary market economy* in which enterprises are separated from the state (the state budget) and equipped with capital assets, the management is an entrepreneurial body, the central plan is replaced by generally valid and legally defined rules of the game (including selection of management through competition, commercial law, general supervision of the business activities of SOEs through audits carried out by independent institutions, anti- monopoly legislation, etc.), and there is a capital market therein, albeit only an obligation market. The *National Property Fund* was to execute ownership rights. In the scope of its economic policy, the government was to use instruments conforming to the market – monetary and fiscal policy. Prices were to be liberalized with exceptional regulation in precisely defined cases. *Denationalization* (privatization) and *capitalization* of the business sphere were to lead towards this system.

The key contributions of Šulc's book could be summarized as follows: First, the characteristic of so-called *dual currencies* (counting and real), which is the key for the analysis of the way in which the whole system functions and the overcoming thereof is the first step towards its transformation. Second, the concept of economic policy as a mutual interconnected and conditioned set of *system-forming* and *regulative* elements. Third, the analysis of the functioning of a *centrally-rationing system* by means of the supply-demand effect when differentiating planned and effective supply and demand, including implementation of the term *investment scissors*. Fourth, the characteristic of the specific type of monopoly in a centrally-rationing system. Fifth, identification of the role of system-forming elements when creating the economic balance of SOEs and the macro-economic balance and the role of *planned corrections* as a key regulative element of the whole system, including built-in regulators as a barrier to the effective behaviour of SOEs and, at the same time, the sources of ineffective management behaviour stereotypes. And finally, sixth, formulation of the conditions of a capital market functioning in a non-capitalist, *regulated monetary-market mechanism*.

Whilst Czech publishing houses refused to publish the book, it was translated into English thanks to financial support by Vladimír Kadlec, and it was to be published by Oxford University Press thanks to the support of Bedřich Levčík (b.1915) and W. Brus. But secret correspondence with the publishing house took too long and the events of the *Velvet Revolution* of 1989 overtook it (Šulc 2009, 97). In the end, the book was published in Czech thanks to Milan Sojka, 20 years after it was written.

Epilogue

The unbearable lightness of economics

The pastoral ideal of the proportional, systematic and smooth functioning of the socialist economy ended at the end of the 1980s. Although capitalism had, from the perspective of the official Political economy of Socialism fallen into an ever-deepening crisis, socialist countries were in fact losing pace with it with ever-increasing speed. Practice fundamentally departed from theory, and the trajectory of economic slump threatened the existence of Socialism itself. The deformed model of Socialism had to be changed.

Members of the *Prognostic Institute*, who had from the 1980s taken part in the formation of prognosis of the economic development of Czechoslovakia until 2020, which was published in mid-1989, were well aware that, instead of a permanently growing standard of living, there is in Czechoslovakia an ever-present disproportionality manifesting itself in unsalable 'dead stocks' on the one hand, and long queues for goods in short supply, accompanied also by clientelism and corruption in the buying and selling process of basic living needs (including toilet paper) on the other hand. It was now naive to assert that such an economy is proportional, whereas the market economy of developed capitalist countries is unrestrained and disproportional. It was more than clear to the economists that socialist planning was unable to secure the proportional development that the market could. Nevertheless, none of these phenomena was considered in the prognosis to be a reason for the collapse of Socialism as a historical and economic reality. On the contrary, the authors expected to open a new period of socialist history, and they still referred to the planning of 'purposeful strategy' as a historical merit of Socialism. They assumed they looked newly at ownership, at competition, the issue of comparative advantages, economic balance, employment, adaptability and the mobility of the workforce, social security, life values and lifestyle, and also at the relationship between the market and the plan; yet that corresponded to the view from the 1960s – the plan regulates the market and the market regulates SOEs. Younger members from the team to a certain degree went against the prevailing mode of thought; V. Klaus spoke of transformation as an investment (Klaus, 1989, 574), during which it is necessary to calculate all costs and profits, and he criticized attempts to 'fight the reform through' and hope that problems emerging in the process would be solved. The depth of inhomogeneity within the *Prognostic Institute* team would appear as early as a few months later, after the *Velvet Revolution*.

The *Velvet Revolution* ended the 40-year long rule of one party and one ideology. The secret of the deep systemic imperfections of the Czechoslovak economy was revealed to the public. The average annual pace of the formation of national income in 1979–1988 was 2.2%; with the exclusion of price fluctuation, growth was at a level of zero. What was viewed in the 1950s as an accelerator of economic growth, i.e. a predominating orientation on the socialist bloc, was now – when Czechoslovakia realized two-thirds of foreign trade with its socialist partners – the reason for adapting the economy to softer conditions and for the loss of competitive ability on the world markets. Even though a notion on the fundamental significance of heavy industry and the necessary preference of its salaries had settled in society, a restructuring of industry based on limiting coal extraction and materially demanding engineering fields on the one side and development of light industry and services on the other side awaited Czechoslovakia. Deep changes in the ownership structure and the democratization of power structure also awaited it. Thus, the road back to capitalism.

Once again, after 40 years, Czech economists would take part in changing an economic system which had never before come to pass. But in the same way as planning did not have a theoretical foundation, neither did the dismantling thereof. No new model based on the confrontation of existing capitalism and the experiences of socialist economies emerged. Theoretical discussions on the form of transformation did not occur. There were two reasons for this: First, the absence of platforms for such a discussion. Indeed, in 1989, Vratislav Šlajer (b.1945) established the *Ekonomické fórum* [*Economic Forum*], according to the newly established political movement *Občanské fórum* [*Civic Forum*] as a space for free discussion among economists on the manner of transformation into a market economy, but the atmosphere for discussion completely disappeared after a few months – some participants went into business, others understood that the time for sharp elbows, which they as theorists did not have, had come. At the start of 1990, the *Prognostic Institute* fell apart as a natural centre for theoretical discussion when its members departed partly into the Czechoslovak Finance Minister Václav Klaus's team and partly into the 'competing' Czech government team with František Vlasák (1912–2005) at the helm. The second reason was also simple: An absence of theoretical concepts that could be discussed. There was only one concept on the table: Šulc's one from his *Economy and State* (2004). Everyone knew it from the *samizdat* edition of his book, and Šulc himself became a member of the above-mentioned Czech government team as early as the first days after the *Velvet Revolution*.

Yet discussions seemed to be opened by two texts which were published in *Hospodářské noviny* [The *Economic News*] in January 1990: An article by Klaus on his doubts on the the quality of Komárek's reconstruction project which had already been written a year previously and which related to the concept of Komárek's prognosis, but which could not be published earlier, and a text by Šulc, who had gone beyond the scope of projects until then and proposed currently possible solutions (Šulc, 2009, 113–114). A key notion of Šulc's proposal (2002) was the denationalization and capitalization of the enterprise sphere on the basis of the *National Property Fund* as the first phase of the transformation, which was to be followed by privatization. The same as in 1945, but in the opposite direction, the transformation was thus to focus on a change in the ownership structure and on the elimination of planning as a tool for controlling the economy. Discussions about this concept did not take place, however, although a marked distinction of the economists themselves occurred; in the public sphere, the appellation 'old boys' (economists connected with the *Prague Spring*) and 'Chicago boys' (referring also to neoliberals) had become common. The latter made it publicly known that the endeavour of the former was a clear effort to preserve Socialism. The former hinted at the fact that the latter did not understand the way the current economy functions, and that they would attempt to transform a planned economy into capitalism of the end of the 19th century, regardless of the fact that capitalism had developed in those 40 years, and that geopolitical conditions had changed. When the expert team of the Czech government, the core of which was the 'old boys', was dissolved on 30 September 1990, it was a sign of the power superiority which the team led by Klaus had gained in that time. David Ellerman, a colleague of Joseph Stiglitz at the World Bank, later referred to them as 'market fundamentalists' proclaiming 'textbook economics' who were 'unleashed' into the real world of policy-making as 'experts' (Myant, Drahokoupil, 2011, 90). The motto of the time became 'capitalism without attributes'.

The selection of the transformation strategy became more a political than an economic issue, and rather (again) an international-political issue. The one chosen was the *Washington Consensus* – the strategy of the IMF and World Bank for helping transitional economies, including requirements for macro-economic stabilization, opening economies in the scope of trade and investments and strengthening of market forces (Myant, Drahokoupil, 2011). This ambivalent hero, once hidden beyond the ocean, had the goal of creating a modern market economy and entirely rejected the communist past. This resonated well with public opinion at the time, in which the communist past was conceived as a deviation from 'our own history' in the framework of Western Europe. It was not unlike the situation during the First Republic, when still at the end of the 1930s, all the failures of the Czechoslovak economy were substantiated by the 300-year Habsburg domination. The so-called *voucher privatization* became the main instrument for transforming ownership structure. Two fundamental systemic changes were added to it at the beginning of 1991: A liberalization of prices, including the abolition of all price subsidies, the implementation of the internal exchangeability of the crown and the liberalization of foreign trade; these measures were preceded by a devaluation of the crown at the end of 1990.

Radical social and economic transformation also affected economics as an academic discipline. On the one hand, it might seem that economics is flowering: It can be studied at 96 faculties of colleges and universities, of which 43 are public, two are state and 51 are private. Each of the faculties offers several subjects of economic study, the largest more than five. Studying economics is possible at every level, on-site or as distance learning. Nevertheless, these changes were not accompanied by changes in the academic body; the *Velvet Revolution* motto 'We're not like them' (meaning the communists after 1948 and 1968) led to a conservation of the personnel structure of the teachers, so changes were manifested only in the change of names of workplaces (Marxism-Leninism institutes in the bounds of which economics had previously been taught disappeared). At the same time, the need to supply the economy with new graduates (again) collided with the lack of teachers; the practice of so-called flying professors, who teach at three or four workplaces throughout the Czech Republic and Slovakia, emerged at the same time and continues to the present. Even assistants without a complete academic education teach. The number of students of economics can be counted in tens of thousands. Seventeen thousand of them study at the largest school, *University of Economics*, which has six faculties.

But on the other hand, it is clear that the core of tuition in the Czech Republic is not economics, but rather business and management. Although standard economics divided into macro-economic and micro-economic theory is part of the obligatory curricula of all fields, ways leading to the expression of their fundamental postulates in the process of historical development and alternative economic theories is given only peripheral attention or none whatsoever, and students fall into false notions on the univocal acceptance of a mainstream approach and the low dynamic of the development thereof (Koderová, 2011). The history of economic thought is an obligatory subject only at one of the six faculties (of Economics and Public Administration) at *University of Economics*.

The impact on economics is devastating. Theoretical economics is almost not cultivated at all. In the public sphere, economics is very often viewed as a field which serves to accumulate wealth, and even after a hundred years, Bráf's criticism of the *Czech disease* still applies. Yet I assert that economic thought in Bohemia and Czech Lands is a valuable part of European thought and the number of thinkers who influenced the development of European economic thought is not as limited as you might think: Founders of cameral sciences; social reformers full of enlightenment and catholic ideas; thinkers who were at the beginning of mathemization of economics or contributed to foundation of the Austrian School; searchers for reconciliation of Liberalism with Socialism, or Marxism with neoclassical economics. In their hands, economics became an inquiry into the nature of human action and the crux of the matters. They themselves were fighting with bureaucratic and ideological obstacles and provincialism and are now hardly resisting falling into oblivion.

Bibliography

Aehrental, A.L.G. von. 1801–1802. *Staatswirtschaftliche Aufsätze in strenger Beziehung auf Zeitumstände, und besonderer Rücksicht auf Böhmen*. Deutschland.

Aehrental, A.L.G. von. 1810. *Über das öffentliche Schuldenwesen*. Leipzig: A. Barth.

Aehrental, A.L.G. von. 1819. *Die Staatswirtschaft nach Naturgesetzen*. Leipzig: F.A. Brockhaus.

Albrecht, C. 2011. Dvě proměny: Počátky a konec Vysoké školy obchodní, 1919–1953. In Doležalová, A. *Učíme ekonomii*, 38–49.

Albrecht, C. 2013. The Influence of Albín Bráf. In Doležalová, A. *Albín Bráf*, 13–20.

Barak, Y. 2015. *Cameralism: A Historiography that Refuses to be a Sonderweg*. Paper presented at the World Economic History Congress in Kyoto, 05/08/2015.

Bata, T. 1990. *Úvahy a projevy*. Praha: Management Press.

Bažantová, I. 2003. Ekonomické názory v humanistickém díle Jana Amose Komenského. *Politická ekonomie* 2, 254–262.

Bažantová, I. 2016. Czech Economist Karel Engliš and his Relation to the Austrian School in the First Half of the 20th Century. *Politická ekonomie* 2, 234–246.

Beccaria, C. di. 1812 (1764). *Dei delitti e delle pene*. Milano: Co. tipi di Luigi Mesori.

Becher, J. J. 1668. *Politische Discurs von den eigentlichen Ursachen des Auff- und Abnehmens der Staedt, Laender und Republicken*. Frankfurt am Main: Zunner.

Bezobrazov, V. P. 1866–1872. *Gosudarstvennyie dochody Rossii*. St. Petersburg:The Saint Petersburg Academy of Sciences.

Bílek, J. (ed.) 2011. *Korespondence T.G. Masaryk - Josef Kaizl*. Praha: MÚA AVČR.

Blažej, Z. 1947. Recenze knihy Lipson E., A Planned Economy or Free Enterprise. London 1946. *Obzor národohospodářský*. XLVI (3), 140–141.

Böhm-Bawerk, E. von. 1959. *Capital and Interest*. Vol. 3. South Holland, Ill.: Libertarian Press.

Bolzano, B. 1837. *Wissenschaftslehre* Sulzbach: J.E. v. Seidel's bookstore.

Bolzano. B. 1847. *Praktische Vorschläge zur Behebung des einem beträchlichten Teile der Bewohner Prag's*. Prague.

Bolzano, B. 1851. *Paradoxien des Undendlichen*. Leipzig : C.H. Reclam .sen.

Bolzano, B. 1937 (1831). *O nejlepším státě*. Plzeň: M. Jašek.

Boreš, et al. 1957. *Problémy nového systému plánování a financování československého průmyslu*. Praha: SNTL.

Borovský, Havlíček, K. 1903. *Politické spisy*. Vol. III/I–II. Praha: Jan Laichter.

Bráf, A. 1883. *Almužna a mzda*. Praha: J. Otto.

Bráf, A. 1907. Vysoké učení obchodní. *Obzor národohospodářský* XII (1), 1–12.

Bráf, A. 1909. *Národohospodářské potřeby české*. Praha: Svépomoc.
Bráf, A. 1913. *Spisy Dra. Albína Bráfa*. Vol.I./1 Praha: Bursík a Kohout.
Bráf, A. 1915. *Finanční věda*. Praha: Nákladem "Sborníku věd právních a státních".
Bráf, A. 1922. *Život a dílo*. Vol. I. Praha: Vesmír.
Bráf, A. 1923a. *Život a dílo*. Vol. II. Praha: Vesmír.
Bráf, A. 1923b. *Život a dílo*. Vol. III. Praha: Vesmír.
Bráf, A. 1923c. *Život a dílo*. Vol. IV. Praha: Vesmír.
Brown, A. 2009. *The Rise & Fall of Communism*. London: The Bodley Head.
Brus, W. 1964. *Modely socialistického hospodářství*. Praha: Academia.
Buquoy, G. von. 1815. *Die Theorie der Nationalwirtschaft nach einem neuen Plane und nach mehrern eigenen Ansichten*. Leipzig: Breitkopf und Härtel.
Burešová, H. 1966. Ekonomický obsah ceny. *Politická ekonomie* 4, 281–289.
Campanella, T. 1638. *Universalis Philosophia Sue Metaphysica Rerum*. Paris.
Chelčický, P. 1966. Postila (1435). In *Drobné spisy*. Praha: Nakladatelství ČSAV.
Chelčický, P. 2011. *Síť víry* (1440–1443). Brno: Host.
Chleborád, F.L. 1869. *Soustava národního hospodářství politického*. Praha: Nákladem vlastním.
Chleborád, F.L. 1884. *Boj o majetek*. Brno: Tiskem a nákladem benediktinů rajhradských.
Chmela, L. 1940. Obecné důsledky celní jednoty pro naše hospodářství. In *Obzor národohospodářský*, XLV (7), 463–468.
Cole, G. D.H. 1947. *Fabiánský socialismus*. Praha: Melantrich.
Černý, B.V. 1940. Tvorba ceny v našem řízném hospodářství. *Obzor národohospodářský*, XLV (6), 374–385.
Čihák, M. 1997. Josef Goldmann: Legenda české poválečné. *Politická ekonomie* 1, 3–24.
Čuhel, F. (Šimek, E.B.) 1896. *Obzor národohospodářský*, I (1), 2.
Čuhel, F. 1907a. *Zur Lehre von den Bedürfnissen: Theoretische Untersuchungen über das Grenzgebiet der Ökonomik und der Psychologie*. Innsbruck: Wagnerschen Universitäts Buchhandlung.
Čuhel, F. 1907b. K nauce o potřebách. *Sborník věd právních a státních*. Praha: Bursík & Kohout, 1–33.
Daněček, J. 1991. Englišova teleologická teorie hodnoty a ceny. *Politická ekonomie* 6, 546–554.
David, Z. 2003. *Finding the Middle Way: The Utraquist's Liberal Challenge to Rome and Luther*. Washington, DC: Woodrow Wilson Centre Press, and Baltimore: Johns Hopkins University Press.
Demokratizace hospodářství a postavení podniků. 1968. *Hospodářské noviny*, special issue no. 16 and 17/1968.
Devátá, M., Olšáková, D. 2010. Ideologizace vědy a školství, 1945–1960. In *Vědní koncepce KSČ a její institucionalizace po roce 1948*. Praha: ÚSD, 73–92.
Devátá, M. 2011. Vysoká škola politických a hospodářských věd a problém (dis)kontinuity výuky ekonomie v letech 1949–1953. In Doležalová, A. *Učíme ekonomii*, 73–92.
Doležalová, A. 1996. *Husovo pojetí pravdy*. Bachelor thesis. Praha: Karlova Univerzita.
Doležalová, A. 2007. *Rašín, Engliš a ti druzí*. Praha: Oeconomica.
Doležalová, A. 2008. *Politické stranictví a ekonomický zájem*. Praha: Národohospodářský ústav Josefa Hlávky.
Doležalová, A. 2010. Nebylo úniku? Kontinuita a diskontinuita v ekonomickém vývoji Československa. In Němeček, J. *Československo a krize demokracie ve střední Evropě ve 30. a 40. letech XX.století. Hledání východisek*. Praha: Historický ústav AV.

Doležalová, A. 2011. *Učíme ekonomii 90 let*. Praha: Wolters Kluwer.

Doležalová, A. 2013a. *Albín Bráf: Politik, národohospodář a jeho doba*. Praha: Národohospodářský ústav Josefa Hlávky.

Doležalová, A. 2013b. Zwischen Autarkie, Emanzipation und Diskriminierung: Die Nostrifizierung in der Tschechoslowakei nach 1918. *Bohemia* 53, 46–93.

Doležalová, A. 2014. Welfare State or Social Reconciliation? Social Question from the Perspective of an Economist (Albín Bráf). In Zudová-Lešková, Z., Voráček, E. *Theory and Practice of the Welfare State in Europe in 20th century*. Praha: Historický ústav AV, 177–198.

Doležalová, A. 2017. The Story of the Poverty: An Interpretation of the Concept of Poverty in Czech Economic Thought in the 19th and 20th century. In Fejtová, O., Hlavačka, M., Horčáková, V., Knotková, V. (eds.) *Poverty, Charity and Social Welfare in Central Europe in the 19th and 20th Centuries*. Cambridge: Cambridge Scholars Publishing, 40–52.

Doležalová, A. 2018a. Bodenreform in der Tschechoslowakei nach dem Jahre 1918: soziale, politische, ökonomische and nationale Dimension dem Eigentumswechseln. In *Eigentumsregime und Eigentumskonflikte im 20. Jahrhundert. Deutschland und die Tschechoslowakei im internationalen Kontext*. Essen: Klartext, 11–44.

Doležalová, A. 2018b. *Jan Viktor Mládek, ekonom*. Praha: Národohospodářský ústav Josefa Hlávky (in print)

Doležalová, A., Holec, R. 2016. Continuity and Discontinuity in the Czech and Slovak Historiographies. In Hudson P., Boldizzoni F. (eds.) *Routledge Handbook of Global Economic History*. London: Routledge, 230–241.

Doležel, K. 1946. *Plánovité hospodářství*. Brno: Vlastním nákladem.

Doležel, K. 1947. Dlouhodobý plán jako předpoklad hospodářské stability. *Obzor národohospodářský*, XLVI (2), 56–70.

Drábek, Z., Janáček, K., Tůma, Z. 1993. *Inflation in Czechoslovakia 1985–91*. Washington, DC: World Bank. International Economics Department WPS 1135.

Droz, J. 1853. *Politické hospodářství*. Praha: Jaroslav Pospíšil.

Droz, F.-X.-J. 1829. *L'économie politique ou principes de la science des richesses*. Paris: Librairie Le Charlier.

Engliš, K. 1909. Počet a osobní poměry chudých v království Českém. *Obzor národohospodářský*, XIV (5, 6, 7), 209–217, 265–271, 314–320.

Engliš, K. 1916. *Sociální politika*. Praha: F. Topič.

Engliš, K. 1919. *Co bude s našimi penězi?* Brno: Polygrafie.

Engliš, K. 1930. *Begründung der Teleologie als Form des empirischen Erkennens*. Brünn, Prague, Leipzig, Wien: Rudolf M. Rohrer.

Engliš, K. 1930. *Teleologie jako forma vědeckého poznání*. Praha: F. Topič.

Engliš, K. 1932a. *Theorie státního hospodářství*. Praha: F. Topič.

Engliš, K. 1932b. *Malá finanční věda*. Praha: Fr. Borový.

Engliš, K. 1933. Noetická kritika Rakouské školy o hodnotě. *Obzor národohospodářský*, XXXVIII (4, 6), 289–303, 361–378.

Engliš, K. 1935. *O řízeném hospodářství*. Praha: Melantrich.

Engliš, K. 1938. *Soustava národního hospodářství*. Praha: Melantrich.

Engliš, K. 1946. *Národní hospodářství*. Praha: Vlastním nákladem.

Engliš, K. 1986. *An Essay on Economic Systems*. New York: Columbia University Press.

Engliš, K. 1992. *Economics. A Purpose Oriented Approach*. New York: Columbia University Press.

Fafl, Z. 1940. Celní unie. *Obzor národohospodářský*, XLV (7), 459–463.

Fišer, D., Kýn, O. 1967. Mnohaleté mezinárodní diskuse o socialismu a trhu. *Politická ekonomie* 7–8, 700–18.

Fišera, F. 1967. O socialitické metamorfóze mzdy. *Politická ekonomie* 4, 337–342.

Frejka, L. 1948. *Rok 1948 v československém hospodářství*. Praha: Orbis.

Frejka, L. 1951. *O ekonomii kapitalismu a socialismu*. Praha: Svoboda.

Funk, V. 1923. *Základy přednášek: Finanční věda*. Praha: Všehrd.

Goldmann, J. 1943. '*Taxation of Tobacco, Beer and Cinema Attendances*'. *Bulletin of the Institute of Statistics*, No 2. Oxford: Oxford University.

Goldmann, J. 1947. *Czechoslovakia: Test Case of Nationalization*. Prague: Orbis.

Goldmann, J. 1949. *Plánované hospodářství v Československu*. Praha: Orbis.

Goldmann, J. 1965. Short- and Long-term Variations in the Growth Rate and the Model of Functioning of a Socialist Economy. *Czechoslovak Economic Papers* 5.

Goldmann, J., Kouba, K. 1967. *Hospodářský růst v ČSSR*. Praha: Academia.

Goldmann, J. 1973. *Od nestability ke stabilitě ekonomického růstu v ČSSR*. Praha: EÚ ČSAV.

Goldmann, J. et al. 1974. *Problémy československé ekonomiky roku 1990*. Praha: EÚ ČSAV.

Goldmann, J. 1975. *Makroekonomická analýza a prognóza*. Praha: Academia.

Goldmann, J. et al. 1978. *Úvod do makroekonomické analýzy a prognózy*. Praha: Svoboda.

Goldmann, J., Kouba, K. 1984. Terms of Trade, Adjustment Processes and the Economic Mechanisms (A quantitative approach). *Acta Oeconomica* 1–2.

Goldmann, J. 1985. *Strategie hospodářského růstu*. Praha: Academia.

Gruber, J. 1914. František Čuhel. *Obzor národohospodářský*, XIX (2), 423–426.

Gruber, J. 1921. Čtvrtstoletí České společnosti národohospodářské v Praze. *Obzor národohospodářský*, XXVI (11), 399–408.

Gruber, J. 1924. Josef Ignác Buček. *Obzor národohospodářský*, XIX (2, 3), 65–72, 111–116.

Gruber, J. 1925. Do třicátého ročníku. *Obzor národohospodářský* XX (1–3), 21–28, 65–72, 111–116.

Habr, J., Jankovský, J. 1990. Profesor Josef Macek. *Politická ekonomie* 1, 525–530.

Havel, J., Klacek, J., Kosta, J., Šulc, Z. 2002. Economics and System Changes in Czechoslovkia. In Wagener, H.J. (ed.) *Economic Thought in Communist and Post-communist Europe*. London: Taylor and Francis, 213–263.

Havelka, M. 2013. 'Česká otázka', 'České myšlénky' a 'Listy politického kacíře'. Trojí perspektiva české politické sebereflexe na přelomu 19. a 20. století. In Doležalová, A., *Albín Bráf*, 33–21.

Havránek, J. 1998. University Professors and Students in Bohemia. In Teich, M. (ed.) *Bohemia in History*. Cambridge: Cambridge University Press, 215–228.

Hayek, F. A. von. 1942. Scientism and the Study of Society. Part I. *Economica* 35(Aug.), 267–291.

Hegel, G.W.F. 1977. *Phenomenology of Spirit*. Oxford: Clarendon Press.

Hejda, J. 1932. *Některé teorie v současné krisi*. Praha: Sbírka přednášek ČSNH.

Heretik, Š. 1955. *Dějiny ekonomických učení*. Praha: SPN.

Herold, V., Müller, I., Havlíček, A. (eds.) 2011. *Politické myšlení pozdního středověku a reformace*. Vol. II/2. Praha: Oikoymenh.

Hicks, J.R. 1947. Keynesova theorie plné zaměstnanosti. *Obzor národohospodářský*, XLVI (4), 145–152.

Horáček, C. 1896. *Počátky českého dělnického hnutí*. Praha: Nákladem České akademie císaře Františka Josefa pro vědy, slovesnost a umění.

Horáček, C. 1903. Význam Františka Ladislava Riegra pro česke písemnictví národohospodářské. *Obzor národohospodářský*, VII (3), 106–113.
Horna, M. 1939. Hospodářské poznámky k teorii životního prostoru. *Obzor národohospodářský*, XLIV (6), 437–440.
Horna, M. 1940. *Problém stálé měny*. Praha: Česká společnost národohospodářská.
Hornigk, P.W. 1753. *Oestereich ueber alles, wann es nur will*. Frankfurt and Leipzig.
Hroch, M. 1968. *Die Vorkämpfer der nationalen Bewegung bei den kleinen Völkern Europas*. Praha: Universita Karlova.
Hrubý, P. 1950. *Politická ekonomie – předsocialistické formace*. Praha: Státní nakladatelství učebnic.
Hudík, M. 2007. František Čuhel. *New Perspectives on Political Economy* 1, 3–14.
Hus, J. 1904. *Sebrané spisy I–V*. Praha: Jaroslav Bursík & Josef Vilímek.
Hus, J. 1947. *Výklad Víry*. Jablonec nad Nisou: Husova jednota biblická.
Jak čeliti nezaměstnanosti? 1938. *Obzor národohospodářský*, XLIII (4), 277–303.
Jevons, W.S. 1871, 1888. *Theory of Political Economy*. London: Macmillan and Co.
Ježek, T. 1967. O potřebě metamorfózy přístupu k teorii mzdy. *Politická ekonomie* 7–8, 674–677.
Johnson, P. 2007. *Intellectuals. From Marx and Tolstoy to Sartre and Chomsky*. New York and London: Harper Perennial.
Jonák, E. 1871. *Základové hospodářství*. Praha: Spolek pro vydávání laciných knih českých.
Jonáš, J. 2013. Albín Bráf a Carl Menger. In Doležalová, A. *Albín Bráf*, 82–88.
Jüngling, L., Nachtigal, V. 1967. Rovnováha na trhu práce. *Politická ekonomie* 10, 893–902.
Kaizl, J. 1879. *Der Kampf um Gewerbereform und Gewerbefreiheit in Bayern von 1799–1868: nebst einem einleitenden Ueberblick über die Entwickelung des Zunftwesens und der Gewerbefreiheit in Deutschland*. Leipzig: Duncker & Humblot.
Kaizl, J. 1882. *Die Lehre von der Überwälzung der Steuern*. Leipzig: Verlag von Duncker & Humblot.
Kaizl, J. 1883. *Národní hospodářství*. Praha: J. Fořt.
Kaizl, J. 1892. *Finanční věda*. Praha: Josef Vilímek.
Kaizl, J. 1909. *Z mého života* I. Praha: Josef Vilímek.
Kalecki, M. 1944. *Studies in Economic Dynamics*. New York and Toronto: Farrar and Rinehart.
Kalecki, M. (ed.) 1947. *Studies in War Economics*. Oxford: Basil Blackwell.
Kampelík, F.C. 1859. *Průmyslné návrhy*. Hradec Králové: F.C. Kampelík.
Kaplan, K. 2000. *Kořeny československé reformy 1968*. Praha: Doplněk.
Kautsky, K. 1889. *Karla Marxe Ekonomické nauky*. Brno: Karel Prokop.
Kavka, M. 1994. Bohemia. In Scribner, B., Porter, R., Teich, M. (eds.) *The Reformation in National Context*. Cambridge: Cambridge University Press 1994, 131–154.
Khavanova, O. 2017. Joseph von Sonnenfels's Courses and the Making of the Habsburg Bureaucracy. *Austrian History Yearbook* 48, 54–73.
Klacek, J., Václav, K., Toms, M. 1968. *Inflace, mzdy a trh: Diskusní úvahy k hospodářské politice*. Praha: Ekonomický ústav ČSAV.
Klacek, J. 1989. Dvě významná období vědecké dráhy Miroslava Tomse. *Politická ekonomie* 4, 403–412.
Klaus, V. 1967. Peníze, cena, ekonomický růst. *Politická ekonomie* 7–8, 633–644.
Klaus, V. 1979. Metodologické problémy makroekonomického modelování. *Politická ekonomie* 7, 697–706.

Klaus, V., Tříska, D. 1988. Ekonomické centrum, přestavba a rovnováha. *Politická ekonomie* 8, 817–30.

Klaus, V. 1989. Imperativy dlouhodobé prognózy a dominantní charakteristiky současné ekonomiky. *Politická ekonomie* 5, 570–579.

Klíma, A. 1965. Mercantilism in the Habsburg Monarchy - with Special Reference to the Bohemian Lands. *Historica* XI, 95–119.

Klimecký, V. 1940. Celní jednota Čech a Moravy s Říší. *Obzor národohospodářský*, XLV (7), 453–458.

Kliment, J. 1938. Individualismus či národní korporativismus? *Obzor národohospodářský*, XLIII (6), 461–462.

Knapp, V. 1998. *Proměny času*. Praha: Prospektrum.

Knies, C. 1930. *Politische Oekonomie vom geschichtlichen Standpunkte*. Leipzig: Hans Buske.

Kocanda, R., Pelikán, P. 1967. Socialistický podnik jako účastník trhu. *Politická ekonomie* 2, 93–102.

Koderová, J. 2006. Pronikání myšlenek rakouských ekonomů do výuky na českých vysokých školách před rokem 1989. *New Perspectives on Political Economy* 1, 60–74.

Koderová, J. 2011. Výuka dějin ekonomického myšlení na VŠE v Praze. In Doležalová, A. *Učíme ekonomii*, 225–233.

Koloušek, J. 1918. *Národní Hospodářství*. Praha: Česká matice technická & Fr. Řivnáč.

Komárek, V. 1989. Prognostická sebereflexe čs. společnosti. *Politická ekonomie* 5, 523–535.

Komenda, B., Kožušník, Č. 1964. Některé základní otázky zdokonalení systému řízení socialistického národního hospodářství. *Politická ekonomie* 3, 219–236.

Komenda, B. 1965: Plánovitá tvorba cen v nové soustavě řízení. *Politická ekonomie* 4, 310–319.

Komenský, J.A. 1901. *Štěstí národa* (1659). Praha: J. Otto.

Komenský, J.A. 1929. *Listové do nebe* (1619). Praha: Karel Reichel.

Komenský, J.A. 1923. *Labyrint světa a ráj srdce* (1623). Brno: Barvič a Novotný.

Komenský, J.A. 1992. *Obecná porada o nápravě věcí lidských II–III* (1662). Praha: Svoboda.

Kornai, J. 1980. *Economics of Shortage*. Amsterdam: North-Holland.

Kosík, K. 1963. *Dialectics of the Concrete. A Study on Problems of Man and World. Boston Studies in the Philosophy of Science, Vol LII.* Dordrecht/Boston: D. Riedel Publishing Company.

Kosta, J. 1995. Die tschechische Wirtschaftforschung in der Instituten der Akademie der Wissenschaften, 1953–1992. In: *Forschung und Lehre Ostmitteleuropas im Umbruch*. Marburg: Herder Institut, 73–78.

Kosta, J. 1996. K ekonomické reformě 1965–1968. In *Studijní materiály výzkumného projektu Československa*. Praha: AV ČR, 21–28.

Kouba, K. 1965. Plán a ekonomický růst. *Politická ekonomie* 4, 292–301.

Kouba, K. 1967. Plán a trh v socialistické ekonomice. *Politická ekonomie* 9, 773–784.

Kouba, K. (ed.) 1968. *Úvahy o socialistické ekonomice*. Praha: Svoboda.

Kožušník, Č. 1964. *Problémy teorie hodnoty a ceny za socialismu*. Praha: ČSAV.

Kožušník, Č. 1967. Zájem podniku na cenových změnách a centrální regulace cen. *Politická ekonomie* 4, 301–314.

Král, A. 1938. Slovensko ve spolkovém státě Česko-Slovenském. *Obzor národohospodářský*, XLIII (8), 731–733.

Krameš, J. 1998. *Kameralismus a klasická ekonomie* v Čechách. Praha: VŠE.

Krameš, J. 2012. *Ekonomie jako předmět výuky na vysokých školách v českých zemích do roku 1918*. Praha: Typograf.

Krameš, J. 2013. Národohospodářské semináře, Albín Bráf a jeho žáci. In Doležalová, A. *Albín Bráf*, 121–133.

Krameš, J. 2016. *Albín Bráf jeho žáci*. Praha: Národohospodářský ústav Josefa Hlávky.

Kroupa, J. 1998. The Alchemy of Happiness: The Enlightenment in the Moravian context. In Teich, M. *Bohemia in History*, 164–181.

Kundera, M. 1967. *Žert*. Praha: Československý spisovatel.

Lacina, V., Hájek, J. 2002. *Kdy nám bylo nejlépe?* Praha: Libri.

Lenin, V.I. 1948. *Imperialism, the Highest Stage of Capitalism: A Popular Outline*. London: Lawrence & Wishart.

Lenin, V.I. 1955. *Spisy*. Vol. 33. Bratislava: SVPL.

Levčík, B., Kosta, J. 1968. Koho reprezentuje socialistický podnik. *Politická ekonomie* 3, 239–247.

Lipson E. 1946. *A Planned Economy or Free Enterprise*. London: A. & C. Black.

Loewenstein, J. 1931. *Diagnosa a léčení světové krise*. Praha: Orbis.

Máče, J. 2001. Laboretismus – specifický směr českého ekonomického myšlení. Politická ekonomie 4, 584–592.

Macek, J. 1915. *Mravní názory Adama Smithe*. Praha: Vlastní náklad.

Macek, J. 1918. *Znárodnění a zlidovění české půdy*. Praha: A. Svěcený.

Macek, J. 1919. Konservatismus, liberalismus a socialismus. *Naše doba* 7, 413–422.

Macek, J. 1923. *Svépomoc na poli hospodářském*. Praha.

Macek, J. 1924. *Demokracie v hospodářství*. Praha: Svaz národního osvobození.

Macek, J. 1925a. *Socialismus*. Praha: Státní nakladatelství.

Macek, J. 1925b. *Základy sociální politiky* I. Praha: Ústřední dělnické knihkupectví a nakladatelství.

Macek, J. 1933. *Zápas s omylem a chudobou*. Praha: Jan Laichter.

Macek, J. 1935a. Politika a hospodářství. In Horák, J. (ed.) *Jan Laichter. Život a dílo*. Praha: Svaz knihkupců a nakladatelů.

Macek, J. 1935b. *Cesta z krize*. Praha: Jan Laichter.

Macek, J. 1943. *Cesty sebevzdělání*. Praha: Jan Laichter.

Macek, J. 1946. *Sociální ekonomika*. Praha: Česká grafická unie.

Macek, J. 1947. Socialismus a svoboda. *Naše doba* 2, 49–53.

Macek, J. 1965. *The Hussite Movement in Bohemia*. London and Prague: Lawrence & Wishart; Orbis.

Maiwald, K. 1937. *Hospodářský život a úvěr*. Praha: Družstevní práce.

Markovski, M. 1987. Jan Maria Novotný and His Collection of Books on Economics. *The Courier* 22/2, 57–65.

Marx, K. 1913. *Kapitál: kritika politické ekonomie*. Sv. 1. Kn. 1, Praha: Nakl. Ústř. děln. knihkupectví.

Marx, K. 1923. *Hodnota, cena a zisk*. Praha: Federace děl. těl. jednot českoslov.

Marx, K. 1929. *Námezdní práce a kapitál*. Praha: Komunistické nakladatelství.

Marx, K. 1961. *Ekonomicko-filosofické rukopisy*. Praha: Státní nakladatelství politické literatury.

Masaryk, T.G. 1895. *Česká otázka*. Praha: Čas.

Masaryk, T.G. 1898, 1946. *Otázka sociální*. Praha: Čin.

Masaryk, T.G. 1925. *Světová revoluce za války a ve válce 1914–1918*. Praha: Orbis: Čin.

Mauss, M. 1990. *The Gift: Forms and Functions of Exchange in Archaic Societies*. London: Routledge.

Medvedev, V.A. 1989. Politická ekonomie socialismu. *Politická ekonomie* 2, 173–218.

Mejstřík, M. 1989. Přínos ke zkoumání nerovnováhy. *Politická ekonomie* 4, 429–431.

Menger, C. 1985 (1883). *Investigations into the Method of the Social Sciences*. New York: New York University.

Menšík, J. 2013. Albín Bráf k metodě ekonomie. In Doležalová, A. *Albín Bráf*, 89–93.

Mildschuh, W. 1927. Z mých vzpomínek na A.Bráfa. In Hobza, L. (ed.) *Bráfův památník*. Třebíč: Spolek absolventů Obchodní akademie, 19–20.

Mill, J. 1857. *Principles of Political Economy: With Some of their Applications to Social Philosophy in Two Volumes*. Fourth edition. London: John W. Parker and Son, West Strand.

Mises, L. von. 1934. *The Theory of Money and Credit*. London: Jonathan Cape.

Mises, L. von. 1949. *Human Action: A Treatise on Economics*. London: W. Hodge and Company Limited.

Mises, L. von. 2003. *The Historical Settings of the Austrian School of Economics*. Ludwig von Mises Institute. [1969] by Arlington House. Online edition.

Mlčoch, L. 1967a. Alternativy chování podniku v decentralizovaném modelu socialismu. *Politická ekonomie* 11, 979–988.

Mlčoch, L. 1967b. Hrubá výroba, hrubý důchod, efektivita a extenzita našeho hospodářského růstu. *Politická ekonomie* 7, 641–662.

Mlčoch, L. 1989. Ochota naslouchat druhým. *Politická ekonomie* 4, 421.

Modráček, F. 1918. *Samospráva práce*. Praha: Ústřední dělnické knihkupectví a nakladatelství.

Modráček, F. 1931. Podstata a cíle družstevního hnutí. In *Družstevnictví a jeho hospodářské a sociální poslání v Československé republice*. Praha: Sociální ústav ČSR.

Molnár, A. 1985. *Na rozhraní věků*. Praha: Vyšehrad.

Mošna, Z., Horálek, M. 1965. Osobní hmotná zaineresovanost v nové soustavě řízení. *Plánované hospodářství* 1, 10–17.

Myant, M., Drahokoupil, J. 2011. *Transition Economies: Political Economy in Russia, Eastern Europe, and Central Asia*. John Wiley & Sons, Inc.

Nachtigal, V. 1969. *Národní důchod Československa*. Praha: EÚ ČSAV.

Návrh nové soustavy řízení národního hospodářství. 1965. Praha: Svépomoc.

Nebesář, J. 1935. *Nové cesty úvěru: veřejné investice a jejich financování*. Praha: Čin.

Nebesář, J. 1939. *Úspory a investice*. Praha: Vydavatelstvo Družstevní práce.

Němec, V. 2011. Vzpomínky studenta. In Doležalová, A. *Učíme ekonomii*, 58–69.

Nikl, M. 1961. O šíření marxistické politické ekonomie v buržoazním Československu. *Politická ekonomie*, 744–761.

Novotný, V. (ed.) 1920. Husův list přátelům v Čechách, no. 129, 10 June 1415. In *M. Jana Husi korespondence a dokumenty*. Praha: Nákl. Komise pro vydávání pramenů náboženského hnutí českého, 270–273.

Peroutka, F. (1933–1936). *Budování statu*. Praha: Fr. Borový.

Šmejkal, M. *et al*. 1962. *Některé otázky dějin ekonomických učení v Československu. Vědecký sborník Vysoké školy ekonomické*. Praha: SNPL.

Petráček, J. 1974. *Kritika buržoazní politické ekonomie* I. Praha: SPN.

Petráček, J. *et al*. 1988. *Dějiny ekonomických teorií*. Praha: SNTL.

Polášek, M. 2010. Josef Macek mezi liberálním socialismem a sociálním liberalismem. *Politická ekonomie* 3, 420–418.

Polášek, M. 2011. Pohled Josefa Macka na charakter ekonomie a její společenskou roli. In Doležalová, A. *Učíme ekonomii* (203–217).

Potužil, F. 1939. Liberalism, socialism a korporativism. *Obzor národohospodářský*, XLIV (5), 365–373.

Pousta, Z. 1998. Univerzita Karlova v letech 1947–1953. In Havránek, J., Pousta, Z. (eds.) *Dějiny Univerzity Karlovy*. IV. 1918–1990. Praha: Karolinum.

Reimann, P. 1932. *Základy marxismu-leninismu*. Praha: Karel Borecký.

Richta, R. 1967. Civilizace na rozcestí. *Společenské a lidské souvislosti vědeckotechnické revoluce*. Praha: Svoboda.

Riegger, J.A. 1787–1799. *Materialien zur alten und neuen Statistik von Böhmen*. Prague and Leipzig: Kaspar Widtmann.

Riegger, J.A. 1792–1795. *Archiv für Geschichte und Statistik von Böhmen*, in three volumes. Dresden: Walther.

Rieger, F.L. 1850. *O statcích hmotných a nehmotných a jich významu i postavení v národním hospodářství*. Praha: František Řivnáč.

Rieger, F.L. 1860. *Průmysl a postup výroby jeho v působení svém k blahobytu a svobodě lidu zvláště pracujícího*. Praha: Nakladatelství Antonína Augusta.

Rieger, F.L. 1910. Rozvrh k přednáškám o politické oekonomice. *Obzor národohospodářský* XV (6), 257–266.

Ringer, F. 1969. *The Decline of the German Mandarins: The German Academic Community 1890–1933*. Cambridge, MA: Harvard University Press.

Robinson, J. 1934 What is the Perfect Competition? *Quarterly Journal of Economic,s* 49 (1), 104–120.

Robinsonová, J. 1975. *Jak porozumět ekonomické analýze*. Prague: Svoboda.

Roscher, W. 1874. *Geschichte der National-Oekonomik in Deutschland*. München: Oldenbourg.

Rothbard, M.N. 2009. Foreword. In Mises, L. von. *The Theory of Money and Credit*. Auburn: Ludwig von Mises Institute, 4–7.

Rusek, A. 1968. Hmotná zainteresovanost a chování socialistického podniku. *Politická ekonomie* 4, 337–346.

Rychetník, L. 1968. Vědeckost a demokracie v řízení národního hospodářství. *Politická ekonomie* 4, 347–354.

Řezník, J. 2011. Ústav pro plánování při Filozofické fakultě Palackého univerzity Olomouci v letech 1949–1953. In Doležalová, A. *Učíme ekonomii* 92–108.

Sabina, K. 1866. *Dějepis literatury československé staré a střední doby*. Praha: A. Štorch.

Saint-Simon, C.H. 1825, 1964. The New Christianity. Dialogues Between a Conservative and an Innovator. In Fried, A., Sanders, R. (eds.) *Socialist Thought: A Documentary History*. Garden City: Anchor Books.

Schindler, E. 1904. Merkantilismus a státní praxe v Rakousku za Leopolda I. *Obzor národohospodářský*, IX (9, 10, 11, 12), 367–372, 415–424, 468–476, 509–518.

Schumpeter, J. 1954. *History of Economic Analysis*. London, Boston, Sydney: George Allen & Unwin.

Scribner, B. 1994. Introduction. In Scribner, B., Porter, R., Teich, M. (eds.) *The Reformation in National Context*. Cambridge: Cambridge University Press.

Sidgwick, H. 1883. *The Principles of Political Economy*. London: Macmillan.

Sedlák, J. 1915. *Mistr J.Hus*. Praha: Dědictví sv. Prokopa.

Smith, Adam Smith with notes by J.R. McCulloch. 1812. *An Inquiry into the Nature and Causes of the Wealth of Nations* (1776). London: Ward, Lock.

Sojka, M. *et al.* 1998. *Dějiny ekonomických teorií*. Praha: VŠE

Současná západní ekonomie, 1989. *Acta Oeconomica Pragensia* 3.

Sousedík, S. 1996. *René Descartes a české baroko*. Praha: Filosofia.

Spencer, H. 1882. *Principles of Sociology*. London: Williams and Norgate.

Svoboda, V. 1947. Poznámky k pojmu a obsahu cenové politiky. *Obzor národohospodářský*, XLVI (4, 5), 152–165, 197–207.

Šauer, L. 1947. Do nových ročníků. *Obzor národohospodářský* 1, 1–4.

Šauer, L., Šauerová, I. 1984. Vysoká škola obchodní. *Acta Polytechnica* 1.

Šik, O. 1949. Reformismus v politické ekonomii. *Nová mysl*, 3, 363–398.

Šik, O., Kazda, J. 1953 *O některých ekonomických zákonech. Ke studiu díla J. V. Stalina Ekonomické problémy socialismu v SSSR*. Praha: SNPL.

Šik, O. 1953. *Socialistická hospodářská soustava a charakter ekonomických zákonů této soustavy*. Praha: Rudé právo.

Šik, O. 1955. *Zákon plánovitého, proporcionálního rozvoje národního hospodářství*. Praha: Rudé právo.

Šik, O. 1962. *Ekonomika, zájmy, politika*. Praha: NPL.

Šik, O. 1964. *K problematice socialistických zbožních vztahů*. Praha: ČSAV.

Šik, O. 1968. *Plán a trh za socialismu*. Praha: Academia.

Šik, O. 1972. *Der dritte Weg; die marxistisch-leninistische Theorie und die moderne Industriegesellschaft*. Hamburg: Hoffmann und Campe.

Šik, O. 1979. *Humane Wirtschaftsdemokratie*. Hamburg: Knaus.

Šik, O. 1989. *Wirtschaftssysteme. Vergleiche – Theorie – Kritik*. Heidelberg: Springer Verlag.

Šik, O. 1990. *Jarní probuzení – iluze a skutečnost*. Praha: Mladá fronta.

Škvorecký, J. 1996. *Republic of Whores*. New York: Ecco Press.

Šmejkal, M., Petráček, J. Šafaříková, V. 1966. *Dějiny ekonomických učení*. I. Praha: SPN.

Štítný ze Štítného, T. 1852. *Knížky šestery o obecných věcech křesťanských*. Praha: Pražská universita.

Štoll, L. 1949. O socialistickou inteligenci. *Tvorba* 42, 981–984.

Šulc, Z. 1998. *Stručné dějiny ekonomických reforem v Československu (České republice) 1945–1995*. Brno: Doplněk.

Šulc, Z. 2002. *Vize a skutečnost české transformace*. Praha: Národohospodářský ústav.

Šulc, Z. 2004. *Stát a ekonomika: příspěvek k teorii hospodářské politiky*. Praha: Karolinum.

Šulc, Z. 2009. *Z jeviště i zákulisí české politiky a ekonomiky*. Praha: Národohospodářský ústav Josefa Hlávky.

Teich, M. 1976. Ignaz von Born als Organisator der wissenschaftlichen Bestrebungen in der Habsburger Monarchie. In Amburger, E., Cieśla, M., Sziklay, L. (eds.) *Wissenschaftspolitik in Mittel-und Osteuropa*. Berlin, 195–205.

Teich, M. 1981. Bohemia: From Darkness into Light. In Teich, M., Porter, R. (eds.) *The Enlightenment in National Context*. Cambridge: Cambridge University Press, 141–164.

Teich, M. 1988. Interdisciplinarity in J. J. Becher's Thought. *History of European Ideas* 9, 145–160.

Teich, M. 1998. *Bohemia in History*. Cambridge. Cambridge University Press.

Teich, M. 2015. *Scientific Revolution Revisited*. Cambridge: Open Book Publishers.

Teichová, A. 1998. *Německá hospodářská politika v českých zemích v letech 1939–1945*. Praha: VŠE.

Toms, M., Hájek, M. 1965. *Dva modely růstu*. Praha: EÚ ČSAV.

Toms, M. 1976. Towards a Marxian Model of Capital Accumulation, Unemployment and Distribution. *Czechoslovak Economic Papers* 16.

Toms, M. 1981. Měření efektů v socialistické ekonomice. Praha: Svoboda.

Traub, H. 1925. *Karel Havlíček Borovský*. Praha: F. Topič.

Třeštík, D. 1968. *Kosmova kronika. Studie k počátkům českého dějepisectví a politického myšlení*. Praha: Academia.

Třeštík, D. 1971. K sociální struktuře přemyslovských Čech. *Československý časopis historický* 4, 537–567.

Tribe, K. 1984. Cameralism and the Science of Government. *The Journal of Modern History* 2, 263–284.

Tribe, K. 2006. Cameralism and the Sciences of the State. In Goldie, M., Wokler, R. (eds.) *The Cambridge History of Eighteenth-Century Political Thought*. Cambridge: Cambridge University Press, 525–546.

Tribe, K. 2009. Strategies of Economic Order. In *Cameralism and the Science of the Government*. Cambridge: Cambridge University Press, 8–31.

Tříska, D. 2011. Léta sedmdesátá a 'Společenství Václava Klause'. In Doležalová, A. *Učíme ekonomii*, 239–240.

Turek, O. 1967. O plánu, trhu a hospodářské politice. Praha: Svoboda.

Ulrych, J. 1937. *Základy marxistické ekonomie*. Praha: Lidová kultura.

Urban, O. 2003. *Kapitalismus a česká společnost*. Praha: Nakladatelství Lidové noviny.

Václav, V. (ed.) 1934. *Laboretismus: soubor přednášek a statí*. Praha: Práce intelektu.

Valenta, F. 1969. *Tvůrčí aktivita, inovace, efekty*. Praha: Svoboda.

Vejvoda, J. 1964. Základní teoretické otázky zbožní výroby ve státním socialistickém sektoru a centrální plánování rozvoje všelidové ekonomiky. *Politická ekonomie* 3, 237–249.

Vencovský, F. 1997. *Dějiny českého ekonomického myšlení do roku 1948*. Brno: Nadace Universita Masarykiana.

Vencovský F., Půlpán, K., et al. 2005. *Dějiny měnových teorií na českém území*. Praha: Oeconomica.

Verunáč, V. 1923. *Dělnická otázka a náš průmysl*. Praha: Masarykova akademie práce.

Verunáč, V. 1928. *Laboretismus: hnutí technicko-mravního pokroku hospodářského. Zásady a směrnice*. Praha: nákladem Parlamentu.

Verunáč, V. 1933. *O hospodářský plán*. Praha: Čin.

Veselý, A.P. 1895. Sociální demokracie a my. In *Pokrok* 18, 12.

Víšek, J.A. 2013. Předmluva. In Doležalová, A. *Albín Bráf*. 8–9.

Vozka, J. 1937 *Bernard Bolzano, první moderní socialista v Čechách*. Praha: Pražská odbočka Dělnické akademie v Praze.

Wagner, A. 1892. *Grundlagen der Volkswirtschaft*. Leipzig: C.F. Winter.

Wakefield, A. 2005. Books, Bureaus, and the Historiography of Cameralism. *European Journal of Law and Economics* 19, 311–320.

Wood, D. 2002. *Medieval Economic Thought*. Cambridge: Cambridge University Press.

Wootton, B. 1936. *Hospodářství s plánem či bez plánu*. Praha: Jan Laichter.

Wootton B. 1947. *Plánování a svoboda*. Praha: Jan Laichter.

Zásady urychlené realizace nové soustavy řízení. 1966. Praha: Státní komise pro řízení a organizaci.

Závodský, P. 1999. Přehled vývoje vysokého ekonomického školství na našem území. *Acta Oeconomica Pragensia* 5, 22–86.

Index

For Product Safety Concerns and Information please contact our EU representative GPSR@taylorandfrancis.com Taylor & Francis Verlag GmbH, Kaufingerstraße 24, 80331 München, Germany